2/06

In Search of
the Promised Land

New Narratives in American History

Series Editors
James West Davidson
Michael B. Stoff

In Search of
the Promised Land

A SLAVE FAMILY IN THE OLD SOUTH

JOHN HOPE FRANKLIN
LOREN SCHWENINGER

NEW YORK   OXFORD
OXFORD UNIVERSITY PRESS
2006

Oxford University Press, Inc., publishes works that further Oxford University's
objective of excellence in research, scholarship, and education.

Oxford   New York
Auckland   Cape Town   Dar es Salaam   Hong Kong   Karachi
Kuala Lumpur   Madrid   Melbourne   Mexico City   Nairobi
New Delhi   Shanghai   Taipei   Toronto

With offices in
Argentina   Austria   Brazil   Chile   Czech Republic   France   Greece
Guatemala   Hungary   Italy   Japan   Poland   Portugal   Singapore
South Korea   Switzerland   Thailand   Turkey   Ukraine   Vietnam

Library of Congress Cataloging-in-Publication Data
Franklin, John Hope, 1915–
    In search of the promised land : a slave family in the Old South / by
John Hope Franklin, Loren Schweninger.
        p. cm. — (New narratives in American history)
    Includes bibliographical references and index.
    ISBN-13: 978-0-19-516087-1 (acid-free paper)—ISBN-13: 978-0-19-
516088-8 (pbk.: acid-free paper)
    ISBN 0-19-516087-8 (acid-free paper)—ISBN 0-19-516088-6 (pbk.: acid-
free paper)
    1. Thomas, Sally, 1787–1850. 2. Thomas, Sally, 1787–1850—Family.
3. Slaves—Tennessee—Nashville—Biography. 4. African Americans—
Tennessee—Nashville—Biography. 5. Nashville (Tenn.)—Biography.
6. Nashville (Tenn.)—Race relations. 7. Thomas family. 8. Rapier family.
9. African American families—Southern States—Case studies. 10. Slavery—
Southern States—Case studies. I. Schweninger, Loren. II. Title. III. Series.

    E444.F825 2005
    929'.2'08996073—dc22   2004061666

9 8 7 6 5 4 3 2 1

Printed in the United States of America
on acid-free paper

Contents

ILLUSTRATIONS

MAPS

FOREWORD

THE FRENCH POLITICAL PHILOSOPHER VOLTAIRE ONCE REMARKED that if God did not exist, man would have to invent him. The aphorism reveals more, perhaps, about the human desire for rational constructs than about the existence of God. On the other hand, the best history uncovers subjects that are simply beyond invention. The family from the antebellum South portrayed here by historians John Hope Franklin and Loren Schweninger breaks nearly all the traditional stereotypes associated with such rational constructs as black/white and slave/free.

How could one invent Sally Thomas, an African American in Nashville who worked tirelessly to insure that her three sons by white men all eventually found freedom—while she remained enslaved? And did so even when that meant buying the freedom of one son and encouraging another to run away to the North, where she would never see him again. Who could invent the white father of her youngest son, James, one of the justices of the U.S. Supreme Court who signed the majority opinion in the *Dred Scott* case, asserting that the Negro "had no rights which the white man was bound to respect"? Who could foretell that, as conditions worsened for African Americans during the 1850s, James Thomas would join his nephew in a quest for a freer country by traveling to

Nicaragua, where the filibustering American William Walker was setting up his own rogue republic? Who could predict that Sally's oldest son, John, in one of the many ironies of the peculiar institution, would raise his first four children as free and his next five as slaves? Who could devise the paths of migration that sent Sally Thomas's descendants on odysseys by covered wagon to California, by steamship to Jamaica, through Bleeding Kansas of the 1850s, into howling snowstorms on the Minnesota prairie, to medical school in Michigan, to a utopian settlement of runaway slaves in Canada, and after the war to the halls of Congress from the second district in Alabama?

Yet these are no inventions. Franklin and Schweninger have uncovered a remarkable story that demonstrates the complexity of African American lives during the antebellum and Civil War eras. The boundaries between slavery and freedom were always harsh and menacing but, as it turns out, sometimes more permeable and flexible than we imagine.

Narrative is the champion of the unpredictable and the ironic; but Oxford's New Narratives in American History is dedicated to more than stories that are diverting curiosities. Our series aims to produce narratives that engage readers *and* serve as lenses into the most illuminating scholarship of our generation. *In Search of the Promised Land* is a prime example of that: a tale unique in its blend of archival richness, narrative twists and turns, and interpretive breadth.

James West Davidson
Michael B. Stoff
Series Editors

Acknowledgments

A NUMBER OF LIBRARIANS, ARCHIVISTS, HISTORIANS, GENEALO-
gists, and friends assisted us in locating important information and
providing illustrations. We offer thanks to Carol Roberts and Ka-
rina McDaniels of the Tennessee State Library and Archives; Amy
Arnold at the State Historical Society of Missouri, Columbia, Missouri; Eppie D. Edwards of the National Library of Jamaica,
Kingston, Jamaica; William Finley, Carolyn Shankle, and Linda Ja-
cobson of Special Collections, Jackson Library, University of North
Carolina at Greensboro; Allen Walker, Baldwin Room, Toronto
Metropolitan Library, Toronto, Ontario; David Bahssin of the Post
Road Gallery in Larchmont, New York; Erica Nordmeier, Ban-
croft Library, University of California at Berkeley.

We wish to express special thanks to several individuals whose
assistance went beyond the call of duty: Ann Webster of the
Mississippi State Department of Archives and History; Carol
Kaplan of the Nashville Room, Public Library of Nashville
and Davidson County, Tennessee; Michael Marleau, an inde-
pendent scholar studying steamboats and the life of Mark Twain;
Joellen El Bashir, Moorland-Spingarn Research Center, Howard
University, Washington, D.C.; and Catherine Kratzer-Yue and

archivist Carmel Barry-Schweyer of the Placer County Museum and Archives, Auburn, California. Special thanks and much appreciation to Bryan and Shannon Prince of North Buxton, Ontario, who shared their personal records with us; Charles Brewer, of Washington, D.C., who provided us with new information about John Rapier Jr.; Emily Schweninger, who composed the captions and drew mock-up maps; Marguerite Ross Howell, who proofread two drafts and created the index; Robert Calhoon, who provided us with information about the religious context of antebellum Nashville; and five anonymous readers for Oxford University Press. Also a special thanks goes to Oxford editor Jim Davidson, who read the manuscript in several drafts and made numerous insightful suggestions.

THE DESCENDANTS OF
SALLY THOMAS

Sally Thomas had three sons: John and Henry, most likely by John L. Thomas, the brother of her owner; and James, nearly twenty years later. James's father was John Catron, later a justice of the United States Supreme Court.

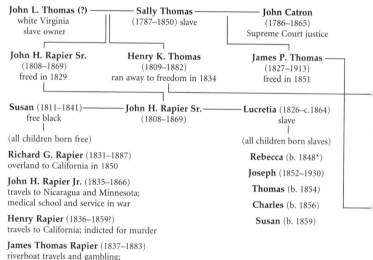

John L. Thomas (?) —————— **Sally Thomas** —————— **John Catron**
white Virginia   (1787–1850) slave   (1786–1865)
slave owner   Supreme Court justice

John H. Rapier Sr.   **Henry K. Thomas**   **James P. Thomas**
(1808–1869)   (1809–1882)   (1827–1913)
freed in 1829   ran away to freedom in 1834   freed in 1851

Susan (1811–1841)—————— **John H. Rapier Sr.** ———— **Lucretia** (1826–c.1864)
free black   (1808–1869)   slave

(all children born free)   (all children born slaves)

Richard G. Rapier (1831–1887)   **Rebecca** (b. 1848*)
overland to California in 1850
                                                                Joseph (1852–1930)
John H. Rapier Jr. (1835–1866)
travels to Nicaragua and Minnesota;   **Thomas** (b. 1854)
medical school and service in war
                                                                Charles (b. 1856)
Henry Rapier (1836–1859?)
travels to California; indicted for murder   **Susan** (b. 1859)

James Thomas Rapier (1837–1883)
riverboat travels and gambling;
conversion experience in Canada

John H. Rapier Sr. moved to Florence, Alabama, where he had children with Susan, a free black, and, after her death, with his housekeeper, Lucretia, a slave.

Henry K. Thomas (1809–1882) ———— **Maria** (c. 1826–c.1895)
free black

(all children born free)

Sarah	**Henry**	**Hannah**	**Jane**	**John**	**Maria**	**Richard**
(b. 1845*)	(b. 1847)	(b. 1849)	(b. 1851)	(b. 1854)	(b. 1857)	(b. 1859)

Henry K. Thomas ran away in 1834 to Buffalo, where he established a barbershop; in 1851 he fled to Canada in the wake of the Fugitive Slave Act.

James Thomas (1827–1913) ———— **Antoinette Rutgers** (1837–1897)
(born free)

James	**Sarah**	**Pelagie**	**Arend John**	**Joseph F.**	**Anthony**
(1869–c.1920)	(b. 1870)	(1871–1939)	(1872–1913)	(1874–1914)	(c.1876–1912)

James Thomas was a barber in Nashville. He traveled widely, including a trip to Central America with nephew John Rapier Jr. Thomas later settled in St. Louis.

*Birth years for children derived from United States and Canadian census returns by subtracting age listed in returns from year of return.

PROLOGUE

It had rained hard the night before, and it was still drizzling and overcast as James Thomas walked briskly along Deaderick Street in Nashville late the morning of March 6, 1851. He passed the State Bank and made his way through the bustling open market toward the public square. Dominating it was the Davidson County Courthouse, an imposing structure whose first-story facade was decorated with finely hewn stone, while an attractive red brick adorned the upper levels. Atop the roof, the town clock rested in a dome, surrounded by eight Ionic columns. Despite its beauty, the courthouse seemed forbidding on this day, shrouded as it was in a gray mist. James Thomas nervously made his way through the front entrance.[1]

There, he was greeted by Ephraim H. Foster, a distinguished lawyer, politician, and planter who had some years before served as a United States senator from Tennessee. The colonel was a "fine looking, wholesome, good humored person, a warm friend to those he liked," Thomas recalled, but toward his enemies he could be menacing. The two men ascended the stairs to the second floor; passing the marshal's office, they entered the courtroom.[2]

The Davidson County Courthouse, Nashville, ca. 1856. (Source: Photograph courtesy of Tennessee State Library and Archives, Nashville, Tennessee.)

The session began promptly at eleven, with a brief report about a previous case. Then the bailiff announced: "In the matter of the freedom of a boy of color named James Thomas." Foster rose and stood before the nine-judge panel hearing the case. In his late fifties, Foster was eager to assist in the emancipation of slaves he deemed worthy of freedom. None, he believed, was more deserving than the twenty-three-year-old mulatto* man standing next to him. Foster had purchased James Thomas when the boy was only six years old, in 1834, at the behest of the boy's mother, Sally, who feared that her son was about to be sold to

---

*In this book the term *mulatto* will be used when contemporaries employed it to describe persons of mixed racial origin.

an unprincipled owner. Thomas had been born in Nashville, in October 1827, and lived all of his life there, Foster explained. As a young boy, he had learned the barbering trade under the watchful eye of slave-born Frank Parrish, who still managed a popular barbershop. Thomas now ran his own barbering business at his home on Deaderick Street.

Foster concluded by saying that the "said Slave has always maintained a most exemplary character,—he is industrious, honest, moral, & humble & polite & in fact has conducted himself as to gain the confidence & the respect, the good wishes and the constant patronage of all who know him. Believing therefore as your petitioner faithfully does, that said Slave James, is a man of great worth in his place & that he would, as a free man, make a valuable, honest, & excellent citizen, he prays your worships, on this his petition to decree the freedom of said negro James, according to acts of assembly in such cases made and provided." After Foster posted a bond for good behavior, the justices ordered that the "said Slave James, otherwise Called James Thomas, be emancipated, and forever set free."

Thomas was elated, of course, and grateful for Ephraim Foster's support. He also realized, however, that politics swirled around the courthouse, and negative comments from a single white person could derail the proceedings. Important as the decree was, Thomas now faced an even greater challenge. Tennessee law required that manumitted slaves immediately leave the state. The only way he could remain was to make a special plea of his own to the judges, a plea that for many blacks fell on deaf ears.

Tall and handsome, with wavy hair and bright brown skin, Thomas now stood before the judges and offered his own peti-

This rare daguerreotype of Ephraim Foster (1795–1854) was taken about the time Foster appeared in court to testify on James Thomas's behalf. Note that Foster appears to have a long scar running back from his widow's peak. This was the band that kept his head perfectly still for up to fifteen minutes. (SOURCE: DAGUERREOTYPE COURTESY OF CHEEKWOOD MUSEUM OF ART ARCHIVES, NASHVILLE, TENNESSEE.)

tion. Reiterating that he had always resided in the city and that he "led a moral & industrious life," he asserted that he had always "deported himself in such manner, as to engage the confidence, the assistance & the good wishes of the Society in which he lives." He also noted that he earned a good livelihood "by faithful attention to his business" and that if he were forced to leave, he would "be greatly damaged by having to Start anew in some Strange Country & rebuild a character he trusts he has already established in Tennessee." When he finished, the judges conferred. After only a few minutes, they ruled that Thomas could remain in the state if he posted his own bond for good behavior.[3]

The entire proceedings took less than an hour. After thanking Foster, Thomas left the courtroom a free man. The event was not important enough to merit attention in the city's leading newspaper, the *Republican Banner and Nashville Whig.* That day's issue ran an article ironically titled, "The Whole Field of Abolitionism Exposed—Abolitionists Look to Supreme Power." It also printed one of the regularly published notices about runaway slaves: "Fifty Dollars Reward. Ranaway from the subscriber bout the 1st of September last, a negro man (black,) named HANNIBLE, about 25 years of age, about five feet 8 inches in height, and rather stoutly built." The next day's issue announced a sale of six "Likely Negroes," two of whom were described as "a little girl" and "a little Girl suitable for a Nurse."[4]

Returning to his house and shop on Deaderick Street, two blocks away, Thomas ruminated on many things. Gaining his freedom was undoubtedly one of the most momentous events of his life. He should have been happy, relieved, delighted—all

In the matter of the freedom of a boy of color named James Thomas

In the County Court for the County of Davidson in the State of Tennessee being June 1851. Present Sample A. McGavock chairman James Marr, R. B. Marr, C. A. Darnell, David Jones, S. B. Davidson ——— Robert Grines, N. S. Berry & David Scout, Esquires, Judges of said Court & Justices of the Peace in said County, the following memorial was presented to wit: Upton M. Foster, a citizen of said County, respectfully shows unto your worships that C. is now and has been since the 30th day of January 18__ the legal owner of a certain mulatto slave called James Thomas who was born in said County of Davidson in the month of October 182_, and has resided therein all his life, When a youth your petitioner State, that said Slave was placed in a barbers Shop where he remained until his back condition his trade and by and having followed its ever since, is the issue an adept in his business, and profitably employed therein.

Your petitioner further Shews, that said Slave has always maintained a good exemplary character, he is industrious, honest, moral, & humble & polite & in fact has demeaned himself as to gain the confidence & the respect, the good will & constant patronage of all who know him, Believing therefore as your petitioner with full does, that said Slave James is a friend of good and that he would as a free man, make a valuable character & especially useful as he prays your worships in his his petition to decree the freedom of said Negro James according to act of assembly in such cases made and provided.
Upton M. Foster

Whereupon present the better than as aforesaid, the said Court having examined the reasons set to in said petition of said Foster and being of opinion that according to the decree, would be consistent with the interest and policy of the State do order this chairman to refund said petition and it is done accordingly.
S. A. McGavock chairman

Whereupon, the premises considered, said Court is ready and willing to accede to said petition, and to emancipate said slave James, on said Foster first entering into bond with good security according to the act of 1831 chapter 112. And upon at the same time the said Foster having entered into bond with Guy Allison his security according to said law, the Court do order therefore there, being present and concurring there in the order, as jointed & decreed the said Slave James, otherwise called James Thomas, be emancipated, and he is set free according to the terms & conditions specified in said act,

In the County Court for the County of Davids on in the State of Tennessee being June 1851
The petition of James otherwise called James Thomas a free man of color Respectfully represents, to the present term of the examplary [illegible] Court he has, by a third [illegible] & [illegible] being in his term, been essentially [illegible] to prove set [illegible] — He petitioner further shews that he is a native of this State, being born and having always resided in said County of Addison & is now about thirty years of age. Your petitioner further Shews, that he has led a moral & industrious life, and has so behaved himself in his [illegible] to secure the confidence, [illegible]

Although the Davidson County Courthouse burned to the ground in 1856, many of the records were saved, including Ephraim Foster's petition on behalf of his nominal slave James and James Thomas's petition to remain in the state of Tennessee. The transcriptions of these documents appear in Appendix 1 on pages 268–272. (SOURCE: RECORDS OF THE DAVIDSON COUNTY COURT, MINUTE BROOK E [MARCH 1851], 134–135, METROPOLITAN NASHVILLE–DAVIDSON COUNTY ARCHIVES, NASHVILLE, TENNESSEE.)

of those things. Yet the excitement he felt was tempered by the knowledge that his mother was not there to share in the triumph of his being a *free* man. Only six months before, he had purchased a plot in the Nashville cemetery and had put up a tombstone with the inscription SALLY THOMAS, 1787–1850. Up until then, he had lived with his mother his entire life, and they had each managed their separate businesses from the same house, she working as a laundress and he as a barber. He missed her greatly and reflected upon all that she had done to bring about this long-awaited day. He also thought about how she, although still a slave, had devoted her life to freeing his two older brothers, John Rapier and Henry Thomas.

Now, on this extraordinary day, James returned to his shop and settled into his regular routine with a heavy heart. Neither the events of the day nor the presence of his jovial customers lifted his spirits. The memory of Sally made him feel sad and lonely.[5]

NOTES

1. The *Republican Banner and Nashville Whig*, the city's leading newspaper, described the weather in a number of towns and cities but did not include Nashville. It was clear from the weather patterns in Clarksville, about forty miles away, and other towns, however, that a front was moving through the area on March 6, 1851. See *Republican Banner and Nashville Whig*, March 5, 6, 7, 8, 9, 11, 1851. For a description of the Davidson County Courthouse, see Robert M. McBride and Owen Meredith, eds., *Eastin Morris' Tennessee Gazetteer 1834 and Math Rhea's Map of the State of Tennessee 1832* (Nashville: The Gazetteer Press, 1971), 213–14; Douglas Anderson, *The Historic Blue Grass Line: A Review of the History of Davidson and Sumner Counties, Together With Sketches of Places and Events Along the Route of the Nashville-Gallatin Interurban Railway* (Nashville: Nashville-Gallatin Interurban Railway, 1913), 42.

2. Loren Schweninger, ed., *From Tennessee Slave to St. Louis Entrepreneur: The Autobiography of James Thomas,* foreword by John Hope Franklin (Columbia: University of Missouri Press, 1984), 29 (hereafter cited as FTS).

3. Records of the County Court, Davidson County, Tenn., Minute Book E (March Term 1851), 134–35, Metropolitan Nashville–Davidson County Archives, Nashville, Tenn.; the 1831 law concerning emancipation can be found in *A Compilation of the Statutes of Tennessee, of a General and Permanent Nature, from the Commencement of the Government to the Present Time,* compiled by R. L. Caruthers and A.O.P. Nicholson (Nashville: Steam Press of James Smith, 1836), 279.

4. The *Republican Banner and Nashville Whig,* March 6, 7, 1851.

5. Sally Thomas's tombstone inscription can be found in Jeannette Tillotson Acklen, comp., *Tennessee Records: Tombstone Inscriptions and Manuscripts Historical and Biographical,* foreword by John H. DeWitt (Nashville: Cullom and Ghertner Co., 1933), 43. The burial plot James Thomas purchased is recorded in Records of the Nashville City Cemetery, Deed Records, James Thomas to City of Nashville, September 10, 1850, Nashville Room, Public Library of Nashville and Davidson County, Nashville, Tenn.

· One ·

SALLY THOMAS
A Life in Bondage

MORE THAN THIRTY YEARS BEFORE JAMES THOMAS WAS FREED, and some ten years before he was born, his mother began a journey of her own. As she sat in a wagon moving slowly along the road leading out of Charlottesville, Virginia, the slave Sally worried about what might become of her two boys riding with her. Sally's owner, Charles L. Thomas, had died in 1814, followed by the owner's wife two years later, which left Sally and her sons as part of the Thomas estate. That her children had not been taken from her brought Sally little solace. As handsome and energetic youngsters, her sons would fetch a good price. Was she being taken to a new location so that her children could be sold?[1]

She had little time to fret, however, as they journeyed up into the high country, amid the cedars, pines, and evergreens, across the Blue Ridge Mountains, and down into the grassy expanse of the Shenandoah Valley. The wagon wended its way southwest, toward Cumberland Gap, and finally into the dense forests of East Tennessee. Along the way, Sally saw other slaves traveling

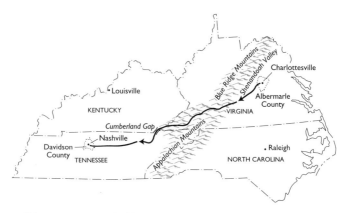

Sally's Journey to Nashville

the same route. Manacled and chained to one another, they trudged along, downcast and dispirited, under the watchful gaze of a slave trader. Neither Sally nor her children were chained. Over a period of several weeks, they came upon an area reminiscent of the rolling hills and dissected countryside they had left behind in Virginia, and eventually reached their destination: the fast-growing Cumberland River town of Nashville, Tennessee.[2]

Born in the year of the Constitutional Convention, Sally was about thirty years old when she made the journey to Tennessee. She had grown up on Charles Thomas's 1,596-acre tobacco plantation, in Albemarle County, Virginia, situated on the north side of the north fork of the Hardware River. She had lived near Thomas Jefferson's Monticello and heard stories about her famous neighbor. She may even have heard that Jefferson was the father of several children by one of his slaves, also named Sally.[3]

Most of the slave women on the Thomas plantation labored alongside the men in the tobacco fields. They worked from sunup to sundown, season after season, year after year. They prepared beds, planted seeds, transplanted shoots, wormed and topped young plants; during the harvest, they hung, stripped, sorted, and bundled the final product. During the winter, the female slaves, like the men, rolled logs, split rails, and put up fencing. In addition, women shucked corn, sewed, cooked, knitted, and dealt with the difficulties of pregnancy, childbirth, and child rearing. While Charles Thomas was neither harsh nor cruel, Sally knew about other whites on neighboring plantations who treated female slaves as roughly as they treated the men, failing to provide them with adequate food and housing, working them long hours in the rain and cold, giving them few respites during pregnancy, and meting out severe punishments for breaking plantation rules.

As an attractive young woman, Sally had drawn the attention of one of the Thomas men, probably John L. Thomas, her owner's brother, and had either suffered or accepted his sexual advances. In 1808, when she was twenty-one, she had given birth to a mulatto son, John; the next year, in October 1809, to a second mulatto son, Henry. As with all slave states, Virginia required that offspring take the status of the mother. Consequently, both boys were born into bondage. In 1814, the inventory of Charles L. Thomas's estate listed "Henry a Boy," valued at three hundred dollars, and "Sally a Woman," assessed at three hundred fifty. Sally's son John went unlisted among the thirty-seven other slaves, but Sally stood out as the most highly valued slave woman on the plantation.[4]

When she arrived in Nashville, the town limits stretched back only a few blocks from the riverfront, and the population included only a few thousand souls. The streets were dusty in summer and muddy in winter; dogs, cattle, milk cows, and hogs meandered in and out of the city limits. Even in those early days, however, it was clear that the town was on the rise as the entrepôt for the Cumberland River Valley, the county seat for Davidson County, and, after 1826, the state capital.[5] The population nearly tripled during the 1810s and almost doubled again during the next decade, with one out of three residents listed as a slave. By 1830, the town boasted about thirty-five hundred white and two thousand black inhabitants year round, but those modest numbers masked the bustling commercial and political activity during the time of the year when court was in session or when the legislature met.[6]

VIRTUAL FREEDOM

One advantage Sally quickly discovered: Nashville offered good opportunities for a few privileged blacks. Even as a slave, Robert Rentfro, better known as "Black Bob," obtained permission from the county court "to sell Liquor and Victuals on his Good Behavior." Later, he bought his freedom and became the proprietor of a popular inn and livery stable at the sign of the Cross Keys on the public square.[7] Freed by her owner, Thomas Malloy, mulatto woman Sophy was also able to arrange for the freedom of her two brothers after Malloy's death. She called upon John Cockrill and entreated him to pay nine hundred dollars to Malloy's estate. Cockrill agreed, and later acknowledged that Sophy had completely reimbursed him.[8] Temperance Crutcher, another slave born and raised in Nashville, purchased her freedom and successfully petitioned to remain in Tennessee as a free woman of color. "Nashville is, and allways has been her home," she explained, "and is the home of her kindred and friends."[9]

Shortly after her arrival, Sally obtained permission from her owner to hire herself out as a laundress, a practice common among urban slaves. This meant she could approach employers, arrange for work to be done, and retain a portion of her earnings. Sometime later, she rented a frame house on the corner of Deaderick and Cherry streets, in the central business district. There she established her business, which specialized in washing and cleaning men's and women's fine apparel. She converted the front room into a laundry, where she manufactured her own soap, blending fats, oils, alkali, and salt in a small vat.[10]

As the city grew during the 1820s, Sally built up a loyal clientele. During the morning, she made her rounds to homes and businesses, collecting sheets, towels, dresses, shirts, trousers, coats, hats, jackets, and undergarments. She then returned to begin the arduous process of sorting and cleaning. She specialized in fine linens and clothing made of velvet, silk, and cashmere. Despite a recession during the early 1820s, the wealth of white residents rose dramatically during the decade. Consequently, the demand for Sally's services increased. As her reputation for high-quality work spread, Sally Thomas, as she now called herself, had more business than she could handle.

Even during these early years, it was apparent that Sally was not a slave in the usual sense. Though she was supervised by a member of the Thomas family, he permitted her to come and go as she pleased, and found such an arrangement advantageous and profitable.[11] Part of the advantage to him was that he did not have to worry about negotiating hiring contracts or receiving his monthly payments. As time passed, Sally became what contemporaries termed a "quasi-slave." The term was used to describe slaves who had been permitted freedom by their master but who had not obtained a formal deed of emancipation from the state[12]—an ambiguous and contradictory position to be in. Sally moved about freely, rented her own house, ran her own business, negotiated her own contracts, bought and sold various items, and possessed her own property. It was, of course, against the law for slaves to act in such a manner, but residents of Nashville valued Sally's services enough that they either did not care or might not have known that she was in fact a slave.

Sally dreamed of someday saving enough money to purchase her children as well as herself out of bondage. But even with her drive and ambition, this seemed highly unlikely. Her income rarely exceeded fifteen or twenty dollars a month. Although she was eventually spared from paying "freedom dues"—the specified amount that slaves paid to owners for the privilege of hiring themselves out—she did have various household and business expenses. Meanwhile, young slave children were selling for as much as three hundred dollars, and handsome, intelligent, "likely" women such as Sally Thomas, despite being older, might bring four or five hundred dollars.[13] Even if she could save enough to purchase her children and herself, it would take many years.

SALLY'S CHILDREN

Her plan for her eldest son, however, did not involve buying him out of slavery. Instead, she arranged for him to work as a personal waiter and "pole boy" for Richard Rapier, a barge captain who navigated the western rivers. Before the United States acquired the Louisiana Territory in 1803, Rapier had formed a partnership with two Nashville men to transport hogsheads of tobacco down the Cumberland, Ohio, and Mississippi rivers to New Orleans, returning with necessities for residents of Nashville.[14] By the time Sally's son joined him, Captain Rapier, a large, fleshy man weighing more than two hundred pounds, was well known to city residents. One newspaper announced in the spring of 1818 that "The Barge General Jackson Has arrived, with a large & General assortment of Groceries"; the "groceries" included tea, cheese, pepper, raisins, sugar, jam, coffee, and sweetmeats. Rapier also brought nails, candles, gunpowder, wine, including Madeira, sherry, port, and claret, and an assortment of fish that included shad, salmon, herring, and cod.[15] Sally admonished her son John, who was about ten years old, to follow the captain's instructions and to work diligently and industriously. She knew that Rapier was an honorable man, and if her son performed his tasks well, she believed he might be able to gain his freedom by self-purchase, or by performing some "meritorious act."

A short time after she made this arrangement, Rapier shifted his operations to Florence, Alabama, located below Muscle Shoals on the Tennessee River.[16] Sally saw John rarely after that, but she learned in 1824 that Rapier had set aside a sum of money, as he disclosed to an Alabama court, "for the purpose of purchasing the freedom of the mulatto boy, John, who now waits on me, and belongs to the Estate of Thomas."[17] In 1826, following Rapier's death, Sally learned that the executors of his estate had carried out the barge master's wishes. They purchased

John from the Thomas estate in Virginia for one thousand dollars. In 1829, the executors obtained permission from the Alabama General Assembly "to emancipate a certain male slave by the name of John H. Rapier."[18]

Sally Thomas was overjoyed. Her eldest son, age twenty-one, was legally free. As Richard Rapier's personal servant, he had also learned to read and write. Her joy was diminished, however, by the challenge she still faced to free the rest of her family. In October 1827, at the age of forty, she gave birth to her third mulatto son, James, who, according to the laws of Tennessee, was also born a slave.

Whatever affection James's prominent white father may have had for Sally, he had little regard for his son. "Now my own father was the Hon C and filled chairs of distinction," James recalled bitterly many years later. "He presided over the Supreme Court (of Tennessee) ten Years but he had no time to give me a thought. He gave me twenty five cents once. If I was correctly informed that was all he ever did for me."

The "Hon C" stood for the "Honorable" John Catron, who had settled in Nashville about the same time as Sally and was almost the same age as she. The son of a German immigrant, Catron had only a common school education but read voraciously. He studied law after his father moved to the tiny village of Sparta, Tennessee, and later transferred to Nashville to practice law. He was appointed to the Supreme Court of Tennessee in the mid-1820s, and to the United States Supreme Court by fellow Democrat Andrew Jackson in 1837. Active in politics, Catron directed the presidential campaign of Martin Van Buren in Tennessee. He never acknowledged his relationship to his son.[19]

In 1831, John Catron (1786–1865) became the first chief justice of the Tennessee Supreme Court. When the United States Supreme Court expanded to nine members, Andrew Jackson appointed Catron, a Democrat, as an associate justice in 1837. He served until his death, in 1865, voting with the majority in Dred Scott v. Sanford, *the case that declared blacks had no rights as citizens.* (SOURCE: PHOTOGRAPH COURTESY OF TENNESSEE STATE MUSEUM COLLECTION, NASHVILLE, TENNESSEE.)

Sally sensed that it would be nearly impossible to save enough money to purchase both her second son, Henry, now a young man and valued on the slave market at a substantial amount, and her son James, who was valued at two hundred dollars even as an infant. Despite this discouraging prospect, she threw her energies into her business. As soon as James became old enough, he, like John and Henry before him, began running errands, keeping water in the kettle for making soap, chopping wood for the fireplace, and delivering cleaned clothes. By the early 1830s, Sally's stringent economy and diligent efforts bore fruit. She had saved several hundred dollars, mostly in Mexican gold coins, which she kept hidden in a tea canister in the loft of her rented home. This Spartan regimen continued unabated until 1834, when she received devastating news. The Thomas estate was about to be broken up and distributed among various heirs, and the estate wanted its human assets returned forthwith to Charlottesville.[20]

"My recolections of Early life are many, but none are so vivid as the one instance where I was [load]ed in a vehicle of some sort bound for Charlottsville," James Thomas began his autobiography, "there to be turned over to one of the rightful heirs of one Thomas, son of old Dr Thomas who had come from Virginia some twenty or more years before." Sally, of course, came too, overcome with grief as she retraced her journey after so many years. For years she had carved out a new life for herself in Nashville, establishing herself as a well-known business person and building up a thriving trade. Would this all now come to an end? Would her sons be sold away from her? Would she be sold to slave traders and taken to some distant land? For the first time in many years Sally felt helpless.

Upon their arrival, the old homestead seemed smaller and the countryside appeared less bountiful than Sally remembered. Many of the whites she had known were dead, and most of her slave contemporaries had died too, or been sold or traded. As it turned out, however, Sally and James were neither sold nor separated, but taken back to Nashville pending the final distribution of the estate. Soon Sally learned that a distant Thomas family relative by marriage, John M. Martin, had inherited her and James. "Mr Martin was a most affable man," James recalled, "full of joke, one of those smiling kind that you cant always judge what is behind the smile." Sally believed that behind his cordial demeanor

During the early twentieth century, James Thomas's children admonished him to stop talking about "the good old times" and write down some of his reminiscences. Accepting their advice, in 1903–1904 he wrote one of the most revealing autobiographies written by a former slave. Pictured here is the first page of the manuscript, eventually published in 1984. Loren Schweninger, ed., From Tennessee Slave to St. Louis Entrepreneur, foreword by John Hope Franklin (Columbia: University of Missouri Press, 1984), 26, 27. (SOURCE: COURTESY OF MOORLAND-SPINGARN RESEARCH CENTER, HOWARD UNIVERSITY, WASHINGTON, D.C.)

Martin was a greedy and reckless young man. She feared he would sell her and her son at a moment's notice, especially if he became hard up for cash. "My mother spent many sleepless nights on account of the turn things had taken,"[21] James wrote.

Henry did not accompany his mother and brother on their journey back to Virginia. In his mid-twenties, tall, athletic, and intelligent, Sally's second son was appraised at far more than she could ever have afforded to pay to buy him out of slavery, even if his new owner had been willing to sell. Sally also knew that Henry was likely to be one of the first slaves sold out of the estate, and would bring a handsome price. After agonizing over his possible fate, she urged him to run away. Sally knew well the dangers of running away, having observed many captured fugitives, chained hand and foot, trudging through the streets with marks of the lash on their backs. She had heard tales about runaways who perished in the wilderness or died at the hands of patrols, slave catchers, or specially bred attack dogs.[22] But sometime in 1834, Henry disappeared from Nashville, where he lived. And then, for Sally, the anxious waiting began—for any news, good or bad.

It would be many months before she learned of Henry's fate. Running at night and sleeping during the day, he avoided the main roads and skirted the tobacco, wheat, corn, and oat fields in southern and central Kentucky. Within two weeks, he reached the fringes of Louisville, where he was spotted, arrested, and jailed. That same night, however, he managed to escape, sneak down to the Ohio River, and unfasten a small boat. Rowing into the swift current, he suddenly heard the roar of "the falls," a drop in the river followed by several hundred yards of turbulent rapids. Entering the white water, Henry considered it a miracle that his boat did not capsize. He made it to the Indiana shore, and soon found a man willing to cut off his chains. He then set off across the countryside, heading northeast and putting as much distance as he could between himself and his pursuers.[23] Although it was a relief to know that Henry was safe and free, Sally would never see her middle son again.

She occasionally did see her eldest son, now known as John Rapier. Following his emancipation in 1829, John opened a barbershop in Florence, Alabama, and married a free black woman from Baltimore named Susan. During the 1830s, John and Susan had four children: Richard, born in 1831 and named after the barge captain; John Jr., born in 1835; Henry, born in 1836 and named after Rapier's fugitive brother; and James Thomas Rapier, born in 1837 and named after his father's youngest slave brother.[24] Living only one hundred twenty miles from Nashville, John Rapier traveled up to see his mother whenever possible, sometimes taking his boys with him. Before the oldest son reached the age of ten, however, Susan Rapier died in childbirth, at the age of twenty-nine. Only the etching on her tombstone, located in the white section of the Florence cemetery, told of her birth on Christmas Day 1811; of her death, along with the death of her two infant children, Jackson and Alexander, in 1841; and of her final wishes: DEPART MY FRIENDS AND DRY UPON YOUR TEARS, FOR I MUST LIE HEAR TILL CHRIST APPEARS.[25]

SALLY'S SON JAMES

Following Henry's escape, Sally turned her attention to protecting her youngest son, James, from John Martin. In 1834, she sought an audience with Ephraim Foster, a prominent lawyer.

Foster had known Aunt Sally, as he called her, for many years and recognized her remarkable qualities. In fact, he had recommended that Sally switch her new baby's name from James, a reference to the apostle, to Andrew Jackson, a reference to Foster's political hero. Wishing to please, Sally called her son James Andrew Jackson, until Foster switched to the Whig Party and supported Jackson's opponent, Henry Clay. Sally now came to Foster, still anxious about her third son's uncertain fate.

"I want you to talk with him [Martin] and learn what he will take for the boy," Sally said. "Maybe we can get Jim or Jackson out of his reach."

"Very good, Aunt Sally," Foster replied, "I will see him and I will let you know what can be done."

A few days later, Foster told Sally that Martin wanted four hundred dollars for six-year-old James, a price that seemed exorbitant. Although she had spent many years putting coins in her canister, Sally had saved only three hundred fifty dollars. She asked Foster if he would lend her the remaining fifty dollars and purchase the boy for her, and promised to pay him back as soon as possible. Foster consented, and the deal was struck. A short time later, she paid off the debt and received a bill of sale, "free papers," for young James.[26]

Even then, however, James was not free. Tennessee law required emancipated blacks to secure a manumission deed from the county court and "thereupon immediately leave Tennessee." Thus, despite having "free papers," James remained in bondage. "Many persons congratulated mother and approved of her thoughtfulness," James recalled. "All the best people of the community gave her credit and thought better of her." Some residents, however, believed she had acted strangely, purchasing her son before purchasing herself.

About two years later, Sally's owner, John Martin, called on Sally and asked if she would sell James back to him for the same amount. In return, he promised to set her free. Sally explained that her son was now on record as belonging to Ephraim Foster; Martin would have to see Foster if he wanted to buy the boy. She, of course, knew that Foster would not consent to such a sale.[27]

Eventually, Sally purchased herself with the assistance of Nashville businessman G. M. Fogg, who lent her part of the two-hundred-dollar price that Martin was asking. She again later paid off the debt. Despite these exceptional efforts, both she and her son remained slaves in the eyes of the law. The deeds in the county courthouse listed James as the property of Ephraim Foster, and Sally as the property of G. M. Fogg. If anything happened to either of them, or if for some reason Foster or Fogg ever needed to dispose of a portion of his property, Sally and James might legally be sold.

Despite this gnawing fear, Sally went about her work with energy and enthusiasm. She taught her son the laundry business, making him her assistant until he was about twelve. She even hired a blacksmith to fashion a special, custom-made lightweight ax so young James could cut up logs to fit their fireplace. Although illiterate herself, she believed it was vitally important that her children learn to read and write. When she could spare him from work, she arranged for James to attend school. James Thomas recalled:

> A portion of the year (some years) the authorities allowed a school to be kept for teaching the children of free persons [of color]. In that school I learned to read and write. It was surprising to a great

many whites to see a colored boy or man with a newspaper. Often they would ask, 'Can you read.' It was a question with many people whether it was the proper thing to have a school for free persons for two reasons. First they might write passes for the slaves. Second it might cause the slave to want the same.[28]

James was right: few free blacks attended school in the southern states at the time. Some states passed laws designed to keep black children illiterate and most slave owners opposed a literate black population. In South Carolina, for example, an 1834 law stipulated that any white person caught teaching a slave to read or write could be fined up to one hundred dollars and imprisoned for up to six months; any free black convicted of the same offense could be fined fifty dollars and receive up to fifty lashes on the bare back. Similar statutes were passed in Virginia, North Carolina, Georgia, and Alabama.[29]

Although Tennessee and several other states did not pass laws prohibiting the teaching of blacks, during the 1830s, James Thomas recalled, the Nashville school was often closed. One night, when James was quite young, Alonso Summer, the school's black teacher, was taken out by a gang of ruffians and whipped nearly to death. Described as a fine scholar, Summer was accused of helping runaway slaves. The leader of the gang, James Thomas noted, was "a son of the most distinguished Jurist in the state."[30] Despite these obstacles, James and a number of other blacks, both slave and free, attended the school over the years.

Such violent episodes underscored the delicate nature of race relations. Sally Thomas understood that any hint of "impropriety" could result in extreme retribution, even for a person like her, who was well-acquainted with many prominent whites. She realized that her reputation as a skilled laundress who offered valuable services enabled her to act in the ways that she did: to approach prominent whites; to outsmart a greedy slave owner like Martin; and to protect her children. She also realized that maintaining her reputation for probity and continuing her outwardly submissive behavior were essential. Sally therefore worked incessantly, driven by the fear that at any moment even their white "protectors" could not prevent her or her son from ending up like so many of the slaves she had observed. Worse still, she worried that she or her son might be kidnapped and sold to the sugar plantations of the Deep South.[31]

So, day in and day out, she watched herself, taking care never to appear arrogant, assertive, haughty, or high-spirited. Any argument over the cost of her services or the behavior of her son could result in a serious incident. Any hostile gesture, display of anger, or refusal to step aside for a white woman could lead to grave repercussions. Few understood this better than Sally Thomas, who, despite her enormous drive and ambition, charted a deferential course with a single goal: freedom for her three boys.

Not only did Sally have to understand the nuances of racial etiquette, she also needed to know the vagaries of the law. In 1839, the Tennessee legislature passed an act making it unlawful for slaves to hire themselves out, own certain types of property, trade certain goods, negotiate contracts, or in any way act as free persons. The law appeared to be aimed directly at quasi-free slaves like Sally Thomas.[32]

It was during periods of heightened racial tension that Sally felt most vulnerable. This was the case on August 17, 1840, the day of the great Whig political convention, when a slave outside of

Nashville named Jake killed his owner, Robert Bradford, an old and respected farmer. On the morning of the convention, Jake, described as a large, raw-boned, and quick-spoken man, refused to go out into the fields. Slaves on many neighboring plantations had been given the day off to go listen to the speeches at the convention and join in the festivities. Jake argued that he should be given time off, too. When Bradford ordered the overseer to tie Jake up and give him a good whipping, Jake drew a knife. James Thomas, who attended the Whig convention, remarked that "Whether he aimed to cut the rope or the Overseer no one knew, but he made a wild thrust which killed Mr Bradford on the spot." Jake fled into the woods and remained at large for months, despite a large reward offered by the governor. Eventually, he was captured, tried, convicted, and hanged. Many owners took their slaves to see the hanging, Thomas noted; this was done to show blacks what might become of them if they became violent.[33]

Despite her fears, Sally knew how much better off she was than the vast majority of slaves who rarely reaped the benefits of their hard work, and had to adopt other tactics: malingering, theft, destruction of property, violence, deception, and flight. Attempts to escape usually ended in failure and sometimes resulted in severe whippings, brutal beatings, incarceration, and even branding. Sally knew slaves whose anger and hatred festered for years; others who seemed depressed and lifeless, unable to recover from the loss of a loved one. She had witnessed slave children sold away from their mothers, prodded aboard steamboats like cattle. She had seen the desperation in the eyes of mothers and fathers and husbands and wives. She knew slaves who cared little about anything beyond a good meal and warm clothing,

A PROCLAMATION,

By James K. Polk, Governor of the State of Tennessee.

To all who shall see these presents, Greeting:

WHEREAS, it has been made known to me that a certain negro man (slave) named JACOB, charged with having committed an atrocious murder on the 17th day of August, (instant,) upon the body of his master, Robert Bradford, late of our county of Davidson, has fled from justice and is now running at large:

Now, therefore, I, James K. Polk, Governor as aforesaid, by virtue of the authority in me vested, do hereby offer a reward of ONE HUNDRED DOLLARS, to any person or persons who may apprehend the said negro man named JACOB, and deliver him to the Sheriff or Jailor of our county of Davidson, in order that justice in that behalf may be had and executed.

IN TESTIMONY WHEREOF, I have hereunto set my hand and caused the great seal of the State to be affixed at the city of Nashville, on this 20th day of August, 1840.

JAMES K. POLK.

By the Governor:
John S. Young, Secretary of State.

DESCRIPTION.

The said negro (JACOB) is about thirty years old, six feet or upwards high, of rather bright complexion, weighs about 160 or 170 pounds, has rather a down look, raw-boned, prominent cheek bones, is very quick spoken, and had on when he escaped, white homespun linsey pantaloons and roundabout coat.

TWO HUNDRED & THIRTY DOLLARS, in addition to the above reward, will be given by the friends and relatives of the deceased for the apprehension of the said boy.

September 7, 1840,—tf

Issued by Tennessee Governor James K. Polk, this notice announced a huge reward (three hundred thirty dollars all told) for the capture and return of the fugitive Jacob [Jake]. The reward was nearly fifteen times the average reward for a runaway in the state. In other respects, however, this notice was similar to many thousands of other runaway advertisements published all across the South. (SOURCE: NASHVILLE WHIG, SEPTEMBER 9, 1840.)

who were casualties of a system that reduced people to eating like animals and living in filth and squalor.

Legally still a slave, Sally Thomas maneuvered within the system with remarkable agility. In about 1839, she arranged for twelve-year-old James to work as an assistant to one of the most prominent physicians in the city, Dr. John Esselman, who attended Andrew Jackson and other prominent Tennesseans. She believed that James could learn a great deal from the doctor, and hoped this might bode well for his future.

Located on Cherry Street, a short distance from Sally's house, Dr. Esselman's office was divided into two parts: the front section contained shelves lined with hundreds of bottles of various medicines; the rear section was an open space containing an "old fashioned split-bottomed chair." The back area seemed like a small theater, with the chair as the only prop standing at center stage. "When a patient came the Dr would take down a bottle or two, mix his pills or what was needed, use his mortar or bottle as the medicine required," James Thomas later explained; he would then escort the patient to the chair in the rear. One of the doctor's specialties was extracting teeth. Jimmy, as the doctor called James, was instructed to hold the patient's forehead tightly while Esselman performed the operation. "When I took hold of the head, the patient was in for a rough deal," James Thomas noted, though the doctor assured his patient the extraction might hurt, though "not much." Esselman

would get out his instrument of torture and carefully role a silk handkerchief around it . . . He would get hold of the tooth. The instrument had a handle the same as a corkscrew. Neither of us let go until the tooth came out and sometimes the jawbone with it. I cant describe the yell that went with the operation.

James also assisted the doctor when it came time to bleed his patients. "The doctor would give them some kind of stick to grasp with the arm straight out from the body," James Thomas wrote. After Esselman applied a tourniquet and punctured the vein, "I would be called to hold the tin pan to catch the blood," which would "spurt about Eighteen inches describing a half-circle where it struck the basin." James remembered taking the pan of blood and pouring it out by the back fence of the yard, where the ducks would come up and fight over it until it was gone.[34]

As much as she wished him to do well and as much as she tried to protect him from those who might do him harm, Sally Thomas was not an overly protective mother. As she grew older, she came to realize that one of the best ways for her children to mature was for them to travel, even though she herself was confined to Davidson County. Consequently, in 1842, when her son James was not yet fifteen years old, she arranged for him to visit New Orleans, booking passage for him on the steamer *Nashville*. Thanks to her friendship with Captain Rapier, Sally had close ties with a number of rivermen, who were also her customers. It would not have been out of the question for her to arrange for one of them to keep a close eye on James, even though he was tall of stature and mature for his years.

Only the sweet smell of magnolias near Port Hudson, Mississippi, and the clouds of mosquitoes at various fueling stations broke the monotony of the journey down the Cumberland, Ohio, and Mississippi rivers. The canebrakes pressed against the riverbank with only an occasional opening for a plantation dock or woodpile landing.[35]

James's first glimpse of the Crescent City, however, remained one of the most vivid memories of his life. More than seventy years later he recalled the panorama of masts that stretched as far as the eye could see, the hundreds of multicolor flags atop vessels from every corner of the globe, and the sweating black dock workers loading and unloading cargo. Climbing over piles of freight boxes, the young man crossed the levee and began making his way through the city. He passed the small curio shops, the busy French Market, the colorful sidewalk cafés, and the tile-roofed Spanish houses that bordered the streets teeming with drays and pedestrians. The city was well-drained, he later wrote, and everyone seemed neatly dressed, polite, and genial. Toward evening he found accommodation, wearily admitting that "the first day's tramp" had furnished him with enough material to talk about for many years.[36]

In succeeding days, he visited the American section, taking in the hotels, theaters, saloons, and gambling establishments. One

----

On his first visit to New Orleans, James Thomas saw many black dock workers. Slaves and free blacks loaded and unloaded tens of thousands of bales of raw cotton each year for export to textile mills in the North and Great Britain. By the 1840s, more than four hundred steamboats were berthed along the city's levee. By the eve of the Civil War, cotton constituted nearly two-thirds of the total export trade of the United States and was bringing in nearly two hundred million dollars per year. Notice the black woman at the bottom left balancing a basket on her head, as black people did in West Africa, and another black woman selling various items from under a canopy. (SOURCE: BALLOU'S PICTORIAL DRAWING-ROOM COMPANION, JUNE 5, 1858, COURTESY OF MICHAEL MARLEAU.)

evening, at nine o'clock, he heard a shot ring out, the curfew for all slaves to be off the streets. Continuing his excursion, he passed several more gambling houses. Inside, he observed well-dressed black waiters serving elegant suppers of fish and game to tables of distinguished-looking white gentlemen, whom he speculated were probably governors, judges, or United States senators.[37]

He was also struck by the variety of the city's black people, who hailed from such diverse locations as the Caribbean, Central America, South America, and Africa. One Sunday afternoon, as he turned a corner in the neighborhood of Esplanade and Royal streets, he came upon a public square where several hundred blacks were dancing, singing, swaying, clapping, and chanting to music he had never heard before. James Thomas recalled:

> [Slaves] were given a (what is now a park) large Square Called Congo green where they indulged in dancing with music made by thumping on the head of a barrel with a skin stretched over it. The performer would thump on it and carry on a chant. Another would beat the sides with two cobs or sticks. The dancers used to wear pieces of tin or some substitute on their legs to make a sort of jingle. I judged it was African music.[38]

These were exhilarating experiences, and after a few weeks, as James began his journey back to Nashville, the sights and sounds of New Orleans swirled in his head.[39]

SALLY'S GRANDCHILDREN: THE RAPIER BOYS

As James Thomas was growing into manhood during the early 1840s and enjoying his first experience of travel, Sally's oldest son was grieving over the loss of his wife. Before Susan's death, John

Rapier Sr. had purchased a young mulatto slave named Lucretia to assist with chores and help take care of his children. Lucretia, however, was only about fifteen, and it was obvious that even with her assistance John could not manage a barbershop and raise four energetic youngsters.[40] In addition, there was no school nearby where he could send his boys. In a quandary as to what to do, he asked his mother if she would take two of the boys.

Within a short time, John Jr. and James Rapier arrived in Nashville. They lived with their grandmother Sally, now approaching her mid-fifties, and would attend the same school their slave uncle James had attended some years earlier. As it happened, it was a perfect time for them to go to school in Nashville. The assault on Alonso Summer had been forgotten. Free black Daniel Wadkins would soon open a school for free blacks and a small number of slave children in a house on Front Street, near the jail. Wadkins taught reading, writing, arithmetic, and geography, but unlike previous black teachers in the city, he taught continuously for fourteen years, from 1842 to 1856. As time passed, he taught larger and larger classes that numbered between thirty and sixty-six students. To avoid public scrutiny, he moved the school's location on at least six different occasions. "Until yesterday we were not aware that there were several schools for free negroes in the city," the editor of the Nashville *Union* noted in 1850, "and all of them in a flourishing condition." Demanding, energetic, and knowledgeable, Wadkins was a man of remarkable ability and courage. He had a profound effect on the Rapier brothers.[41]

"My two sons that are with mother are well when I last heard from them," John Rapier Sr. wrote from Florence, Alabama, in

1843. "John and James are well please with thir grand mother and Do not want to come home So James writes."[42] Two years later, he added that James, who was seven, "reads well for a little Boy" and John Jr., who was nearly ten, "writes very plain for a boy of his age and practice and has as much taste for reading as any child I know off and very good in arithmetic."[43] An observer later noted that John Jr. became the protégé of a distinguished lawyer in the city; following a fire in the lawyer's home, John received many damaged books, which he "eagerly devoured."[44]

John Rapier Sr. kept Henry, his third son, at home. The father lamented that Henry cared little about learning or school and that he never seemed to be out of trouble of one kind or another. Rapier sent the oldest boy, Richard, to live with John's own brother, Henry, who, following his escape, had settled in Buffalo, New York, opened a barbershop, married a young woman named Maria, and taken the surname of Thomas.[45] Sally's second son was now known as Henry K. Thomas. John Rapier Sr. urged his son Richard to study his lessons well so that he could be held up as an example to his younger brothers. "I am in hopes you will show me that you have not Been in Buffalo all this time for nothing," Rapier wrote; he was well-pleased with his son's penmanship and hoped that his other studies were "as much improved." He wrote Richard, "you are Blessed if [you] will look at your situation that you have kind relation who are anctious to see you grow up an ornament to society." The father admonished his son to do all that his uncle and aunt asked him to do for they had his best interests at heart and would never ask him to do anything that was improper. Indeed, he asked Richard to treat Henry's wife, Maria, who was still in her teens, as if she were his own mother.[46]

With three of his boys away from home, John Rapier Sr. pondered what might become of them if anything should happen to him. As a free person of color, he feared that they could be enslaved, or might not receive a share of his property after his death. While whites, including widows, had built-in protections against such eventualities, free blacks did not. Consequently, Rapier petitioned to the Alabama General Assembly, asking lawmakers to protect his children. His standing among whites as a person of integrity, honesty, and industry served him well as the assembly enacted a law stating "That the following named children of John Rapier, a free man of color, viz: Richard, Henry, John and James, be, and they are hereby ligitimated, as the children of John H. Rapier, and capable both in law and equity of receiving and inheriting the estate of the said father, to all intents and purposes as though they had been born in lawful wedlock."[47]

Though he was worth several thousand dollars, John Rapier Sr.'s financial condition did not improve during the 1840s. The barbering business was slow, especially during the severe depression that took place early in the decade. The ideal location of his shop, which he operated from his white frame house on Court Street, in downtown Florence, mattered little in the face of an economic downturn that hit those in the service sector particularly hard. In 1843, Rapier complained that he had never seen such hard times in Alabama; produce was worth practically nothing; cotton prices were down from nine to four and a half cents a pound; and male slaves brought only four hundred fifty dollars each, while female slaves brought only three hundred fifty, half of what they had been before the depression. With banks closing their doors, many people were losing farms and homes.

Alabama bank notes were discounted forty percent, and the state had recently increased taxes, and included, Rapier complained, a new one-dollar capitation tax on free men of color. Despite the downturn, Rapier sent his mother and brother small amounts of money to help defray his sons' expenses. To conserve his own resources, he planted a large vegetable garden. Bragging to his son Richard in Buffalo, Rapier wrote, "i have a fine prospect of a good garden at the present most of the things are up and growing."[48]

In raising her children, Sally had succeeded against difficult odds. Her goal of maintaining her independence while protecting her family was fraught with difficulty. Despite her quasi-free status, she had feared the worst when she and James were taken to Virginia to be distributed among the heirs of the Thomas estate. Even after returning to Nashville, she and her youngest son might have been sold without the intervention of her white friends, especially Ephraim Foster. It was in part her good fortune and in part her ability to maintain her reputation for honesty and integrity that provided her with a measure of protection. Even under the best of circumstances, she recognized the fragile nature of her status. It would be a simple matter for her to be taken up and sold. In such an eventuality, she feared the worst for young James.

Notes

1. FTS, 2, 28; Records of the County Court, Albemarle County, Va., Deed Book 6 (July 14, 1814), 26, County Courthouse, Charlottesville, Va. There were a number of Thomases who owned slaves named Sally in Albemarle County during the period, but only one family fits the description provided by James Thomas in his recollections. John M. Martin served as executor of the will of Margaret Thomas, wife of Charles Thomas; Martin

also acted as guardian of the couple's children after Margaret's death. For material on the white Thomas family in Virginia, see Records of the County Court, Albemarle County, Va., Indenture, Charles L. Thomas to John L. Thomas (Charles's brother), Deed Book 19 (May 9, 1814), 236–39. This created a trust estate for Charles's mother, Frances Thomas. Bill of Sale, Charles L. Thomas to Mary Thomas (Charles L. Thomas's daughter) for the slave Betsey, Deed Book 19 (May 9, 1814), 459; Inventory, Estate of Charles L. Thomas, deceased, Will Book 6 (July 14, 1814), 26–27; Last Will and Testament of Margaret Thomas, Will Book 6 (December 14, 1815), 184; Estate of Charles L. Thomas, deceased, Will Book 6 (October 23, 1816), 193–95; Administrator's Accounts, Estate of Charles L. Thomas, Will Book 9 (1817–1827), 179–91; Division of Land, Estate of Charles L. Thomas, Will Book 9 (May 6, 1826), 267–68; Decree, Division of Slaves, Will Book 9 (November 17, 1825), 260; Deed of Gift, Charles Lewis Thomas (Charles's son) to John L. Thomas, Deed Book 32 (January 2, 1835), 89–90; Edgar Woods, *Albemarle County in Virginia* (Charlottesville, Va.: The Michie Company Printers, 1901) 223–24, 392. This study indicates that one of Charles L. Thomas's sons, Charles Lewis Thomas, and one of his daughters, Frances Elizabeth Thomas, migrated to Tennessee. William L. Norford, *Marriages of Albemarle County and Charlottesville, Virginia, 1781–1929* (Charlottesville, Va.: Jarman Printing, 1956) 128, 202, 223.

2. For a description of the slave trade and frontier Nashville, see Donald R. Wright, *African Americans in the Early Republic, 1789–1831* (Arlington Heights, Ill., Harlan Davidson, Inc., 1993), 8–12; Walter Johnson, *Soul by Soul: Life Inside the Antebellum Slave Market* (Cambridge, Mass.: Harvard University Press, 1999), 7–122; Anita Shafer Goodstein, *Nashville 1780–1860: From Frontier to City* (Gainesville: University of Florida Press, 1989), 205.

3. Annette Gordon-Reed, *Thomas Jefferson and Sally Hemings: An American Controversy* (Charlottesville: University of Virginia Press, 1997).

4. The paternity of the two boys cannot be determined with certainty. They were both of mixed racial origin. Considering how well Sally and the boys were treated, and her naming her firstborn John, it is probable they were the children of John L. Thomas, Charles L. Thomas's brother, who lived in Henrico County. Sally's son John was born in 1808. See Records

of the Probate Court, Will Records, Lauderdale County, Ala., vols. 5 and 6 (June 3, 1824), 117, County Courthouse, Florence, Ala.; *Acts of the Eleventh Annual Session of the General Assembly of the State of Alabama* (Tuscaloosa: McGuire, Henry and Walker, 1830), 36. Her son Henry was born on October 21, 1809. See Mary Louis Sheffield Ragland, transcriber, "Fisher Funeral Home Records, Vicksburg, Mississippi, September 9, 1878–April 1, 1883," Mississippi Department of Archives and History, Jackson, Miss.

5. The state capital moved several times during the early decades of the nineteenth century, from Knoxville to Nashville in 1812, back to Knoxville in 1815, then to Murfreesboro in 1817, and back to Nashville in 1826. It was not until the spirited legislative session of 1843 that Nashville's status as the state capital became permanent, even though the legislature had met in the city since 1826.

6. The population of Nashville, 1800–1860, was as follows:

Year	Total	Percentage growth	White	Black	Slave	Free black
1800	345	—	191	154	151	3
1810	1 100	219	—	—	—	—
1820	3 076	180	2 054	1 022	964	58
1830	5 566	80	3 554	2 012	1 808	204
1840	6 929	24	4 406	2 523	2 114	409
1850	10 165	47	7 626	2 539	2 028	511
1860	16 988	67	13 043	3 945	3 226	719

Source: Goodstein, *Nashville 1780–1860*, 205, 81.

7. Goodstein, *Nashville 1780–1860*, 205, 81; in 1799, the Tennessee Assembly passed a law forbidding any slave from moving about to conduct any type of business without "a pass from his or her master, mistress, or overseer, expressing the time when, and the business for which they go." *Acts Passed at the First Session of the Third General Assembly State of Tennessee, Begun and Held at Knoxville, on Monday the Sixteenth Day of September, One Thousand Seven Hundred and Ninety Nine* (Knoxville: Roulstone and Wilson 1799), 70–71. Nonetheless, "Black Bob" continued to sell liquor and food.

See Legislative Records, Petition of Inhabitants of Davidson County to the Tennessee General Assembly, 1801, Tennessee State Library and Archives (hereafter TSLA); Anita Goodstein, "Black History on the Nashville Frontier, 1780–1810," *Tennessee Historical Quarterly* 30 (Winter 1979): 412–13. For the population of Davidson County see *Aggregate Amount of Persons within the United States of America . . . in the year 1810* (Washington, D.C., 1811), 77; *Fifth Census; or, Enumeration of the Inhabitants of the United States [in] 1830 . . .* (Washington, D.C.: Duff Green, 1832), 111.

8. Legislative Records, Petitions and Memorials, John Cockrill to the Senate and House of Representatives, 1821, TSLA.

9. Legislative Records, Petitions and Memorials, Petition of Temperance Crutcher to the General Assembly of Tennessee, 1837, TSLA.

10. FTS, 30.

11. It was not until Charles L. Thomas's mother, Frances, died in the mid-1830s that the estate was finally broken up, although the land and slaves were distributed among children, including minors, during the mid-1820s. Records of the County Court, Albemarle County, Va., Administrator's Accounts, Estate of Charles L. Thomas, Will Book 9 (1817–1827), 179–91; Decree, Division of Slaves, Will Book 9 (November 17, 1825), 260; Division of Land, Estate of Charles L. Thomas, Will Book 9 (May 6, 1826), 267–68; Deed of Gift, Charles Lewis Thomas (Charles's son) to John L. Thomas, Deed Book 32 (January 2, 1835), 89–90.

12. Helen Catterall, ed., *Judicial Cases Concerning American Slavery and the Negro*, 5 vols. (Washington D.C., Carnegie Institution, 1929; reprint ed., New York: Octagon Books, 1968), 2:479, 499, 504, 514, 417, 534, 538, 542, 474, 593. The term was used by lawyers and judges. Indeed, Tennessee (and other states) developed a theory of the "twofold nature of emancipation," requiring both the assent of an owner and the assent of the state. After the assent of an owner (which could not be withdrawn), a slave ceased to be under "the dominion of the master," but did not become legally free until the state or county passed a law permitting this status. Thus, there was a period when a black person was a "*quasi* slave."

13. John Hope Franklin and Alfred A. Moss Jr., *From Slavery to Freedom: A History of African Americans*, eighth edition (New York: McGraw Hill, 2000), 145.

14. Records of the County Court, Davidson County, Tenn., Partnership of Richard Rapier, Lemuel T. Turner, and James Jackson, Deeds, Vol. C (July 1801), 405, in Metro-Davidson County Archives, Nashville, Tenn.; *Tennessee Gazette and Metro District Advertiser Repository*, March 29, 1808; *Clarion*, September 27, 1808; *Imperial Review and Cumberland Repository*, May 5, 1808; *Democrat Clarion and Tennessee Gazette*, May 19, 1812, May 31, 1814.

15. The *Clarion and Tennessee State Gazette*, April 28, 1818. Some months later, another paper announced that the *General Jackson* was about to sail back to the Crescent City with a load of tobacco. *Nashville Whig and Tennessee Advertiser*, November 21, 28, 1818.

16. Jill Knight Garrett, *A History of Florence, Alabama* (Columbia, Tenn.: Jill Garrett, 1968), 10; "List of Purchasers of lots in Florence at the first sale held, July 27, 1818," Coffee Papers, Alabama Department of Archives and History, Montgomery, Ala. The first advertisement for Richard Rapier and Company appeared in the *Alabama Republican* on April 10, 1819, June 12, 1819.

17. Records of the County Court, Lauderdale County, Ala., Will Records, Vol. VI (June 3, 1824), 117.

18. *Acts of the Eleventh Annual Session of the General Assembly of the State of Alabama* (Tuscaloosa: McGuire, Henry and Walker, 1830), 36. The sum of one thousand dollars was an extremely large amount to pay for a slave, even one as talented and bright as John Rapier.

19. FTS, 60. Catron was born a year before Sally Thomas, in 1786, and arrived in Nashville in 1818. Timothy S. Huebner, *The Southern Tradition: State Judges and Sectional Distinctiveness, 1790–1890* (Athens: University of Georgia Press, 1999), 41–42.

20. FTS, 30.

21. FTS, 28; Records of the County Court, Albemarle County, Va., Administrator's Accounts, Estate of Charles L. Thomas, Decree, Division of Slaves, Will Book 9 (November 17, 1825), 260; Division of Land, Will Book 9 (May 6, 1826), 267–68; Deed of Gift, Charles Lewis Thomas (Charles's son) to John L. Thomas, Deed Book 32 (January 2, 1835), 89–90. It is not clear how John M. Martin became the owner of Sally and James. He was guardian of one of the Thomas children and described as a "kinsman" of Charles L. Thomas.

22. For what were termed "negro dogs," bred specifically to hunt runaway slaves, see Frederick Law Olmsted, *A Journey in the Seaboard Slave States, with Remarks on Their Economy* (New York: Dix and Edwards, 1856), 160, 161; Charles Stearns, *Facts in the Life of Gen. Taylor; The Cuba Blood-Hound Importer, the Extensive Slave-Holder, and the Hero of the Mexican War* (Boston: self-published, 1848), 14.

23. FTS, 4, 29, 32.

24. Richard was born December 13, 1831, John Jr. on July 28, 1835, Henry in 1836, and James on November 13, 1837.

25. Loren Schweninger, *James T. Rapier and Reconstruction* (Chicago: University of Chicago Press, 1978), 15–16.

26. FTS, 29–30.

27. Ibid., 30; *A Compilation of the Statutes of Tennessee, of a General and Permanent Nature, from the Commencement of the Government to the Present Time* (Nashville, Tenn.: Printed at the Steam Press of James Smith, 1836), 279. The statute requiring emancipated slaves to leave the state was passed in 1831.

28. Franklin and Moss Jr., *From Slavery to Freedom*, 179

29. *Acts and Resolutions of the General Assembly of the State of South Carolina, Passed in December, 1834* (Columbia, S.C.: E. F. Branthwaite, 1834), 13; Peter Kolchin, *American Slavery 1619–1877* (New York: Hill and Wang, 1993), 129.

30. FTS, 32; Goodstein, *Nashville 1780–1860*, 151; G. W. Hubbard, *A History of the Colored Schools of Nashville, Tennessee* (Nashville: Wheeler, Marshall, and Bruce, 1874), 4, cited in Goodstein, *Nashville 1780–1860*, 241, 55*n*.

31. United States Manuscript Population Census (hereafter USMSPC), Davidson County, Tenn., Second Division, 1850, 308. The census lists those in prison and their crimes. "Negro stealing" was quite common.

32. For general laws in Tennessee concerning slaves and free blacks, see *The Statute Laws of the State of Tennessee, of a Public and General Nature* (Knoxville: F. S. Heiskell, 1831), 314–30; for the law prohibiting self-hire and quasi-freedom, see *Acts Passed at the First Session of the Twenty-Third General Assembly of the State of Tennessee, 1839–40* (Nashville: J.

George Harris, Printer to the State, 1840), 82–3; *Statute Laws of the State of Tennessee of a General Character; Passed Since the Compilation of the Statutes by Caruthers and Nicholson, in 1836, and Being a Supplement to That Work,* compiled by A.O.P. Nicholson (Nashville: Published by J. G. Shepard, 1846), 286–87. The penalty, upon conviction, was five dollars for each offense. If Sally Thomas had been convicted of breaking this law, it would have been not only expensive but also embarrassing for her white customers. Similar laws in other states did not specify female slaves. See Helen Catterall, ed., *Judicial Cases Concerning American Slavery and the Negro,* 5 vols. (Washington, D.C.: W. F. Roberts Co., 1932), 2:161–62; John Hope Franklin, "Slaves Virtually Free in Ante-bellum North Carolina," *Journal of Negro History,* 28 (July 1943): 308–9; Clement Eaton, "Slave Hiring in the Upper South: A Step Toward Freedom," *Mississippi Valley Historical Review* 46 (March 1960): 672; Legislative Records, Presentment of the Grand Jury for Sumter District, S.C., Fall 1849, no. 29, South Carolina Department of Archives and History, Columbia, S.C.

33. *Nashville Whig,* August 26, 1840; John Hope Franklin and Loren Schweninger, *Runaway Slaves: Rebels on the Plantation* (New York: Oxford University Press, 1999), 1.

34. FTS, 38–39.

35. Ibid., 106–7.

36. Ibid., 106, 108–9.

37. Ibid., 110–111.

38. Ibid., 109; John Blassingame, *The Slave Community: Plantation Life in the Antebellum South* (New York: Oxford University Press, 1972; rev. ed., 1979), 23, 37–39.

39. Thomas apparently was not affected by the law prohibiting free blacks from entering the state. *Acts Passed at the Second Session of the Fifteenth Legislature of the State of Louisiana Begun and Held in the City of New Orleans December 13, 1841* (New Orleans: J. C. De St. Romes, State Printer, 1842), 308–18; FTS, 113.

40. USMSPC, Lauderdale County, Ala., Florence, 1840, 107. The census listed only Rapier as the head of household and the gender, status, and ages of others in the household. One female slave was listed as between the ages of ten and twenty-four. Later census returns gave Lucretia's ap-

proximate age as being fourteen or fifteen. See USMSPC, Lauderdale County, Ala., Florence, 1850, 293; and 1860, pp. 38–39.

41. Goodstein, *Nashville 1780–1860*, 150–52; Nashville *Union,* September 20, 1850, quoted in ibid., 152; Merton England, "The Free Negro in Ante-Bellum Tennessee" (Ph.D. diss., Vanderbilt University, 1941), 32.

42. John Rapier Sr. to Henry Thomas, February 28, 1843, Rapier-Thomas Papers, Moorland-Spingard Research Center, Howard University, Washington, D.C. (hereafter RTP). John Rapier Sr. was taught to read and write by barge captain Richard Rapier.

43. John Rapier Sr. to Richard Rapier, April 8, 1845, RTP.

44. W. J. Wilson discussed this in the eulogy he delivered at the Reunion Club in Washington, D.C., in May 1866. *The Christian Recorder* (Philadelphia), June 16, 1866.

45. A. M. Sumner to Henry Thomas, May 26, 1836, RTP.

46. John Rapier Sr. to Richard Rapier, April 8, 1845, RTP.

47. *Acts Passed at the Annual Session of the General Assembly of the State of Alabama; Begun and Held in the City of Tuscaloosa, on the First Monday in December, 1844* (Tuscaloosa: John M'Cormick, 1845), 164. The act was approved January 21, 1845.

48. John Rapier Sr. to Richard Rapier, April 8, 1845, RTP.

· Two ·

FROM SLAVERY TO FREEDOM

Sally Thomas was so well-known in Nashville by the 1840s that many residents thought she was free and owned her own home. She was respected by whites as an industrious, dependable, intelligent, and skillful laundress; she was admired by blacks as a devoted mother and grandmother who had made great sacrifices to protect her family. In fact, she was such a fixture in the city that when the United States census marshal arrived at 10 Deaderick Street in the summer of 1840, he listed her by name as the head of the household. It was extremely rare for slaves to be cited in such a manner; in fact, census takers were instructed only to check a box designating an age range for each slave. For example, the unnamed male slave in Sally Thomas's household, listed as between the ages of ten and twenty-three, was her twelve-year-old son James.[1]

The year after the census taker cited her as a resident of Nashville's Third Ward, Sally's two grandchildren, John and James Rapier, arrived in the city to begin their schooling. Sally nurtured her grandsons as she had nurtured her own children, guiding and protecting them during most of the next decade. She also provided a room, helped pay for their board, and sometimes paid their tuition of one dollar per month.

It was relatively easy to maintain contact with her Alabama son, John Rapier Sr., who visited the Tennessee capital periodically and wrote letters to his sons in Nashville. More problematic was maintaining contact with Henry, her fugitive son in the North. It would be suspicious even for a free black, much less a slave, to receive mail from the land of abolitionism. Not even someone as well-regarded as Sally Thomas was willing to take such a risk. Instead, she followed Henry's activities through letters smuggled into the South and delivered to her son John Rapier Sr. Conversely, she sent news to Henry in letters smuggled out of the South written by her Alabama son. "I have not wrote to mother as you request me as yet," John Rapier Sr. explained to his brother Henry Thomas on one occasion, "but I shall See her in the corse of ten or Twelve days and then I Show your letter to her." He added that the letter he was writing would be posted by a trusted white man, Mr. Fox, "who is going on to that place I meane to cincinnati." Addressed to Mr. H. K. Thomas, Buffalo, New York, and written in Florence, Alabama, the letter was postmarked Cincinnati, Ohio, in March 1843.[2]

Meanwhile, Sally continued to operate her cleaning business as she had done for nearly a quarter century. She worked ceaselessly, surmounting the economic downturn of the early 1840s and taking in more work in later years. There were certain occupations that southern whites, especially slave owners, felt blacks performed better than whites; indeed, they felt that slaves and free blacks had a birthright to engage in cleaning, serving, waiting, cooking, barbering, and laundering. Sally took advantage of these attitudes and continually expanded her customer base. This, coupled with her graceful demeanor and concerted efforts to please her customers, earned her a steady income. Her youngest son later described her as energetic, hardworking, intelligent, gracious, diligent, and successful. Her youthful appearance belied the fact that by 1845 she was now approaching her sixtieth year. "[M]other looks as young as she did 8 years ago and works as hard," her son John observed after a visit to Nashville, "and hardly take the time to talk to you."[3]

Despite her status as a slave, she remained the central figure in the Thomas-Rapier family, helping to free her children, offering them advice and counsel, supporting their activities and goals, even helping to raise John's children while they attended school. She was proud that both of her older sons managed businesses, had acquired property, and cared deeply about their families.

Yet, everywhere she looked there were unsettling reminders that at any moment she or any member of her family might be taken up and sold as slaves. Permanently etched in her memory was her trip to Charlottesville, Virginia, in 1834, when she and her youngest son, James, narrowly escaped being "disbursed" with other chattel property from the Thomas estate. The thought of being separated from her six-year-old son had caused her unspeakable grief on that occasion. She knew that once such a separation took place it would be impossible for her to retrieve her young one. What was worse, she would always have wondered where he was and how he was doing.

THE DOMESTIC SLAVE TRADE

From that time forward, Sally focused more closely on the movement of slaves. As a young woman, she had witnessed blacks arriving in Nashville from Virginia and North Carolina bound for the Lower Mississippi River Valley. There had been a constant stream of slaves trudging along the streets, either accompanied by their owners or pressed along by traders. The demand for laborers in the Deep South had been so great during the 1830s and 1840s that it seemed that no number of "prime" or "likely" blacks could satisfy the region's voracious appetite for human chattel.

Lined up two abreast, with a chain running the length of the line, or chained together with iron or wooden collars, the slaves were driven into the city from the east and out of the city southward, along the old Indian and buffalo trail known as the Natchez Trace. They followed the route toward the Tennessee River and Muscle Shoals, crossing the Tombigbee River, then turning south and making their way between the Pearl and Black rivers to the slave-trading center of Natchez, Mississippi. For five hundred miles the Trace twisted like a giant snake through heavy forests, across ridges and valleys, swamps and streams. Some owners and traders thought the journey helped "prepare" slaves for the heat and humidity they would face on the vast cotton and sugar plantations of the Deep South.[4]

Those who conducted the slave trade in Nashville—dealers, agents, traders, auctioneers, and factors—were especially active around the first of the year. In fact, as Sally Thomas well knew, New Year's Day was the busiest of the year. People flocked to the city from the surrounding countryside to settle accounts, hire slaves for the coming season, and buy and sell human beings. Beginning in the morning and continuing throughout the day, the auctioneer sounded his gavel, "knocking down" men, women, and children. Before each transaction, potential buyers examined the field hands, house servants, and artisans, by feel-

Used as a roadway by Native Americans for centuries, the Natchez Trace became the most important overland route for transporting slaves from the Upper South to the Lower Mississippi River Valley during the antebellum period. Tens of thousands of blacks trudged along this path, through the dense forests and swamps, on their way to a lifetime of toil on the cotton and sugar plantations of Mississippi and Louisiana. Many among them would never see their loved ones again. (SOURCE: PICTURE IN LYLE SAXON, *FATHER MISSISSIPPI* [NEW YORK: THE CENTURY CO. 1927], 160.)

ing, poking, squeezing, prodding, handling, and scrutinizing the human property for sale. They felt arms, legs, necks, breasts, buttocks; they inspected skin, scalps, and teeth. They examined the women as well as the men, children as well as adults.

"What am I offered for this Negro Wench," or "this Likely Negro Man[?]" the auctioneer cried. Some sellers refused to separate families, but most cared little about keeping husbands and wives, parents and children, brothers and sisters, or other kin together. Selling family members as a group cut into profits. It was easier and more profitable to sell individual slaves. A typical advertisement in the Nashville *Republican Banner* proclaimed, "For Sale, A Negro girl 17 years of age, House servant and Seamstress," and "ALSO—a Negro boy about 12 years of age."[5]

Sullen and silent, with a small bundle of their belongings before them, slaves experienced the wrenching pain of being separated from loved ones. Some women broke down, pleading with their owners not to sell them without their children; some men became belligerent when they discovered they would be sold without their wives or children. But other blacks, Sally's son James later recalled, "felt a degree of indifference." They felt that they could not be sold to a crueler or more brutal master than the one who had put them up for sale. "Among those sold were all colors," James Thomas added, referring to slaves, like him, who were the sons and daughters of white men. "How many hundred of thousands of mixed bloods in the country were auctioned off while their fathers were fighting wordy battles for the oppressed and downtrodden of some far off people the record doesn't show."

Toward the end of the day, the slave traders, who had often bought human chattel on speculation, began preparing to transport them to distant markets. "Death and the Nigger trader were both feared and about equally dreaded," James Thomas wrote. From Nashville, the traders drove coffles of slaves down the Natchez Trace or herded them aboard steamboats going down the Cumberland, Ohio, and Mississippi rivers. Prices in Alabama, Mississippi, and Louisiana were sometimes half-again greater than they were in the Upper South. Thomas knew of cases where a child was sold off in order to discipline the mother, or a mother was sold to punish her child. Slave traders often did not want babies or small children. "The trader would draw the line on a child," James Thomas observed. " 'I'll take the Negro Wench' but I don't want that child. You can keep it. It will only be in the way." The trader, James Thomas believed, was "devoid of feeling."

Traders were especially interested in purchasing "fancy stock," attractive young women of mixed racial origin. They bought them at low prices in the Upper South and sold them for large sums in New Orleans. "People buying that kind of property were at liberty to feel the woman and ask her questions," James Thomas commented. Traders dressed the women in fancy clothes, kept them in comfortable steamboat compartments. Upon their arrival, the future concubines were placed in special holding areas in the Crescent City. Among the young women were a number of nearly white quadroons. As it happened, the wives of some of the men who bought such "fancy stock" refused to allow the light-skinned black women in the house, or demanded that they be resold.[6]

Despite being in her fifties during the 1840s, Sally Thomas herself would have brought a good price. So too would her son James, now in his teens, and grandchildren John and James

BOYD & LYLES

GENERAL-AGENTS
&

DEALERS IN NEGROES
& C.
CASH ADVANCES MADE ON NEGROES CONSINGHED US
No. 50 Cherry Street Nashville Tenn.

Like most slave brokers, the Nashville firm of Boyd & Lyles advertised in newspapers and with broadsides, posters, and letterheads. This envelope imprint appears to show the two brokers discussing the value of a black family. Their offices on Cherry Street were located in the central business district; the Tennessee Capitol stands on the hill in the distance. General agents such as Boyd & Lyles bought, sold, conveyed, mortgaged, traded, and transported slaves; they also served as moneylenders and loan agents and were not averse to scouring the countryside in search of "likely" men, women, and children. (SOURCE: COURTESY OF TENNESSEE STATE MUSEUM COLLECTION, NASHVILLE, TENNESSEE.)

Rapier, who, despite their youth would have fetched several hundred dollars each if kidnapped and carried away. Because of this reality, the slave trade weighed heavily on Sally's mind. The images of slaves being bought, sold, and traded, coupled with the knowledge that some free blacks disappeared and were never heard from again, reminded her how vulnerable she and her sons and grandsons were. Her gnawing fear grew worse every time she heard the auctioneer's gavel or saw a youngster sold away from his mother.

JAMES THOMAS: THE BOYHOOD YEARS

Despite his mother's anxiety, James Thomas felt safe from being sold on New Year's Day. He was not only watched over by his mother but also protected by her white patron, Ephraim Foster. Nevertheless, James received strict instructions as to how to deal with questions from traders and speculators. If he were asked his owner's name he should always respond by saying, "Mrs. Sally Thomas." "I have had many times some fellow to say to me 'boy who do you belong to?' Had I have said Mother, I would have to answer questions. Instead I said Mrs Thomas. 'What Mrs Thomas.' Mrs Sally Thomas. Does she want to sell you. I cant say. Tell her I will buy you if she will sell you.'"[7] If the ruse were discovered, James and Sally could fall back on the protection of Foster. James Thomas affirmed that Foster "proved to be a staunch friend as long as he lived and his family were also good friends to me." He did "all that he said he would do." Sally was cautioned to keep James out of trouble and make sure he walked a straight line. If good advice and switches were any indication, her son ruefully recalled, she kept up her end of the bargain. As a result, James, less than most slaves, feared being sold and separated from his mother during his youth. Nonetheless, he understood that one improper incident or misstep could result in disaster.[8]

When not helping his mother at the laundry or running errands for white gentlemen, James moved deftly between the two racial worlds. He was a bright and inquisitive youngster, known and well-liked by many residents, black and white. He was also adventurous, visiting the slave quarters on nearby plantations, attending black religious gatherings, listening to speeches at political rallies, and venturing into the back alleys along the riverfront. Of mixed racial origin, he personified, in a sense, the two worlds of race. His background and experiences, aided by his remarkable memory, afforded him a unique opportunity to observe and comment on every aspect of the South's peculiar institution. Few understood better than he how the two races were inextricably bound, with slavery both bringing them together and driving them apart.

Such was the case with religion. The black population, both free and slave, fervently embraced Christianity. James noted that this zeal created services that combined animated participation with lively doctrinal debates. With members of the congregation standing up, sitting down, pointing, shouting, and remonstrating, arguments about the meaning of Scripture could go on for hours. Did admission into the faith require complete immersion? Should every word in the Bible be considered literal truth? Could man communicate directly with God? Some slaves and free blacks professed to be Campbellite Baptists; others saw themselves as strong Methodists; still others said they were members of the Ironside Baptist Church, whose members included different sects and denominations. Whatever their differences, James Thomas said, all blacks believed that Christ died on the Cross to save people from sin and that God was "no respecter of persons, the black and white have the same chance for salvation."[9]

It was this concept that drew blacks in Nashville to the preaching of white minister Jesse Ferguson, who, in 1847, took over the pulpit of the Vine Street Christian Church. The twenty-eight-year-old preacher and church magazine editor attracted two hundred black and five hundred white worshipers to his church on Sundays by preaching that grace came from inner reverence rather than outward professions of faith. Christian ideals, especially the "old, pure, divine system taught in the New Testament," should be felt in one's heart.[10]

In Nashville, there was also what was called "the African church," where slaves and free persons of color worshiped without white supervision. Following Sunday-morning services, where white ministers instructed servants to obey their masters, slaves gathered in the afternoon and evening for their own spiritual fulfillment.[11] At these gatherings, black preachers exhorted their followers to disobey their masters, to seek freedom in this life as well as the next, and to listen to the words of the Lord who gave Moses the power to lead his people: "I *am* the LORD thy God, which have brought thee out of the land of Egypt, out of the house of slavery."[12]

Slave owners sought to prevent slaves from hearing such "radical" doctrines. They argued that black preachers were "dangerous to the public weal & safety" and "injurious to the great mass of Negroes who attend such worship."[13] Whites enacted laws

Jesse B. Ferguson (1819–1870), minister, reformer, editor, was the most captivating preacher in Nashville during the late 1840s and early 1850s, especially among the downtrodden. James Thomas called him a "brilliant young man." (SOURCE: COURTESY OF DISCIPLES OF CHRIST ARCHIVES, NASHVILLE, TENNESSEE.)

prohibiting slaves from assembling by themselves without written permission from an owner, overseer, or employer.[14] But neither the public outcries nor the restrictive laws seemed to have their desired effect.

One thing was certain, James Thomas concluded, there was no such thing as a black atheist.[15]

Just as slaves debated the Scriptures, they also discussed politics. The black man "began talking politics," James Thomas wrote, "about the same time he began preaching." During the 1830s, the recharter of the Second Bank of the United States sparked debate. Designed to stabilize the currency and stimulate trade, the bank was not a government entity but rather a private corporation controlled by wealthy businessmen and political leaders. Many working-class people perceived it as a vehicle for the wealthy to exploit the masses. Many slaves also opposed the bank, but for a different reason. To black Tennesseans, the "Monster Bank" made it possible for slave traders to borrow unlimited funds to carry on the traffic in human flesh. Consequently, slaves felt an affinity with President Andrew Jackson, not because Jackson's plantation, the Hermitage, was located in Davidson County, but rather because, in 1832, he vetoed the bill to recharter the bank.

While blacks supported Jackson on this issue, they were quick to point out his duplicity when it came to slavery. Following the 1815 Battle of New Orleans, where blacks had fought alongside whites against the British, Jackson reneged on his promise to free the slaves who had fought so courageously. The Americans defeated the British decisively, but the general only acknowledged the services of blacks "in words of kindness," James Thomas noted contemptuously, and told them "to go home and be good boys." When he died in 1845, James Thomas added, the former President failed to free even his most loyal personal "body servant."[16]

Jackson's chief opponent during this period was Henry Clay, of Kentucky. Clay became a leader in the Whig Party, which was born out of a hatred of Jackson's perceived tyranny, much in the same manner that the Whig Party in England arose in opposition to the tyranny of King George III. As a United States senator, Clay opposed Jackson at every turn and was especially incensed by the latter's attack on the bank. On August 17, 1840,

Andrew Jackson. (Source: Octavia Zollicoffer Bond, *Old Tales Retold, or, Perils and Adventures of Tennessee Pioneers* [Nashville: Smith & Lamar, Publishers, 1906], following 222.)

Henry Clay spoke on behalf of William Henry Harrison, the Whig presidential candidate, before an estimated forty thousand people at the party's great convention in Nashville. "I managed to get out to hear him," James Thomas recalled, for he was there among the several thousand slaves and free blacks interspersed in the crowd. James was twelve years old at the time. He and the other slaves had observed "stump orators" before—those who took off their coats, rolled up their sleeves, and preached the political gospel according to one side or another. But, James Thomas observed, Clay was different. He was smooth and articulate. "None of the spread Eagle such as I had been seeing and hearing. After his speech, he left the platform looking as fresh as when he came, wearing the same smile."

James Thomas must have thought it strange when Clay asserted that the Whigs, unlike the Democrats, were the true purveyors of democratic ideals handed down from Thomas Jefferson, ideals that asked only if a candidate was capable and honest, and supported the Constitution. At this and other gatherings, blacks listened intently, especially when the political debate involved racial matters. They were usually not disappointed, James Thomas noted, as "it seemed impossible not to discuss the Negro. He was always discussed."[17]

It may have seemed odd to some that slave owners would permit their slaves to attend such events, but blacks living on plantations around Nashville often counted on such diversions, as the incident with the slave Jake and his owner, Robert Bradford, indicated. Nor were public addresses and conventions the only places where slaves could hear political discussions. "Servants kept a close Ear on political conversations and arguments," James Thomas wrote. House servants, waiters, cooks, even gardeners and horse tenders listened to members of their owner's family discuss the expansion of slavery in the territories, the growth of abolitionist sentiment, and the birth of the Liberty Party. "When they were in waiting they would keep around to listen," James Thomas wrote; later, they would repeat to other slaves the arguments they had heard, doing so "in almost a whisper." Slaves knew not only the issues of the day, but also how emotional and distressed their owners became when speaking about slave escapes, violence, arson, and possible revolt.[18]

As with religion and politics, blacks found relief from the drudgery of slavery by engaging in a spirited social life— especially during the Christmas holidays. Even though each year authorities in Nashville posted notices in mid-December about regulating the movements of slaves, free Negroes, and mulattoes during the holiday season, the black population moved about the city freely, gathered for social occasions, and stayed out past curfew. "I was at the hermitage during the Christmas week and they (the Genls men and women of all work) commenced dancing in the morning," James Thomas wrote. "Some played cards, while others would seek some isolated spot for Cock fighting." Slaves at the Hermitage visited friends and loved ones on neighboring plantations, or socialized in their quarters, eating and drinking in the brick and log buildings provided by their famous owner. Andrew Jackson owned more than 135 slaves, and they all joined in the Christmas festivities, including the field hands, or, as James Thomas called them, the "men and women of all work."[19]

At other times of the year, social activities were more difficult. Some owners forbade slaves to leave their plantation, except on rare family visits. The long hours and drudgery in the fields often left blacks with little energy to visit friends, even those within the slave quarters. But conditions in Davidson County were probably better than in most parts of the Deep South, where the clearing and tilling of new lands resulted in the vigorous buying, selling, and trading of slaves. In fact, in Nashville, James Thomas said, many of the "old time blacks" were genuine sports. They gambled at chuck-o-luck, cards, cockfights, and horse races. They were always present at Clover Bottom, Jackson's private racetrack. "I've seen them lose or win fifty dollars often on a race," James Thomas wrote, noting that many of the trainers, stableboys, and jockeys were black. On Sunday afternoons and evenings following the races, slaves gathered in secluded areas.

They barbecued pigs and chickens, drank whiskey, and made the woods "ring with noise." At the end of the party, the ground was covered with bones and feathers and "trampled as if there had been a political meeting."[20]

Mingling with various groups of blacks at religious, political, and social gatherings, young James endured the prejudice many dark-skinned blacks felt toward persons of mixed racial ancestry. These blacks called mulattoes "No Nation," "Mule," and "yaller Hammer." Ordinary slaves never "took much stock in the 'Yaller' Nigger," as mulattoes were called, and chastised them for their mixture of black and white blood. Dark-skinned slaves, James Thomas asserted, took pride in their racial purity, and often claimed that their ancestors were from royal families in West Africa.[21]

Despite the color prejudice of blacks, and despite his privileged situation, James sympathized with the plight of ordinary slaves. Perhaps as a result of his mother's influence, he understood their pain and suffering. Even as a boy, however, he could not rid himself of his strong aversion toward poor whites—in his opinion, the dregs of southern society. In this, he followed the lead of the white gentry, who "wanted nothing to do with a white man that could not rise above that," who could not acquire skills and accumulate property. White gentlemen, James Thomas observed, refused to hire poor whites as waiters, servants, laundresses, or barbers; nor would they hire them as masons, carpenters, or coopers. James watched as such whites passed through Nashville, sitting atop rickety wagons loaded with their worldly goods—chairs, tables, hoes, shovels, tools, pots, pans—and surrounded by ragged, half-starved children and mangy dogs.

Despite his contempt for poor whites, James also feared them, believing they harbored a special hatred for blacks. After all, the city's poor whites hunted runaway slaves, served on patrols, and broke up slave gatherings. They often drank to excess, and if they happened to encounter a town slave out after curfew they could become violent. Indeed, James Thomas noted, one reason the legislature passed a law requiring whites to be present at black gatherings was not only to protect whites against slave conspiracies but also to prevent the slaves from being attacked by landless whites. James Thomas feared that many poor whites, lacking a respectable family name and rejected by the planters with whom they sought to ingratiate themselves, would want to make good on their threat "if I could get hold of that nigger I would take the nigger down a peg or two."[22]

BARBERSHOP

About 1841, at age fourteen, young James Thomas left Dr. Esselman's office and began working as an apprentice barber for Frank Parrish, a quasi-free slave who operated a popular bathhouse and barbershop on Deaderick Street, across from the *Banner and Whig* newspaper office. Parrish stood six feet tall and was described as a fine-looking man, an elegant dresser, and gentlemanly and polite. Like James Thomas, he was the son of a white father and a slave mother. Following his owner's death, the widow, Catherine Parrish, permitted Frank to start a business. Though she knew that he was her deceased husband's illegitimate son, she appeared not to be embarrassed by this fact. Other white women were neither as accepting of their husband's mixed-race children nor as magnanimous toward their partners' infidelity. Indeed, the pain and suffering white women experienced when their husbands took a slave woman to bed often remained for a lifetime.[23]

As early as 1836, Frank Parrish advertised that his bathing establishment offered private "apartments" for ladies and warm- and cold-water baths and showers for ladies and gentlemen. During the summer, the bathhouse remained open from six in the morning until ten at night. Next door was Parrish's barbershop, boasting a staff of assistants and a display case filled with collars, suspenders, fancy soaps, perfumes, and the "BEST CIGARS AND TO-BACCO" in the city.[24]

James learned a great deal under Parrish's tutelage, not only about cutting hair and shaving beards but also about the subtleties of racial etiquette. Many of Parrish's customers were members of the slaveholding aristocracy, and James observed how Parrish dealt with rich slave owners, remaining deferential without being obsequious, engaging in conversation without being contentious, and accepting criticism without being offended. Within a short time, Parrish bragged that his new assistant had "no superior in his business."[25] "James [is] still with Frank Parrish and has the character of a good Barber, So a Gentleman told me," James's brother, John Rapier Sr., wrote after visiting Nashville in 1843. "He is well thought of by the Gentlemen." He had social skills and manners "to please almost anyone who does not let their prejudice go to [far] on account of color."[26] Two years later, Rapier added that James was still with Parrish and was doing quite well with "the promise of twelve dollars per month."[27]

After a five-year apprenticeship, James Thomas opened his own barbershop. The nineteen-year-old slave established his business at 10 Deaderick Street, in the house where he had grown up and where his mother still ran her laundry business. The location was ideal. Within a few steps of several banking houses, newspapers, and law firms, and the market, courthouse and state capitol, the shop was convenient to bankers, merchants, lawyers, politicians, and other professional men. Soon, James counted among his customers a number of prominent Tennesseans, including former United States Senator Ephraim Foster; six-term governor William Carroll; dry-goods merchant and businessman Elias S. Hall; slaveholder William Harding, owner of the famous Belle Meade estate; and minister and politician William G. "Parson" Brownlow. "I shall always remember Parson Brownlow as a peculiar man," James Thomas wrote. Statesman, editor, and preacher; thin-visaged; and having full eyes and a swarthy complexion, Brownlow remained unflappable even during the most turbulent campaigns. Preaching before one hostile audience in a hotly contested election, he calmly drew his pistol from underneath his coat and placed it on the lectern alongside the Bible.[28]

"The old time barber shop," James Thomas recalled, "was the best of all places to learn the ways and peculiarities of the old time Gentleman." No one seemed in a hurry. Everything was discussed. Topics included the advancement of cotton on the Liverpool market, the magnetism and sporting tastes of Andrew Jackson, the price of acreage along the Mississippi, the disrespectful attitudes of the younger generation, and the growing tensions between the North and South. During discussions, James usually remained silent, although sometimes he ventured an opinion or asked a question. Once, he asked a young Virginian about the Wilmot Proviso, a controversial proposal in 1846

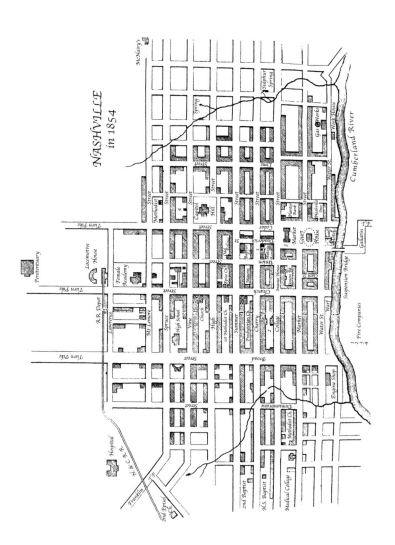

NASHVILLE
in 1854

to exclude slavery from certain territories in the Southwest that had been acquired from Mexico during the Mexican War. Southerners opposed any measure that would give Congress the right to tamper with slavery in the territories. "The set back I got from him for asking such a question caused me to be careful as to who I plied questions to with regard to politics," James Thomas recalled. He was informed that a slave barber had no business eavesdropping on a white man's conversation.[29] On another occasion, General William Giles Harding was in the shop and asked James if he had a relative living in Buffalo, New York. When James responded that he did, Harding complained that James's brother Henry had treated him "in a gruff manner." The shop quickly became silent, and James could do little more than apologize for his brother's rudeness.[30]

During the 1850s, James listened to discussions of Illinois senator Stephen A. Douglas's proposal that settlers in Kansas and Nebraska be free to decide for themselves whether slavery should be permitted in the territories. The proposal was called "popular sovereignty." James learned, too, about "Bleeding Kansas," where proslavery and antislavery forces waged war against one another over the expansion of slavery; he watched as the Re-

---

Even at this late date, residents of Nashville could walk fifteen blocks and be on the outskirts of town. Sally and James Thomas lived four blocks from the Cumberland River, in the heart of the central business district, on the southeast corner of Deaderick and Cherry Streets (follow Cherry Street to dot near center of the map). It was an ideal location, only a block from the market and two blocks from the courthouse. (SOURCE: COURTESY OF TENNESSEE STATE MUSEUM PHOTOGRAPHIC ARCHIVES, NASHVILLE, TENNESSEE.)

William "Parson" Brownlow (1805–1877), minister, politician, anti-secessionist, began his career as a circuit-riding Methodist preacher. During the Civil War, he was charged with treason by the Confederacy for his loyalty to the Union; after the war, he became the first Reconstruction governor of Tennessee. (SOURCE: COURTESY OF TENNESSEE STATE MUSEUM COLLECTION, NASHVILLE, TENNESSEE.)

publican Party was born out of the conflict. Those who frequented the shop never tired of denouncing abolitionists for their naïveté and duplicity; nor did they tire in their praise of southern whites for their intimate knowledge of the black man's character.[31]

Tactful, articulate, and sociable, James Thomas built up a thriving trade. He took advantage of the leisurely pace of southern life, the desire of gentlemen to meet and discuss politics, and the reputation of his shop as a first-class establishment. "The old timer would walk in, take of[f] his coat, hand it to the boy, take off his hat (all his papers would often be in his hat), take of[f] his stock [scarf] and put it in the hat," James Thomas recalled. "The boy would brush hat and coat while [the] shave was going on." By 1850, Thomas had hired two assistants, twenty-three-year-old Albert McKay and nineteen-year-old Silas Hall, free persons of mixed race; they cut hair, trimmed and shaved beards, brushed off coats and hats, and swept and mopped the floors. Both lived with James above his shop, as did James's nephew James Rapier, who was still attending school. In 1853, James Thomas placed his business card in the city's first business directory: "JAS. THOMAS, Barber Shop, 10 Deaderick st."[32] A number of his customers visited the shop daily. Not even the most inclement weather kept them away. "We had quite a snow storm yesterday, afternoon," Ellen Fogg wrote her friend Ephraim Foster. "Mr Fogg is exceedingly kind and amiable to us, goes to the barbers every day, returns to us in the evening with his face very smooth and curls nicely arranged."[33]

Charging twenty cents for a haircut, fifteen cents for a shave, his "tonsorial establishment" provided Thomas with a continual and comfortable income. At a time when day laborers earned a dollar a day and skilled artisans not more than two or three dollars a day, Thomas, in a good week, could take in twenty-five dollars and more. As a free black he could now invest his savings, and he soon had saved enough to buy some real estate. Although, even as a slave, he had purchased a ten-dollar burial plot in the city cemetery for his mother, he now joined another black man, Willis Hickman, in buying a lot for three hundred fifty dollars at a court-ordered sale. It was a handsome piece of property, fronting one hundred feet on Ewing Street and stretching back one hundred fifty feet to an alley. The deed listed James Thomas as a free man of color and Hickman as "a man of color." As Hickman was almost certainly a slave, it was necessary for someone to hold his property as a trustee. The person who promised to "hold one undivided half of said lot no. 143 as Trustee for said Willis Hickman," and to permit Hickman to "transfer & convey the Same to any person" was none other than United States Supreme Court justice John Catron—James Thomas's father.[34]

Despite such success, Thomas faced stiff competition. Also advertising in the city's first business directory were several other free persons of color, including John Williams under the sign of "WILLIAMS & ROLLINS, BARBERS, 21 N. Market st"; Nelson Walker, who ran a shop on Deaderick Street a short distance from Thomas's business; and Thomas's friend and mentor, Frank Parrish, who could now regale his customers with stories about Western Europe and the Middle East. In 1851, with his master, Edwin Ewing, and a group of Tennessee slave owners, Parrish had toured England, Scotland, the Germanies, Persia, and Egypt.[35] "Everywhere in Europe and the Orient, Frank was taken for the principal man of the Party," James Thomas mused. "All rushed to look after him (according to Mr Ewings letters), supposing those other fellows were mere followers in his train." Parrish protested that he was not the head man, but the foreigners refused to believe it and heaped more attention on him.[36] Now located on the Public Square, Parrish's barbershop became more popular than ever. The competition between the two barbers, however, remained amicable. James Thomas greatly admired and respected his older mentor.[37]

As young James grew to maturity and started his own business, Sally Thomas continued her clothes-cleaning enterprise. She worked in the house that was now both a laundry and a barbershop. She, too, boasted a large circle of slave and free black friends and was also well acquainted with a number of whites who frequented her laundry or engaged her services. As time passed, she grew less apprehensive that she or her son might be sold away from Nashville. Nonetheless, she remained on guard and vigilant, especially during periods of slave unrest or rumors of a slave conspiracy. However much she and her son had become part of the fabric of the city, their color made them vulnerable. No matter how much she struggled to carve out a place for herself and James, Sally knew better than anyone that her privileged status was fragile and tenuous.

Notes

1. USMSPC, Davidson County, Tenn., Nashville, Third Ward, 1840, 278; Byron and Barbara Sistler, eds., 1840 Census, *Tennessee Transcribed and Indexed* (Nashville: Byron and Barbara Sistler, 1986), 527.

2. John Rapier Sr. to Henry Thomas, February 28, 1843, RTP.

3. John Rapier Sr. to Richard Rapier, April 8, 1845, RTP.

4. Harnett T. Kane, *Natchez on the Mississippi* (New York: William Morrow & Co., 1947), 5–6, 61–64; Frederic Bancroft, *Slave Trading in the Old South* (Baltimore, Md.: J. H. Furst Co., 1931; reprint ed., New York: Frederick Ungar Publishing Co., 1959), 288; Walter Johnson, *Soul by Soul: Life Inside the Antebellum Slave Market* (Cambridge, Mass.: Harvard University Press, 1999), 7, 122; Wright, *African Americans in the Early Republic,* 8–12.

5. Nashville *Republican Banner,* December 29, 1841, January 5, 1842.

6. FTS, 59–61.

7. Ibid., 80.

8. Ibid., 31.

9. Ibid., 66–69.

10. Jesse B. Ferguson, "Public Worship of the Lord," *Christian Magazine* 1 (1848); 42–43; Jesse B. Ferguson, quoted in Enos E. Dowling, *An Analysis of the Index of the Christian Magazine 1848–1953* (Lincoln, Ill.: Lincoln Bible Institute Press, 1958), ii. The authors wish to thank Robert Calhoon for sharing the above material with them.

11. FTS, 67–68; see also, Michael A. Gomez, *Exchanging Our Country Marks: The Transformation of African Identities in the Colonial and Antebellum South* (Chapel Hill: University of North Carolina Press, 1998), 256–57, 264–67.

12. Holy Bible, King James Version, Exodus 20, 2.

13. Petition of the Citizens of Hardeman County to the Senate and the House of Representatives of the State of Tennessee, December 3, 1857, Legislative Petitions, TSLA. This and other legislative petitions concerning slavery are on microfilm. See Loren Schweninger, ed., and Robert Shelton, assist. ed., *Race, Slavery, and Free Blacks: Series I, Petitions to Southern Legislatures, 1777–1867* (Bethesda, Md., University Publications of America, 1999), microfilm edition, reel no. 14, frames 562–65. A 450-page guide, compiled by Charles E. Smith, accompanies the microfilm.

14. *A Compilation of the Statutes of Tennessee, of a General and Permanent Nature, from the Commencement of the Government to the Present Time* (Nashville: R. L. Caruthers and A.O.P. Nicholson, 1836), 677. The law was passed in 1803.

15. FTS, 63, 66–67.

16. Ibid., 69–70.

17. Ibid., 57; Epes Sargent, *The Life and Public Services of Henry Clay, Down to 1848*, ed., Horace Greeley (Philadelphia: Porter and Coates, 1852), 203. There is no extant copy of Clay's August 17, 1840 speech, but there are summaries. See Robert Seager II, ed., Melba Porter Hay, assoc. ed., *The Papers of Henry Clay*, 10 vols. (Lexington: University of Kentucky Press,

1988), 9:439–43; Daniel Mallory, comp. and ed., *The Life and Speeches of the Hon. Henry Clay . . .* (Hartford, Conn.: Silas Andrus and Son, 1853), 427–31. Apparently, Clay did not mention the formation of the Liberty Party, founded in April 1840 as part of the antislavery movement in the North.

18. FTS, 70.

19. Ibid., 59.

20. Ibid., 41, 66. Clover Bottom was owned by Jackson and several other planters in the vicinity. William Robertson, *The History of Thoroughbred Race in America* (Englewood Cliffs, N.J.: Prentice Hall, 1964), 41. For comparison with the Deep South, see Ann Patton Malone, *Sweet Chariot: Slave Family and Household Structure in Nineteenth-Century Louisiana* (Chapel Hill: University of North Carolina Press, 1992).

21. FTS, 70, 98.

22. Ibid., 89, 71.

23. See Elizabeth Fox-Genovese, *Within the Plantation Household: Black and White Women of the Old South* (Chapel Hill: University of North Carolina Press, 1988); Deborah Gray White, *Ar'n't I a Woman?: Female Slaves in the Plantation South* (New York: W. W. Norton, 1985; revised ed., 1999); Drew Gilpin Faust, *Mothers of Invention: Women of the Slaveholding South in the American Civil War* (Chapel Hill: University of North Carolina Press, 1996).

24. Nashville *Republican*, April 21, 1836; J. Merton England, "The Free Negro in Ante-Bellum Tennessee," 215, 267–70; Goodstein, *Nashville 1780–1860*, 77.

25. Nashville *Daily Republican Banner*, April 9, 1841. Though Thomas is not mentioned by name, the date of the article suggests that Parrish was describing him.

26. John Rapier Sr. to Henry Thomas, February 28, 1843, RTP.

27. John Rapier Sr. to Richard Rapier, April 8, 1845, RTP.

28. Elias Hall was acquainted with many politicians. See Elias Hall to John Overton, July 7, 1823, April 12, 1827, John Claybrooke Papers, TSLA; FTS, 4, 73 [Carroll], 82 [Brownlow].

29. FTS, 84.

30. Ibid., 34, 78.

31. Ibid., 73, 143–54.

32. USMSPC, Davidson County, Tenn., Nashville, 1850, 117; *The Nashville General Commercial Directory* (Nashville: The Daily American Book and Job Printing Office, 1853), 68.

33. Ellen S. Fogg to Ephraim Foster, Foster-Woods Papers, TSLA. G. M. Fogg is mentioned in Thomas's autobiography, but not as a customer. Considering the Fogg family's connection with Ephraim Foster, it is likely that Fogg was one of James Thomas's customers. In the 1850 census, G. M. Fogg, age forty-nine, was listed as the head of household; Ellen, age twenty-nine, and two children, G. M. and Ellen, ages seven and five, were listed in the same household. USMSPC, Davidson County, Tenn., Nashville, 1850, 132.

34. Records of the Davidson County Court, Warranty Deeds, Book 18 (June 1, 1854), 366–67.

35. *The Nashville General Commercial Directory* (Nashville: The Daily American Book and Job Printing Office, 1853), 68–69.

36. FTS, 92.

37. Frank Parrish was twenty-five years older than James Thomas. Parrish later moved his business to the basement of the St. Cloud Hotel. In 1853, at age forty-eight, he purchased his freedom, though he had been living as a quasi-free bondsman since childhood. Records of the Davidson County Court, Minute Book E, 1850–1853 (October 4, 1853), 563–64; *Nashville Business Directory* (Nashville: Smith, Camp and Co., 1857), 167; ibid., 1859, 121; ibid., 1860, 240. For his various business transactions, see Records of the County Court, Davidson County, Tenn., Warranty Deeds, Nashville, Book 19 (December 23, 1854), 251–52; ibid., Book 22 (October 9, 1855), 330.

· *Three* ·

TRAVELS IN THE
NORTH AND WEST

SALLY THOMAS'S SON'S REPUTATION AS AN EXCELLENT BARBER spread even beyond Davidson County. In 1848, Sally listened as James told her how he had been summoned to a hotel in Nashville by Maury County slave owner Andrew Jackson Polk, brother of Episcopal clergyman Leonidas Polk and a distant relative of the President, James Knox Polk. Two years before, A. J. Polk had married the wealthy and attractive Rebecca Vanleer, a member of a prominent iron-manufacturing family. "They were," one family member said, "the handsomest couple I have ever seen." In 1847, with Rebecca's money, Polk purchased from his brother the beautiful plantation Ashwood Hall, with its formal gardens, orchards, greenhouses, and a spacious mansion house.

Now Polk was planning an extended summer trip to the North and asked James Thomas if he would accompany him as his personal body servant. He promised to pay him liberally and explained that they would have an extended stay in New York

City. "In those days a man that had been to New York," James Thomas recalled, "had been somewhere worth talking about." Nonetheless, Thomas told Polk that he did not think he could go at this time. He had recently opened his own business and feared he might lose some of his customers. "Don't tell me about your business," retorted Polk. "I'll buy it and shut it up."[1]

It was not long afterward that the two men boarded a stagecoach and began their journey northward over a rutted and dusty road. Following much the same route that Thomas's brother Henry had traversed some fourteen years earlier—through the tobacco, corn, and wheat country, to Louisville—they transferred to a steam packet going up the Ohio River, to Cincinnati. Crossing northward to Buffalo, they boarded a boat on Lake Ontario, shipped to Oswego, and transferred to a stage going from Oswego to Rome, where they caught a train for Albany. As much as Thomas wished to see his brother in Buffalo, it was too risky; he arrived and departed the city in Polk's close company. From Albany, they boarded the steamboat *Allida,* and, as the band played "Oh, Susannah," the two men began the last leg of their journey down the Hudson River.

Tall, good looking, impeccably dressed, and gripping a gold-headed walking cane, the twenty-three-year-old Polk was a striking figure. As he strolled the deck, passengers would stop and stare, whispering to one another. James Thomas, too, as he put it, "came in for a share of attention." At age twenty, with his bright brown coloring and wavy hair, he felt many eyes following him. When Polk went below deck, passengers came up to Thomas and questioned him about his traveling companion. Was he related to the president? Did he own a plantation? How

The popularity of steamboat travel grew rapidly during the middle decades of the nineteenth century, as the steamboat's reputation spread for quick, reliable, and even luxurious service, for those who could afford first-class accommodation. Thomas, Polk, and their fellow passengers had a perfect view of the Palisades of the Hudson, a wall of rock extending as far as the eye could see and jutting skyward between fifty and two hundred feet. (SOURCE: ENGRAVING IN N. P. WILLIS, *AMERICAN SCENERY; OR, LAND, LAKE, AND RIVER: ILLUSTRATIONS OF TRANS-ATLANTIC NATURE* [NEW YORK: R. MARTIN & CO., 1840, REPRINTED ED., IMPRINT SOCIETY, BARRE, MASS., 1971], 20–21.)

many slaves did he own? "When I said about three hundred, some would pucker their mouths and let out a low whistle." They asked James if he were Polk's slave. When he replied that he was not, several refused to believe it and urged him to run away. Polk was apparently well aware of the scrutiny visited upon him and his companion, as evidenced by one incident in which Polk made a public display of asking Thomas to take his walking cane, his watch, and his billfold (bulging with money) while he took a nap. "I had nothing to do," Thomas said, "but rest on the head of the cane and answer currious peoples questions until we neared New York."[2]

Upon their arrival, they registered at the Astor House, the city's first luxury hotel. Located on Broadway at Barclay Street, the hotel boasted a front entrance flanked by Doric columns, a handsome reception area, three hundred rooms, and privately supplied running water.[3] Polk instructed the management to make sure his companion was made comfortable. "I never saw Mr Polk, only in the morning," James Thomas recalled. "He would go out among the horse men and other fanciers." Polk did give Thomas money to entertain himself and to buy his meals. "Your funds must be low," he remarked to Thomas, handing him a ten-dollar bill. Polk's only admonition was for Thomas to dress well and "Don't let these fellows down you." Otherwise Thomas was left on his own to take in as much of the city as he could during the next several weeks.[4]

Thomas was shocked by the city's noise, bustle, and mass of humanity. He had never seen so many people going and coming at one time. "I fell in with some dashing fellows," Thomas remarked, "who took me around and told me I was a southern 'blood.'" He soon learned, however, that blacks were not welcome in many places. He was told that he would not be admitted to most museums unless he was with a white person or accompanying white children. The same was true for the omnibus. If "a colored face got inside of an Omnibus," Thomas said, the white passengers would jump off at the next stop. One evening, he passed the hall where the Campbell Minstrels were performing. He bought a ticket, went in, and took a seat. Within a few minutes an official tapped him on the shoulder and informed him that "some of our people are not satisfied with you here and I will have to return you your money." Thomas rose and departed.[5]

Not only did he experience the humiliating experience of being asked to leave a theater, but he also soon discovered that blacks in New York City were often ridiculed and made fun of while walking down the street. They were "grinned at and hooted at," or someone would say "black cloud risin," or throw a rock, or, in some cases worse: blacks would be "jumped on and roughly handled." This all seemed very strange. In the South, Thomas observed, slaves and free blacks attended various events without fear of expulsion, and whites "never laughed at [the] Negro because he was a Negro but would laugh at his pranks and foolishness at times."[6] Thomas reflected, "I felt as though I would like to meet another man that would have the affrontry to advise me to run away to live in New York."[7]

As a result, he spent most of his time socializing with his new black friends or conversing with fellow servants staying at the Astor House. The guests at the hotel included United States senator Daniel Webster; San Francisco hotel proprietor J. J. Bryant; and General Thomas John Wood, recently back from the Mexican War, where he had distinguished himself at the Battle of Buena Vista. Thomas noted how the servants of these men often discussed the political, economic, military, and racial views of their employers, assuming an "authority on certain points." On one occasion, when Thomas remarked that Tennessee senator John Bell was one of "the ablest men in the senate," he was quickly corrected by Webster's servant, who called Bell "a very common Man" while extolling his boss, Webster, as a "Giant force as a statesman and as having no equal." During these and other discussions, Thomas noted, Irish servants who waited upon them were awestruck when they heard the names of leading politicians.[8]

After a number of weeks, Thomas and Polk began their journey home. As they passed through Washington, D.C., Thomas commented on the heat, the dust, and the unpaved streets. From Washington, they proceeded to Richmond, Virginia, where he observed "more slave dealers than I ever saw at once." About every five minutes, some ugly fellow, loudly dressed, would approach him and say "who do you belong to boy?" He told them to speak to "that Gentleman and I would point to Mr Polk." The slaves about to be sold were mostly young people, and it seemed to make but little difference with them where they might be sent.[9] After visiting Polk's sister in Raleigh, North Carolina, the travelers continued westward, taking with them on their homeward journey an elderly slave who wished to see old friends who had been transported from North Carolina to Tennessee many years before but who were still owned by the Polk family.[10]

Arriving back in Nashville, Polk paid Thomas liberally for his services. "I had a few pictures to hang up, some New York clothes, and had to answer many questions as to what I had seen and how I liked the people I had seen north," Thomas recalled.[11] And, as he had after returning from New Orleans, he shared his experiences with his mother, Sally Thomas, who found great satisfaction in knowing that her slave son had traveled to so many places and seen so many exciting things.

A major slave-trading center in the east, Richmond, Virginia, boasted any number of brokers, traders, merchants, dealers, and agents, who specialized in buying and selling human property. Slaves were held in private jails until they appeared on the auction block wearing their best clothes and carrying small bundles of their personal belongings. Potential buyers inspected the slaves' arms, legs, teeth, eyes, and backs; they also examined women as "breeders." (SOURCE: FREDERIC BANCROFT, SLAVE TRADING IN THE OLD SOUTH [BALTIMORE: J. H. FURST CO., 1931], FRONTISPIECE.)

In 1851, James Thomas again accompanied Polk on a summer trip to the North, but this time the slave master brought along his wife, Rebecca, his two young children, and Kitty, the children's slave nurse. The party of six traveled first to New York City, where Thomas looked up his sporting friends from three years earlier. One of the first things he did was go to Genin's Department Store, where he purchased a tall white hat with a long nap, known as a Jenny Lind hat.

Among the guests staying at the hotel was a Nashville physician whose wife had brought her quadroon maid, a tall, handsome girl named Jessie, who asked Thomas to take her for a walk on Broadway. Jessie wore a light, gauzy dress with printed figures on it—a dress, James Thomas said, that would have attracted little attention in New Orleans. He wore his new hat. "Talk about cake walk," Thomas wrote. "Jessie insisted on looking at sights in the show windows, at the same time kept talking. All that Barnum had in his museum turned out on broadway, couldnt have turned more people around for a second look."[12]

After four or five weeks in New York City, Thomas and the Polk family traveled to Saratoga, registering at the United States Hotel. The people there appeared stiff and formal compared with guests at a "southern watering place," Thomas observed, but the hotel offered an "elegant bill of fare, service unsurpassed." The maître d' was Mason Morris, a black man who moved like a ballet dancer between the tables, seating hundreds of guests. In an emergency, he might be persuaded to stop what he was doing to hand a spoon to a lady who needed one, but seldom would he be distracted from placing guests at the correct tables to do the same for a man.[13] After Saratoga, they journeyed to Boston, spending a week at the Revere House, where they celebrated the Fourth of July in the cradle of the Union. That evening, Polk instructed Kitty not to join the fireworks celebration. In addition, she was not to call him "master." With her brightly colored head scarves and neckerchiefs, Polk feared that street toughs would not let her pass unmolested. If "those people knew you belong to me they would come and carry you off and you would never see [your husband] Isaac again."[14]

Built in 1824, the United States Hotel provided not only luxurious accommodation, but also live theater, concerts, a museum, and spectacular natural sights. Saratoga was famous for its mineral springs and spas. Visitors drank the mineral waters, or took the "water cure," by soaking and bathing, hoping to fortify themselves against illness. During the decades before the Civil War, many well-to-do southerners traveled to Saratoga during the summer months. (SOURCE: PRINT FOUND IN GEORGE WALLER, SARATOGA: SAGA OF AN IMPIOUS ERA [ENGLEWOOD CLIFFS, N.J.: PRENTICE-HALL, INC., 1966], 92.)

In August they were at the Ocean House in Newport, Rhode Island. The guests included, among others, United States senator Stephen A. Douglas, who served as patron of the final dress ball of the summer season. The topic of the day was the debate about slavery. French novelist Victor Hugo published an open letter condemning slavery in the United States and elsewhere, while John H. Latrobe, of the American Colonization Society, published a defense of the peculiar institution. In a two-column article, Latrobe asserted that it would not be long before all the free blacks in the United States emigrated to West Africa.[15]

Before beginning their return journey, Polk and his party attended the state fair in Rochester. Rebecca Polk asked her husband if she might take the children to see the escaped slave and now prominent abolitionist "Mr Fred Douglass whom she knew," but Polk absolutely refused to permit such a visit. He feared that as a large slaveholder he might become the subject of an article in Douglass's newspaper *The North Star*.[16] They returned through Baltimore, across the mountains to Wheeling, Virginia, and on to Louisville, where Polk rented rooms at the elegant Galt House Hotel.

During their stay, Thomas took the opportunity to visit the hotel's barbershop. There he met the head barber, free black Stratford Goins. While Thomas and Goins were engaged in conversation, an elderly gentleman entered the shop and took a seat. "[W]here is my boy?" meaning his slave, he asked Goins. "I don't know Governor. The last I heard of him, he was in Cincinnati." "[T]he great fault of your race is their ingratitude," the man asserted. "That boy went and came when he pleased. If he wanted anything, he came to me for it. Now, I'm sick and cant help myself. He never comes near me." Later, Thomas learned that the customer was Robert Letcher, a former governor of Kentucky.[17]

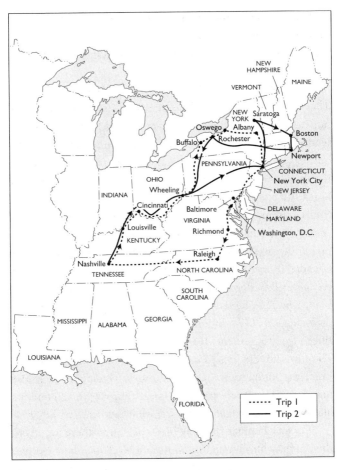

Sojourns to the North

The final leg of their journey took Thomas along the route his older brother Henry had followed to freedom seventeen years before, across the Kentucky countryside and into Tennessee.

NASHVILLE'S BLACK COMMUNITY

Thomas considered himself a good deal better off than most northern blacks. At home he earned a good livelihood, and attended various religious, political, and cultural functions without fear of expulsion. As a boy and young man, he listened to the stirring sermons of Jesse Ferguson and Alexander Campbell, heard the political speeches of Henry Clay, James K. Polk, and Andrew Johnson, and witnessed thoroughbred horse racing at Andrew Jackson's Clover Bottom. An amateur musician—he played the fiddle and attempted to play the flute—Thomas had attended concerts featuring Norwegian violinist Ole Bull, Italian composer Ernesto Camillo Sivori, and Swedish opera star Jenny Lind, who sang her famous "Echo Song" in a special Nashville performance. "My position in the front wing brought me ten or fifteen feet from where Miss Lind had taken her position," James Thomas said. She possessed "a splendid bust and shoulders, a fine clear complexion, light eyes, and an abundance of golden hair dressed over her ears." Her voice "flowed with a limpidness and purity of tone that carried the whole audience with her."[18]

Nor was Thomas the only black person at these events. At the Campbellite church, the white and black members received the sacrament together; at political rallies, slaves and free people of color would "slip around and mix with the crowd"; at Jenny Lind's concert, blacks sat close to the stage. Such intermingling and seeming lack of animosity between the races,

An international star, with the famous P. T. Barnum as her manager, Jenny Lind (1820–1887), known as the Swedish Nightingale, arrived in Nashville in late March 1851, a few weeks after Thomas gained his legal freedom. It was a spectacular event. For sale were Jenny Lind bonnets, gloves, coats, parasols, combs, jewelry, and (as in New York City) hats. Nashville's Willard's Restaurant boasted a "Jenny Lind Room"; the first ticket was auctioned off at two hundred dollars. (SOURCE: CHARLES G. ROSENBERG, *JENNY LIND IN AMERICA* [NEW YORK: STRINGER & TOWNSEND, 1851], FRONTISPIECE, COURTESY OF SPECIAL COLLECTIONS, JACKSON LIBRARY, UNIVERSITY OF NORTH CAROLINA AT GREENSBORO.)

Thomas asserted, were in sharp contrast to race relations in the North.[19]

Moreover, Thomas was part of a vibrant black community. While the number of legally free blacks in the city remained relatively small, increasing from only 409 in 1840 to 511 in 1850, among the more than two thousand slaves were several hundred who hired themselves out and claimed the status of virtual freedom. They included Sarah Estell, the manager of a popular ice cream shop in a small log cabin near the McKendree Church; Jerry Stothard and Peter Lowery, hack drivers who owned their own coaches and horses, and who eventually purchased themselves and their families out of bondage; and hackman James Wilson, who advertised low prices, prompt service, and coaches always ready.[20] Construction boss York Freeman, though a slave, earned a good living building houses in Davidson County.[21] Slaves also hired themselves out as confectioners, coopers, wagoners, mechanics, brickmasons, stonemasons, seamstresses, nurses, laundresses, and barbers.[22]

Perhaps the most celebrated slave in Tennessee was Jack Macon, known simply as "Doctor Jack." Owned by William H. Macon of Maury County, Jack was permitted to move about the countryside as an itinerant physician during the 1830s and 1840s. His patients of many years were so enthusiastic about his talents that they petitioned the state legislature for an exemption after lawmakers, in the wake of the Nat Turner Revolt of 1831, passed a law prohibiting slaves from practicing medicine. Doctor Jack was an extraordinary physician, his patients testified, who possessed "great medical skills" particularly when treating "obstinate disease of long standing." Several of his patients contended that Jack was far superior to white physicians. His followers agreed with the words of "An old observer," who may well have been Doctor Jack himself:

I believe that nature has wisely (& graciously) formed roots, & herbs, to meet every complaint incident to the human species, & that [if] men would study to grow acquainted with them & their uses, & would drench less with drugs, the world would be people'd a great deal sooner, & mankind would enjoy a great deal more health & strength.

After practicing for many years, Macon moved to Nashville and opened an office a few blocks from Thomas's barbershop. Now in his seventies, he placed his business card in the city's first business directory: "JACK, Root Doctor, Office—20 North Front St."[23]

Legally emancipated blacks also fared well in Nashville. Many among them, like Thomas, were persons of mixed ancestry. Some were given financial assistance by white relatives. Most free blacks sustained themselves by learning a trade or a skill. They purchased small plots of land, accumulated personal property, started small businesses, and bought loved ones out of slavery. Slave-born Thomas J. Barber, for example, not only purchased himself but paid five hundred fifty dollars for his three children, James, Ellen, and Mary Frances. Following the death of his slave wife, the mother of his children, he married a young term slave (to be emancipated at a future date) named Myra. Barber petitioned the General Assembly to emancipate her earlier, since her owner had recently died and the executor of his estate was willing to set her free. He also asked the assembly to recognize in law the freedom of his children.[24] Although the legislature did not grant his requests, Barber continued to live with his wife and children.[25]

The interracial cooperation between industrious blacks and prominent whites could be seen in many aspects of Nashville's economic, political, social, and cultural life. The city and surrounding countryside emerged as one of the most prosperous areas in the entire South, and Nashville became the service center for a wide area. But it was more than an economic center that caused free blacks and upper-class whites to come together. Prosperous whites relied on the many talented and literate blacks for a wide range of services, including entertainment. "The leading dancing master of Nashville when I was a boy was a colored man by the name of [Jordan] McGowan," James Thomas recalled. "He instructed many of the leading people of the city [in] the polished art of dancing." McGowan, a free black, established a music school, gave private lessons, conducted a dance band, and booked engagements on nearby plantations. Rachel Gains, a Davidson County slave, recalled how her owner sent for McGowan and his string band about every two weeks. The band would arrive early Friday evening, and the plantation hands would dance in the grape house late into the night. As a teenager, James Thomas took violin lessons from McGowan. "James will make a man of musick I think," his brother John wrote in 1845; "he seems very fond of it."[26]

Quasi-free slaves and legally freed blacks in Nashville maneuvered within the system and achieved a remarkable measure of autonomy and independence. They did so despite a legal structure designed to restrict their movements and curtail their activities. Newly emancipated blacks, for example, were required to post a "good behavior bond" and obtain residency permission from the county court, or immediately leave the state. During the 1830s and 1840s, even in the aftermath of the Nat Turner Revolt, however, city blacks often ignored or circumvented these regulations and other coercive statutes.[27]

They were able to do so in large measure because of the acquiescence of whites. A number of Tennesseans, including slave owners, held genuinely liberal sentiments regarding blacks. The most conspicuous in Nashville was Thomas's legal owner, Ephraim Foster. As early as 1818, Foster had appeared before the Davidson County court seeking the manumission of the African-born slave Simon, who was "sober, industrious, hardworking, and a firm believer in the Christian religion." Later, he posted a one-thousand-dollar security bond for Anna, a slave who was also honest, industrious, sober, and "strictly obedient to heredity."[28] Other whites favored gradual emancipation, and a few, especially in the early decades of the century, advocated immediate abolition.[29] Even those sharing the views of Thomas's father, John Catron, who castigated free blacks as "indolent," "thieving," and "depraved," seemed willing to indulge a few slaves or free Negroes whom they deemed worthy and industrious.[30]

Thomas could call upon his white acquaintances and friends in times of crisis. One frightening incident occurred in late 1850 or early 1851, when he discovered he had been robbed. The most valuable item taken was the bill of sale that Ephraim Foster had signed when Sally purchased James from Foster many years before. Thomas immediately went to the Davidson County Courthouse and asked the recorder of deeds to look up the bill of sale. There could not, of course, be a bill of sale registered to Thomas's slave mother. As it stood, the recorder said, "you are the property of Eph Foster and if he dies his heirs can sell you." Thomas went to the colonel and told him about being robbed and how things "stood on the record." Foster immediately called upon his son Robert, an attorney, and told him that if he died that night for him to make sure that the record was set straight. Foster also told his son that he had no claim on James as a slave. "You will be protected James," Foster promised, "and when the court convenes, I will make you a free man."[31] And so he did, on March 6, 1851.

THE CHANGING ATTITUDES
OF WHITES

It was ironic that following his formal emancipation, Thomas became increasingly dissatisfied with Nashville. The sectional conflict created a hostile environment for slaves and free people of color. Of course, white attitudes toward blacks had always been mixed and ambiguous, but with the passage of the Fugitive Slave Act in 1850, the publication of Harriet Beecher Stowe's *Uncle Tom's Cabin* in 1852, and the eruption of violence in Kansas over the expansion of slavery in 1854–1855, Tennessee whites became more aggressive, enforcing old laws and enacting new ones to control the perceived threat in their midst. In 1854, the legislature passed a law requiring slaves freed by will or contract to "be transported to the western coast of Africa." If funds were not provided for this purpose, the court should hire the slave out "until a fund sufficient for the purpose aforesaid shall have been raised." Further, slaves who had already acquired a right to freedom, but who had not been emancipated by the court, would be subject to the provisions of the act.[32] Within the next few years, additional statutes prescribed the death penalty for a slave who set fire to a barn, stable, crib, outhouse, gin house, manufacturing establishment, bridge, steamboat, or lighter, or any slave aiding, abetting, or advising "an insurrectionary movement."[33]

Increasingly, blacks were being routinely stopped and interrogated. If they could not provide satisfactory proof of their status or a travel pass from their owner, they were arrested and jailed. In 1852, matters became so serious, with numerous arrests and incarcerations, that the assembly enacted a law to protect slaves moving about in a town or city without a pass. They should not be summarily arrested and jailed, the lawmakers said; they should be asked to give a reasonable account of themselves and placed in some safe location until their story could be checked. This would prevent the recurring abuses (and "property damage") caused by arresting and jailing innocent slaves as runaways. Another 1852 law declared that free black children whose parents could not support them should be bound out to a suitable white person, and free black adults who became disorderly should be hired out by the county court for not less than one nor more than five years. If the person refused to be hired, or ran off from an employer, he or she would be imprisoned "at the discretion of the court."[34] After passing these and other statutes, the legislators fashioned an act encouraging free blacks to choose an owner and become slaves"[35]

James Thomas followed closely the passage of these laws and the national political debate that spawned them. In fact, he acquired a thorough understanding of the political issues of his day. He understood the arguments over the expansion of slavery into the territories, the bitter debates between proslavery adherents and northern abolitionists that led to the death of the Whig Party and the birth of the Republican Party, and the hatred that southern slaveholders felt toward what became known as "Black Abolitionists" who might wish to tamper with their "peculiar institution." In all of these debates and conflicts "the Negro," James Thomas explained, was somehow at the center, and however much each side claimed this was not the case—for the South it was a matter of states' rights and for the North a matter of "free soil" and "free speech"—blacks took center stage in the emotional sectional conflict. With each new crisis, Thomas saw the position of free people of color deteriorate in Tennessee and elsewhere, pushing him and others like him back toward bondage. Despite his business success and his long history in the community, Thomas felt threatened.[36]

Any decision to leave Nashville, however, would have to be weighed against closing a successful business, leaving his white friends and protectors, and abandoning a thriving black community. The death of Ephraim Foster in 1854 was a severe blow, although Foster's son Robert promised to act in Foster's stead. Thomas had a number of black friends and acquaintances in Nashville, people he had known all of his life and who had watched him grow into young manhood. They included his former mentor Frank Parrish, Parrish's slave wife, Sarah Jane, and a young family member, Ann Parrish; school teacher and minister Daniel Wadkins; musician and bandleader Jordan Mc-Gowan; slave preacher Alfred Williams, who was interested, as was Thomas, in daguerreotypes; hack driver and livery operator Peter Lowery and his son Samuel Lowery, who became pastor of the Colored Christian Church. "I do not wish you to think for a moment That I have forgotten you for I think of you all the time," Ann Parrish wrote Thomas on one occasion when he was away from the city. "Mr Parrish Is still very unwell with his leg," she wrote. It had been severely bitten by a dog. "I fear he will never get entirely well. He sends his respects to you."[37]

Such friendships made any decision to leave Nashville extremely difficult for Thomas. And where would he go even if he left? He had witnessed firsthand the hostility of whites toward blacks in the North; he had seen the Negro traders and speculators in Baltimore, Washington, D.C., Richmond, New Orleans, and other southern cities; he had watched slaves on the auction block being led away in chains to destinations they could only imagine with fear and anxiety; he had heard rumors that many free blacks and slaves who emigrated or were sent from the United States to West Africa quickly perished from exposure and disease or were killed by natives. Nor was he certain that there might not be some easing of the political tensions that created such a hostile environment for black Americans in Tennessee, although he doubted such would be the case. Should he remain in comfortable and familiar surroundings, or should he venture into the unknown? The journey from slavery to freedom did not prepare him for these new circumstances. Nor did it prepare him for the events that were soon to unfold.

A Fugitive Slave in the North

As Sally Thomas's youngest son became increasingly dissatisfied with Nashville, her second son, the fugitive slave Henry, made a place for himself in Buffalo, New York. During the late 1830s and early 1840s, as in many other parts of the country, Buffalo experienced an economic downturn. By the mid-1840s, however, the city had regained its earlier prosperity and was attracting immigrants from different parts of the United States and Europe. Like both of his brothers, Henry opened a barbershop. He soon boasted a string of loyal white customers. His first shop, located on Commercial Street, was a modest success, but after moving to the basement of the elegant Niagara Hotel, his earnings rose dramatically. He began purchasing real estate, including a lot on Cedar Street in 1842, for one hundred dollars, and, in 1847, a tract of land along Buffalo Creek, about a mile from the Lake Erie harbor, also for a hundred dollars. The land had been part of the Seneca Indian Reservation. Both pieces of property more than doubled in value within a few years.[38]

Unlike his free black brethren in the South, Henry Thomas could speak out on the issues of the day. In Buffalo he followed with interest national events, including the military campaigns of Mexican general Santa Anna in the War for Texas Independence and the struggles of the Creek and Seminole Indians in Alabama, Georgia, and Florida.[39] He followed, too, the failures of the Whig and Democratic Parties, the rise of the Liberty Party, and the arguments of various groups of abolitionists.

In 1845, Thomas traveled to the village of Geneva, New York, to participate in what was called a "free suffrage convention." He and former Virginia slave Austin Stewart presided over the meeting. The delegates complained that the property qualification for blacks to vote in New York was unfair and discriminatory. White men were not subject to the same restriction. Moreover, they argued, propertyless immigrants could vote within a short time after their arrival, while blacks in a similar situation were refused the franchise. The free black delegates vowed to agitate for equal suffrage. They promised to use their "time, talent, and substance" to achieve this goal. They concluded that elective franchise was "a mighty lever for elevating, in the scale of society, any people;" without it, they considered themselves only "nominally free."[40]

Henry Thomas's leadership at the Geneva convention marked his debut as a political activist in the antislavery and black convention movements in the North.

Despite this activity, he could not rid himself of the anxiety that one day his past would catch up with him and a slave catcher would appear at his front door. His deep love for his young wife, Maria, a free black, and their two small children, Sarah and Henry, made this an especially worrisome concern. He was only too aware that his fugitive status put both him and his family in jeopardy. On one occasion, William Giles Harding, owner of the great Belle Meade estate near Nashville, traveled all the way to Buffalo to retrieve one of his runaway slaves. When he learned that a black man from Nashville lived in the city, Harding went to Thomas's shop to make inquiries. "I went to ask him if he knew anything about a boy who ran off from me," Harding recounted. "I told him I only wanted to see him. I had come to Buffalo for that purpose." Henry, however, gave Harding "a very cold and indifferent reply." The incident served to remind him that he, too, could become the object of such a search.[41]

Thomas's worries during the 1840s turned into anxiety and fear following the passage of the Fugitive Slave Act. The new law, part of the broad Compromise of 1850 over slavery, instructed Superior Court judges to appoint "commissioners" to arrest and imprison any person "held to service or labor" in one state, who escaped to another state, and to return them "to whom such service or labor shall be due." The commissioners were entitled to ten dollars compensation for each slave returned and five dollars compensation in cases where the proof did not, in the opinion of the commissioner, warrant such delivery. In short, the commissioners would work with local law enforcement officials to capture and return fugitives. "In no trial or hearing under this act," the law read, "shall the testimony of such alleged fugitive be admitted in evidence;" nor would there be a trial by jury. Anyone who interfered with this process faced a fine of up to one thousand dollars and up to six months' imprisonment. The words *slave* and *slavery* were absent from the new law, just as they had been omitted from the United States Constitution.[42]

Shortly after its passage, Henry Thomas and other blacks in Erie County gathered to denounce the new act in a "large and enthusiastic meeting" at Clinton Hall, in Buffalo. Thomas was the first to speak. He and the other delegates condemned the law as unconstitutional and in violation of every principle of the rule of law. Slave owners and slave catchers could claim any black person as their property. Those accused were presumed guilty until proven innocent. The commissioners were "probably without learning or experience in matters of law," and once a judge decided on a case, the decree could not be appealed, even if the judge erred. Affidavits taken hundreds of miles away and describing persons "held in service" in the vaguest terms could be presented as "conclusive evidence." In sum, the members said, the new law "might be more properly styled a bill to extend Slavery over the free States and encourage the kidnapping of freemen."[43]

Henry Thomas helped draft these resolutions, but the meeting and later protests against the law did little to allay his anxiety. Then, in August 1851, the Buffalo *Commercial Advertiser* trumpeted a disturbing headline: "ARREST OF A FUGITIVE." "Deputy Marshal Gates this forenoon arrested the second cook of the steamer

Buckeye State," the paper reported, "on a charge of being a 'fugitive from service'—the Agent or the owner, who resides in Louisville, Ky., having made the necessary affidavits to obtain process, &c." The fugitive, named Daniel, attempted to escape but was struck on the head and subdued. "He is a fine, athletic negro," one observer noted, "of great value, doubtless, to his owner."[44] With the help of abolitionists, Daniel was released and quickly crossed the border into Canada. But the successful escape only deepened Henry's anxiety. Should he flee across the border, too?

When black representatives from the United States and Canada met in Toronto a month later, Henry joined such prominent black leaders as former slaves Henry Bibb and James D. Tinsley, and free blacks Mary Ann Shadd, Isaac D. Shadd, and Martin R. Delany, an active supporter of emigration. The fifty-three delegates condemned slavery, praised the British government, and advocated immigration to Canada. They denounced the Fugitive Slave Act as "an insult to God, and an outrage upon humanity." Henry Thomas left the meeting convinced it was too risky to remain in the United States. In the fall of 1851, he closed his barbershop, put his property up for sale, and moved his family to the all-black community of Buxton, Canada West.[45]

THE CALIFORNIA GOLD RUSH

John Rapier Sr., in Alabama, felt deeply about family ties, and he used them in times of need to help raise his children. He had sent John Jr. and James to live with their grandmother Sally for a number of years, and he had sent Richard (called Dick) north to live with his uncle Henry in Buffalo, where he could pursue his education. By the late 1840s, Dick Rapier had completed his studies and obtained a rudimentary education in reading, writing, mathematics, and language. At eighteen years old, however, he was not interested in settling down. A year and a half before Henry Thomas took his family to Canada, young Dick returned to Nashville. He had not been there long before he heard tales of fortunes being made in the goldfields of California and, even more tantalizing, word that a number of Nashville residents were heading west to seek their own fortunes. One was a twenty-six-year-old businessman named Madison Berryman Moorman. When Rapier applied to join the expedition, Moorman took him on.

Moorman came from an unusual background, and his racial attitudes were even more unusual. The grandson of a Virginia Quaker who had been "read out of meeting" for taking up arms during the American Revolution and who had also emancipated all his slaves, the younger Moorman also opposed slavery and, unlike the great majority of his countrymen, accepted friends without regard to color.

Moorman had organized a company to mine and pan gold from the mountains and streams of California. Its members included a general superintendent, two assistant superintendents, including Moorman, a treasurer, engineer, physician, two druggists, two slaves, named Walker and John, described as "cash stock," and "Dick Rapier, col'd."

Dick Rapier's meager personal finances, coupled with Tennessee law, prohibited him from investing in Moorman's company, but he was hired on as one of the six "Outsiders." His job would be to manage the mules on the overland journey across the western plains.

As the steamboat *Sligo No. 2* pulled away from the wharf on the afternoon of April 27, 1850, laden with livestock, disassembled wagons, machinery for crushing quartz and extracting gold, and sundry other supplies, Sally Thomas, her son James Thomas, and her grandson James Thomas Rapier were among those who crowded the wharf area. They and the others assembled waved their handkerchiefs and shouted as the last bell rang, a cannon fired, and the mate cried, "Draw in the staging!" Richard Rapier and the other passengers gathered on the hurricane deck to watch the City of Rocks, as Nashville was called, slowly fade into the distance.[46]

Sixty-two hours later, they arrived in St. Louis for a brief stopover,[47] before steaming to the confluence of the Mississippi and the Missouri rivers, and then up the muddy Missouri, shifting the course from time to time to avoid waterlogged trees drifting down the river in their path.[48] A week of preparation was needed to ready them for the overland journey, but on May 14 their wagons began rolling west. Rapier no doubt had his hands full: he had charge of between forty and fifty mules as he and the others set out across the plains.[49]

Paralleling the Kansas River for about one hundred miles, they turned northwest toward Fort Kearney. Fording small creeks and streams, they moved across the flat land, covering about twenty or twenty-five miles a day. In the evenings, they arranged the wagons in a "hollow square," picketed the mules (Rapier's job), and posted guards. Wherever possible, they purchased fresh meat, usually beef, from other journeyers. Once, they bought a string of catfish from a friendly Indian. "Our fish were nicely fried and the heads souped," Moorman noted in his diary, "upon which, all hands feasted most bountifully." After supper the men smoked pipes and cigars with "no small degree of cheerfulness around our camp fire."[50]

By June they were on the high plains, having sold five wagons and three thousand pounds of provisions at Fort Kearney and having put most of their supplies on pack mules. On the other side of the fort, they came upon a horrific sight: a row of camps whose inhabitants were gravely ill or dying. "The number of fresh graves had multiplied frightfully," Moorman observed, "and upon every grave board was written '*Died of* CHOLERA.'" The disease was particularly terrifying because it struck with astonishing speed: a person might be hale and hearty in the morning, yet vomiting and doubled over in pain within a few hours, and dead that evening. Radical dehydration left the skin wizened and also discolored, as the capillaries ruptured. As much as they tried to avoid the contagion, several members of Moorman's party came down with fevers and chills; Rapier and Moorman, however, avoided any illness, and no one in their party died.[51]

Beyond the cholera camps, along the South Platte River, they traveled parallel to huge herds of antelope and buffalo that fed on the tall grasses in the riverbed. The Platte was shallow, rapid, and muddy, and the bed stretched six miles across in some places. The wild flowers were "beautiful and delicate," and the cedars and pines on the sand hills in the distance looked like toy soldiers.[52]

At Fort Laramie, the company left three men, weak from illness, and proceeded toward the Black Hills, an arid, grassless region covered with low, stunted pines. As evening approached, the men pressed on, unable to find a campsite with grass and water. Rapier, with Moorman, had to bring up the rear and "stay back with the tardy mules."[53] As the sun set, the two men reached the summit of one of the highest peaks of the Black Hills. The contrast in the view was startling: behind them, a land entirely dry and desolate; ahead, a forest of deep-green pine trees bathed in the golden hues of the setting sun. "I & my colored friend Dick," Moorman reported, "with our almost worn down charge [of mules], made the best head way we could over the hills & through the deep defiles & gorges, through the darkness." They caught up with the company at eleven that night, having traversed forty-six miles of rough, mountainous terrain.[54]

With so little grass available in South Pass, Rapier had to improvise. He, Moorman, and a few others, including the slave Walker, drove the mules nearly eight miles off the trail so they could feed. Nights were so cold they awoke the morning of July 9 to find ice "one quarter of an inch thick" covering the top of their water barrel. When they entered the City of the Great Salt Lake on July 20, they had traveled twenty-two hundred miles from Nashville.[55]

They found the Mormons hospitable and friendly, and the location one of unexpected beauty, with lofty snow-covered mountains in the distance. They bought supplies of flour, beef, and mutton, and on Sunday morning, Rapier's friend Moorman listened to a sermon by Brigham Young, which he said was "protracted and disconnected."[56] They boarded with local families for five days until it became too expensive, and then made a dash across the Great Salt Lake Desert, via a shortcut known as Hastings Cutoff. The route offered seventy-five miles of ovenlike temperatures and scant water, but it shaved three hundred miles off the usual route to California.

Traveling mostly at night, the party suffered through extreme heat, choking dust, brackish water, coupled with lack of sleep and sheer exhaustion. It could not have been easy for Dick Rapier to goad his suffering mules across the white-salt wasteland, but he had no choice. To slow down would have meant death, and several stragglers in the group barely survived.[57]

Entering Humboldt Valley, they confronted a group of hostile Indians. From the beginning of the trek they had come in contact with various Indian tribes, including the Wyandotte, Kaw, Pottawatomie, Pawnee, and Sioux, most of whom had been friendly. Shortly after midnight on August 12, however, the men awoke to gunfire and someone yelling "Indians!" They leaped to their feet, grabbed their guns, extinguished the fire, and, with gunfire passing overhead, rushed out to protect themselves. The mules were exposed to the attack, and Rapier was joined by others in herding them within the camp's inner circle. "All the animals were soon in *cor[r]al*," Moorman wrote, "during the performance of which the wild savages made the whole valley ring with their frightful yell." The Indians remained close by throughout the night but did not attack again.[58]

Moving along the Humboldt Valley west and south, Moorman's group followed the river until it disappeared into the sands of another desert. They accomplished their second desert crossing in under two days. Without sleep, water, or food except

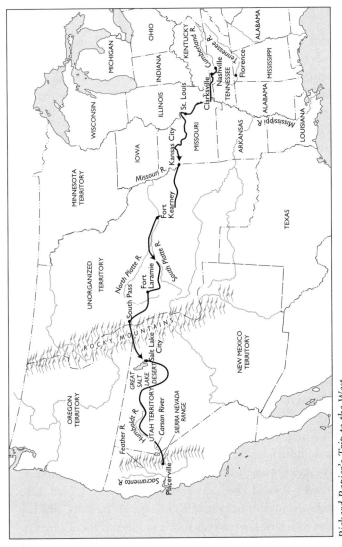

Richard Rapier's Trip to the West

bread, they pressed on, observing over the last thirty miles hundreds of dead and dying animals and abandoned wagons. "Men were fainting, for want of water, under the fatigue and hardships of the miserable waste," Moorman wrote, "and the amount of human suffering is indescribable."

Finally, in late August, after moving up the Carson River, they got their first glimpse of the Sierra Nevada mountain range.[59] Moorman and four others decided to proceed on foot to their initial destination of Placerville, California, while Rapier and the remainder of the company followed with the pack mules and a single wagon. Rapier arrived in Placerville the second week of September, nearly four and a half months after leaving Nashville. He was taken aback by the crowds of mean-looking miners thronging the streets; they wore long, unkempt beards, slouch hats, and brightly checkered shirts. He was also struck by the variety of stores, restaurants, hotels, gambling houses, brothels, and "doggeries." He learned that the town's nickname of Hangtown was coined when a black cook, described as a "nice chap," was hanged for stealing some of his employer's gold.[60]

It did not take Rapier long to discover that digging and panning for the precious metal was even more difficult than the 2,700-mile journey he had undertaken to reach the Promised Land. Indeed, by the fall of 1850, some of the rivers and mines were already exhausted. Among the tens of thousands of prospectors who flooded into California, the 1852 census listed 2,206 blacks and mulattoes, including a number of "servants" who had come with their masters only to acquire their freedom once California entered the Union.[61] Only six weeks after they arrived,

The gold rush attracted prospectors from as far away as the Caribbean, Central and South America, and China. Although few among them were abolitionists, most Californians opposed slavery because they feared that the system's cheap labor would create unwanted competition. Among those who joined the gold rush were slaves (with their owners) and free blacks. (Observe the black prospector to the far left.) (Source: Lithograph courtesy of Bancroft Library, University of California—Berkeley.)

the Tennessee gold prospectors went their separate ways, finding "the mines too poor to support" them.[62]

Rapier left his friends and journeyed to the Feather River in the Sacramento River Valley, where he eventually purchased some land and began farming. A few years later, he was joined by his younger brother Henry Rapier, but they quarreled and Henry went off on his own. "Dick said nothing a Bout his Brother

Henry not as much as to call his name," the boys' father, John Rapier Sr., fretted. "I am Sorry to See Brothers have so littel respect for each other for it is not rite for them to act that way."[63] The father later heard that Henry had become a professional gambler. This could only lead to a life of liquor and loose women, the father grieved. "I would not be Sirprise," he lamented, "to hear of his death." Dick, however, remained in California, planted a crop of wheat and barley, and settled into the routine of a commercial farmer.[64]

THE EPIDEMIC'S SHADOW

Sally Thomas was her usual lively self when she waved good-bye to her eighteen-year-old grandson Dick Rapier as he departed for California goldfields. In the spring of 1850, at age sixty-three, she was vibrant, energetic, and ebullient. Despite her vigorous activities picking up dirty clothing, washing it, and delivering the clean garments, she maintained a youthful appearance. Indeed, her vitality seemed almost limitless. But the same cholera epidemic that frightened Dick Rapier's party outside Fort Kearney came also to Nashville that year, as well as to other major cities in the South and Midwest. And as the deaths struck, with savage speed, so did the fear.

Late in that summer of 1850, Sally began to feel queasy. She tried to rest, hoping against hope that her illness was only the flu and would soon pass. But within hours, she began vomiting and experiencing severe muscle cramps and diarrhea. Her facial features became contorted, and her skin darkened. It was the inexorable, fatal progression. In the midst of a full-blown epidemic, few city residents even noticed her passing.[65]

About a week later, the United States census taker arrived at 10 Deaderick Street. With Sally Thomas gone, he listed her twenty-two-year-old slave son, James, as the head of the household and noted that her twelve-year-old grandson, James Thomas Rapier, was living at the same residence.[66] Her son and grandson laid Sally Thomas to rest in the Nashville City Cemetery during the same week of the passage of the Fugitive Slave Act.[67] While they both felt anxious about the future, they grieved deeply at the loss of the woman who had held the family together for so many years. Although her death came suddenly, the legacy of a mother determined to free her three sons and keep her family together remained alive for generations.

N o t e s

1. FTS, 121; Mary Polk Branch, *Memoirs of a Southern Woman: "Within the Lines" and a Genealogical Record* (Chicago: Joseph G. Branch Publishing Co., 1912), 79; Jill Knight Garrett, "St. John's Church, Ashwood," *Tennessee Historical Quarterly* 29 (Spring 1970): 14.

2. FTS, 121–22.

3. Gloria Deák, *Picturing New York: The City from Its Beginnings to the Present* (New York: Columbia University Press, 2000), 280.

4. FTS, 122–23. It was not unusual for southerners to travel to the North during the summer months in the period leading up to the Civil War. See John Hope Franklin, *A Southern Odyssey: Travelers in the Antebellum North* (Baton Rouge: Louisiana State University Press, 1976).

5. FTS, 124.

6. Ibid.

7. Ibid.

8. Ibid., 122–23.

9. Ibid., 125.

10. Ibid.

11. Ibid.

12. Ibid., 127. John N. Genin (1819–1878), a New York City merchant, used many advertising gimmicks to attract shoppers to his store, including naming hats after famous people.

13. FTS, 128; George Waller, *Saratoga: Saga of an Impious Era* (Englewood Cliffs, N.J.: Prentice-Hall, 1966), 161.

14. FTS, 128–29.

15. Ibid., 128–30.

16. Ibid., 130; Frederick Douglass, *Narrative of the Life of Frederick Douglass, an American Slave: Written by Himself* (Boston: Anti-Slavery Office, 1845).

17. FTS, 125. In Thomas's autobiography, the return route for the second trip was placed after the return route of the first and thus out of sequence. Thomas reported that the governor called Stratford Goins "Henry."

18. Ibid., 5, 6, 43–45, 47, 52–53.

19. For a comparison of the economic plight of blacks in the North and the South, see Ira Berlin, "The Structure of the Free Negro Caste in the Ante-Bellum United States," *Journal of Social History* IX (1976): 297–318.

20. For Sarah Estell, see "Old Days in Nashville, Tennessee, Reminiscences of Jane Thomas," reprints from the Nashville *Daily American,* 1895–1896, in Jane Thomas Papers, TSLA; for Stothard and Lowery, see Legislative Papers, Petitions of Samuel Seay to the Tennessee General Assembly, November 2, 1837, November 4, 1839, TSLA; Records of the Davidson County Court, Minute Book 1850–1853 (1851), 135–37, 144, 175, 192; for James Wilson, see *Nashville General Business Directory*, 1853, 22.

21. Records of the Davidson County Court, Wills and Inventories, Vol. 9 (July 7, 1832), 596; ibid., Warranty Deeds, Book 2 (March 12, 1849), 389–90; ibid., Book 7 (January 25, 1845), 247; *Nashville General Business Directory*, 1853, 13.

22. Loren Schweninger, "The Free-Slave Phenomenon: James P. Thomas and the Black Community in Ante-Bellum Nashville," *Civil War History* 22 (December 1976): 293–307.

23. Legislative Petitions, Petition of Residents of Maury, Bedford, Giles, Hickman, Williamson, and Lincoln Counties to the General Assembly, ca. 1832, no. 11-1832-1a-4, reel 12, TSLA; Testimonials Concerning Doctor Jack, 1829–1831, no. 294-1831-1-7, reel 12, ibid.; Petition of Citizens of Tennessee to the Legislature, August 1843, no. 189-1843-1-2, reel 17, ibid.; *Journal of the House of Representatives of the State of Tennessee at the Twenty-fifth General Assembly, Held at Nashville, on Monday the 25 Day of October, 1843* (Knoxville: Tenn.: E. G. Eastman and L. Gifford, 1844), 180; *Journal of the Senate of Tennessee at the Twenty-fifth General Assembly, Held at Nashville* (Knoxville, Tenn.: E. G. Eastman and L. Gifford, [1844]), 190; Petition of the Ladies of Tennessee to the Legislature, August 1843, no. 189-1843-3-4, reel 17, TSLA; Loren Schweninger, "Doctor Jack: A Slave Physician on the Tennessee Frontier," *Tennessee Historical Quarterly*, LVII (spring/summer 1998), 36–41; *The Nashville General Commercial Directory* (Nashville: Daily American, 1853), 36; *Nashville City and Business Directory, for the City of Nashville* (Nashville: E. G. Eastman & Co., [1859]), 87. In 1860, at age about eighty, Jack Macon died in Nashville of "old age." Records of the Nashville City Cemetery, 1846–1860, May 16, 1860, Nashville Room, the Public Library of Nashville and Davidson County, Nashville, Tenn.

24. Legislative Petitions, Petition of Thomas J. Barker to the Tennessee Legislature, ca. 1841, TSLA.

25. *Acts Passed at the First Session of the Twenty-third General Assembly of the State of Tennessee, 1839–40* (Nashville: J. George Harris, 1840); *Acts Passed at the First Session of the Twenty-fourth General Assembly of the State of Tennessee, 1841–42* (Murfreesboro: D. Cameron & Co., 1842).

26. FTS, 69; George P. Rawick, ed., *The American Slave: A Composite Autobiography,* 19 vols. (Westport, Conn.: Greenwood Press, 1972), 16:17; John Rapier Sr. to Richard Rapier, April 8, 1845, RTP.

27. *A Compilation of the Statutes of Tennessee of a General and Permanent Nature from the Commencement of the Government to the Present Time* (Nashville: Steam Press of James Smith, 1836), 277–79; *Acts Passed at the*

First Session of the Twenty-third General Assembly of the State of Tennessee (Nashville: J. George Harris, 1840), 82; J. Merton England, "The Free Negro in Ante-Bellum Tennessee," *Journal of Southern History* 9 (February 1943), 50–51; *Statute Laws of the State of Tennessee of a General Character; Passed Since the Compilation of the Statutes by Caruthers and Nicholson, in 1836* (Nashville: J. G. Shepard, 1846), 168–70.

28. Records of the County Court, Davidson County, Tenn., Minute Book, October 1816 to January 1818 (February 2–3, 1818), 457; ibid., Minute Book, April 1819 to October 1821 (October 1821), 208, Metropolitan Nashville–Davidson County Archives, Nashville, Tenn.; Ephraim H. Foster to Jane Foster, July 30, 1847, Foster-Woods Papers, TSLA.

29. Legislative Petitions, Petition of James Upton, Hugh Bagle, and David Logan, et al., to the Tennessee General Assembly, 1817, TSLA; ibid., Petition of George Crouch and Jacob Ellis, 1833, TSLA; ibid., Petition of John Gibson, January 7, 1842, TSLA.

30. James Patton, "The Progress of Emancipation in Tennessee," *Journal of Negro History* 17 (January 1932): 67–68; Records of the County Court, Davidson County, Tenn., Wills (June 29, 1865), 20:31–36.

31. FTS, 30–31.

32. *Acts of the State of Tennessee, Passed at the First Session of the Thirtieth General Assembly, for the Years 1853–4* (Nashville: McKennie & Brown, 1854), 121.

33. *Public Acts of the State of Tennessee Passed at the First Session of the Thirty-second General Assembly, for the Years 1857–8* (Nashville: G. C. Torbett & Co., 1858), 18–19 [setting fire to barns]; 94–95 [aiding "an insurrectionary movement"].

34. *Acts of the State of Tennessee, Passed at the First Session of the Twenty-ninth General Assembly for the Years 1851–2* (Nashville: Band & McKennie, Printers, 1852), 120; free black children bound out, ibid., 235; disorderly free blacks, ibid., 237; resist with force, ibid., 719–20.

35. *Public Acts of the State of Tennessee Passed at the First Session of the Thirty-second General Assembly, for the Years 1857–8* (Nashville: G. C. Torbett & Co., 1858), 55–56 [free blacks volunteering for slavery]. In 1858, the law allowed the children of free blacks volunteering for slavery to

remain free if they so chose. In 1860, this law was amended, giving mothers an opportunity to make the decision for their children. *Public Acts of the State of Tennessee, Passed at the First Session of the Thirty-third General Assembly for the Years 1859–60* (Nashville: E. G. Eastman & Co., 1860), 117.

36. FTS, 80–81.

37. James Thomas to John Rapier Jr., October 3, 1856, December 23, 1856, RTP; USMSPC, Davidson County, Tenn., Nashville, 1850, 155; ibid., Second Ward, 1860, 343 [Julia Sumner]; George Rawick, *The American Slave: A Composite Autobiography*, 18:4 [Alfred Williams]; Records of the County Court, Davidson County, Tenn., Wills (November 28, 1854), 16:428–29 [Sarah Jane Parrish]; D. Porch, trans., *Davidson County, Tennessee, 1850 Census* (Fort Worth: American Reference Publishers, 1969), 253 [Ann Parrish]. In the census, Parrish was listed as an illiterate mulatto barber, age forty-five; Ann was listed as a twenty-year-old literate mulatto. No family relationship was indicated. Parrish's slave wife, Sarah Jane, was not listed. The correspondence cited in RTP as "anonymous" to James Thomas was almost certainly [Ann Parrish] to James Thomas, May 27, 1857, RTP.

38. Records of the Erie County Court, Land Deeds, Liber 99 (July 20, 1842), 354, County Hall, Buffalo, N.Y.; ibid., Liber 167 (December 24, 1847), p. 59; Assessment Records, Buffalo City Court, 1844, Fourth Ward, n.p., Buffalo, N.Y.; ibid., 1851, Fourth Ward, 1117. The description of the Buffalo Creek Reservation property is found in Records of the Erie County Court, Land Deeds, Liber 131 (October 15, 20, 1852), 463, County Hall, Buffalo, N.Y. For residency in Buffalo, see A. M. Sumner to Henry Thomas, May 26, 1836, RTP; *Buffalo City Directory* (Buffalo: Horatio N. Walker, Publisher, 1844), 213; ibid. (1847–48), 158; ibid. (1851–52), 289.

39. A. M. Sumner to Henry Thomas, May 26, 1836, RTP.

40. *National Anti-Slavery Standard*, October 30, 1845. For a description of Geneva, N.Y., see *The Liberator*, October 10, 1845. Austin Stewart served as president, and Thomas as first vice-president, of the convention.

41. FTS, 34, 78.

42. Mark V. Tushnet, "Fugitive Slave Act of 1850," in Randall M. Miller and John David Smith, eds., *Dictionary of Afro-American Slavery* (New York: Greenwood Press, 1988), 276.

43. Buffalo *Daily Republic* [Buffalo, N.Y.], October 4, 1850. The delegate listed as Henry *R.* Thomas at a second mass meeting on October 17, 1850 was in fact Henry *K.* Thomas, who again was appointed to a select committee to prepare the order of business. The second meeting "Resolved, that the fugitive slave bill, passed by Congress, not only violates the sacred guarantees of the Constitution, but is Anti-Republican, Anti-Christian, and unworthy of the support of enlightened freemen." *North Star* (Rochester, New York), October 24, 1850.

44. Buffalo *Commercial Advertiser*, August 15, 16, 19, 1851; Buffalo *Morning Express*, August 30, 1851; New York *Daily Tribune*, September 2, 1851.

45. "Proceedings of the North American Convention, Convened at St. Lawrence Hall, Toronto, Canada West, September 11–13, 1851," in C. Peter Ripley, ed., et al., *The Black Abolitionist Papers, Volume II, Canada, 1830–1865*, 5 vols. (Chapel Hill: University Press, 1986), 2:149–69. See also: Victor Ullman, *Look to the North Star: The Life of William King* (Toronto: Umbrella Press, 1969), 108.

46. Irene D. Paden, ed., *The Journal of Madison Berryman Moorman 1850–1851* (San Francisco: California Historical Society, 1948), vii, viii, 1; Rudolph M. Lapp, *Blacks in Gold Rush California* (New Haven: Yale University Press, 1977), 29.

47. Paden, *Journal of Madison Berryman Moorman*, 2–4.

48. Ibid., 4, 92.

49. Ibid., 6–7. The settlement, called Kansas, was twelve miles above Independence, Mo. Prior to 1850 it was called Kansasmouth or Kawsmouth, near the confluence of the Kansas or Kaw and Missouri rivers. It expanded in 1850 to become the Town of Kansas; in 1853 it became the City of Kansas; and in 1889, Kansas City. In 1899, it legally absorbed Westport, originally four miles inland from Kansasmouth. Ibid., 92. The number of mules is mentioned in ibid., 20.

50. Ibid., 11, 14.

51. Ibid., 18. The single death among those in the group occurred from cholera after they arrived in California. The description of cholera is found in William McNeill, *Plagues and Peoples* (Garden City, N.Y.: Anchor Press, 1976), 231.

52. Paden, *Journal of Madison Berryman Moorman*, 20, 23–24.

53. Lapp, *Blacks in Gold Rush California*, 29.

54. Ibid., 31–32.

55. Ibid., 30, 46–48.

56. Ibid., 48–52.

57. Ibid., 56–57, 115. The distance to Sacramento City was reduced from eight to five hundred miles. Most emigrants, however, took the longer, less dangerous route. The Hastings Cutoff was rarely used after 1850. Using "several Vitameters," Moorman estimated the desert crossing at ninety miles.

58. Ibid., 7, 10, 16, 64–65.

59. Ibid., 76–78.

60. Richard Keen, *Account of a Journey Overland to California from Logan, Indiana, in 1852, and of the Return Voyage via Panama to New York*, July 24, 1852, cited in Paden, *Journal of Madison Berryman Moorman*, 129; Lapp, *Blacks in Gold Rush California*, 83.

61. In 1852, the total population of slightly more than a quarter-million included 171,841 whites, 31,266 "Indians domesticated," 54,803 foreign born, 1,678 blacks and 528 mulattoes. *The Seventh Census of the United States: 1850* (Washington: Robert Armstrong, 1853), 982. Also see Lapp, *Blacks in Gold Rush California*, 31.

62. On October 19, 1851, Moorman wrote that the company "suspended" operations, but this suspension in fact ended the company's activities as originally conceived. Paden, *Journal of Madison Berryman Moorman*, 85.

63. John Rapier Sr. to John Rapier Jr., December 13, 1856, RTP.

64. John Rapier Sr. to John Rapier Jr., September 15, 1856 [comment on death], December 13, 1856, August 6, 1857, RTP; Richard Rapier to James Thomas, December 14, 1877, RTP.

65. See Jane Ellen Cheatham to Ephraim H. Foster, July 5, 1850, Foster-Woods Papers, TSLA.

66. USMSPC, Davidson County, Tenn., Nashville, 1850, 177. The census taker arrived on September 16, 1850.

67. Deed of Purchase, James Thomas to the Corporation of the City of Nashville, September 10, 1850, Nashville Room, Public Library of Nashville and Davidson County, Nashville, Tenn. The Fugitive Slave Act became law on September 18, 1850.

· *Four* ·

In Search of Canaan

In Nashville, the last day in December 1855 was cold, windy, and rainy. The sky was laden with thick, black clouds, and the icy drizzle seemed to chill the soul as much as the body. For some time following Sally's death, her youngest son, James, had been considering whether to remain in Tennessee or seek a new home. The increasing racial tensions, growing sectional conflict, and strident antiblack pronouncements caused him grave concern—concern that was heightened by the death of his friend and white patron, Ephraim Foster.

Thomas had lived in Nashville all his life; he did not want to consider leaving if he could avoid it. But the wish to find a haven where conditions were better for blacks—a "Promised Land" or Canaan, as the Bible would have called it—tugged at him. And he was willing to consider a region beyond the borders of the United States. Indeed, having traveled in the segregated North as well as having lived in the slave South, James Thomas was open to more adventurous possibilities.

Was it chance that brought a visit from his twenty-year-old nephew John Rapier Jr. on that gloomy day in December? Perhaps not, given the unsettled times, for Rapier, too, was troubled by the growing white hostility toward blacks. James Thomas was particularly fond of his nephew, who was only eight years his junior; the two had lived together when John had come to his grandmother Sally's to attend school in Nashville. And now young Rapier brought word of a newspaper article about William Walker, a Nashville native who had invaded Nicaragua. Walker and a band of filibusters, the term then used to describe Americans who took part in fomenting revolutions in Latin America, had captured Granada and were preparing to organize a new government. He was offering emigrants two hundred fifty acres of free land as well as free passage to Central America.[1]

James Thomas had known William Walker since boyhood, as they were nearly the same age. Even so, when young John Rapier announced that he planned to join the filibusters and hoped his uncle would too, Thomas hesitated. How committed was Walker to his declarations that he was fighting in defense of liberty? How much did he care about the native inhabitants? How dangerous would it be to venture into an area where warring factions were fighting one another? But his nephew persisted, arguing not only that the cause was just but also that Central America was a region of unsurpassed beauty. In the end, Thomas agreed to go.[2]

During the next few weeks, he closed his barbershop, took leave of his friends, wound up his affairs in Nashville, and headed for the Crescent City. Once reunited in New Orleans, John Rapier Jr. and James Thomas went to the wholesale grocery firm of Dyas & Company, where they asked the owners, R. I. and Robert Dyas, to help them place their names on a steamboat passenger list. "It was necessary in those days when about to travel, particularly in the direction of free Territory on any Rail Road, steam ship, stage or anything Else," James Thomas recalled, "to have some reputable [white] person or persons to Identify the applicant as free, as a measure of protection." Without such protection, the owners of a shipping company might be held liable for taking away someone's property. A Dyas assistant went with Thomas and Rapier when they signed the ship's list. On the morning of February 12, 1856, they boarded the steamer *Daniel Webster,* bound for Greytown (San Juan del Norte), Nicaragua.[3]

Bound for Nicaragua

After a few days at sea, an officer of the ship confronted the two men and demanded their papers. Thomas explained that they had been vouched for, but the captain had no record to that effect. "I have been the centre of attraction on more than one occasion," James Thomas wrote. "They were not pleasant to me and I don't believe anybody would relish such things." To have about forty or more people "gawking at you as though you had stolen a horse and questions by the purser and Captain to us was annoying." After examining their papers, including letters and other documents, the officers "let the matter drop."[4]

Arriving in Punta Arenas, at the southern tip of Nicaragua, they switched to a smaller boat for their voyage up the San Juan River. The world closed in on them as they journeyed upriver, passing the sugar cane plants, the thickets of plantain and casaba, and the groves of orange, banana, and lemon trees. Crocodiles wriggled off the shore into the river; at times, the chattering of the monkeys nearly drowned out all conversation, and the swarms of mosquitoes drove the men from the deck on several occasions. At El Castillo, they saw the relics of "the broken power of Spain," John Rapier Jr. reported, including a dilapidated prison, where rotting stocks and yokes had been used for torture. "For these ruthless Spaniards were licentious," Rapier wrote bitterly, "and neither age, patriotism, youth, beauty nor virtue was a safeguard against their brutal passions."[5]

Crossing Lake Nicaragua, they docked at Granada, the oldest Spanish city in Central America, founded by conquistador Hernández de Córdoba in 1524. As they trudged up the mile-long road to the center of the city, with the mountains rising in the background, they mingled with "a sprinkling of pure Castillians," several blacks and mulattoes, as well as a number of Indians and "Ladinos," as Rapier called them. The men wore loose, white cotton trousers and broad-brimmed sombreros; the women, walking erect with earthen water jugs on their heads, wore brightly colored skirts and loose-fitting halters.[6]

Growing up in Nashville, James Thomas had seen William Walker on many occasions. He was a quiet, modest, and unobtrusive young man, Thomas wrote, who regularly attended the Christian Church that permitted black and white worshipers to receive the sacrament on the same floor at the same time. Weighing only one hundred thirty pounds and slight of build, Walker was almost effeminate in appearance, with a fair complexion, light hair, and freckles. Thomas sized him up when he delivered a letter entrusted to him by the general's father. "He read the letter and looked as though in deep thought several minutes," Thomas recalled. The letter was the first word Walker had received from home in some time.

Thomas was struck that Walker remained unpretentious despite his rank of commander in chief of a triumphant army. "He

Travels of James Thomas and John Rapier Jr. to Nicaragua

had a horse, a uniform in good order, one pair of boots, a scarcity of linen, his sword, one pistol besides his horse pistols, military hat, nothing shiny on him but the spurs and buttons on his coat." Beneath his jacket he wore a necklace with a picture of his only sister Alice in a gold case.[7]

Thomas and Rapier also met Walker's brother Norvell, a recruiting agent, and Kentucky-born Parker H. French, Walker's one-armed confidant. French had recently returned from Washington, D.C., where he had failed to obtain recognition of the new government from the Department of State.

During the next few weeks, Thomas and Rapier discovered that their romantic ideas about Central America were far from reality. The daily reveille was followed by a death march, Rapier wrote, "as a cart emerged from the gates of the hospital piled high with plain and rudely constructed coffins, often to the number of half a dozen." Upon rising each morning, the soldiers would ask "who died last night?" The medical staff was poorly trained and poorly equipped, and the hospital ill-supplied. It consisted of one long, narrow room, stifling hot with little ventilation, and about twenty beds. Two-thirds of the deaths were from infection, diarrhea, dysentery, or malignant fevers. On the day Thomas and Rapier visited, two soldiers had died that morning; another was delirious, writhing in sweat and begging to go home to his mother. The "wild roar of Lake Nicaragua," Rapier wrote, "is [an] eternal funeral dirge."[8]

Just as ominously, Thomas and Rapier discovered that Walker's plan did not include any strategy for uplifting the peasants of the country. Rather, he intended to conquer the surrounding nations and reintroduce slavery in the region. "The in-

Physician, lawyer, journalist, and America's best-known filibusterer, William Walker (1824–1860) embodied the idea of Manifest Destiny. Born and raised in Nashville, he sympathized with the South and sought to establish new territories in Mexico and Central America to maintain a balance of power with the North. He led expeditions to Baja California and Mexico; then to Nicaragua, where he declared himself president. He was eventually executed by the Honduran government. (SOURCE: WILLIAM O. SCROGGS, *FILIBUSTERS AND FINANCIERS: THE STORY OF WILLIAM WALKER AND HIS ASSOCIATES* [NEW YORK: MACMILLAN COMPANY, 1916], FRONTISPIECE.)

troduction of Negro-slavery into Nicaragua," Walker explained, "would furnish a supply of constant and reliable labor requisite for the cultivation of tropical products." Thomas and Rapier received this news with dismay. The only reasonable course of action seemed clear. On April 9, 1856, less than two months after arriving, Thomas informed the general that he and his nephew would return to the United States.

As they departed, word came that an invading army from Costa Rica had decisively defeated Walker's forces. His peasant army, equipped mostly with machetes, had lost half of its troops, or more than a thousand men; Walker had lost three of his top aides, and his native troops began to disappear. Nonetheless, Walker remained in the country and, in July 1856, declared himself president of Nicaragua, resulting in recognition by the United States. Eventually, however, he was defeated by a combined force of Central American states and the betrayal of a former friend, Cornelius Vanderbilt, whose Accessory Transit Company controlled Walker's supply lines. In May 1857, the "grey eyed man of destiny" surrendered to the United States Navy.[9]

"When I was going to Nicaragua people would ask, what are you going there for? I thought it strange to put that question to me when such grand opportunities were presented according to the papers," Thomas later recalled with chagrin. But by the time he left Central America he felt betrayed. Instead of a land of opportunity, he witnessed only death and destruction.[10] In Greytown, Thomas and Rapier arranged passage on a small Jamaican trading schooner bound for Aspinwall, the Caribbean terminus of railroad crossing the Isthmus of Panama.[11] Arriving in Aspinwall, they felt that they had finally returned to civilization. There were hotels, restaurants, boarding houses, and other businesses. Gold-seekers from California filled the streets, fresh from their eastward journey on the forty-seven-mile railroad line that took them from the Pacific Ocean to the Atlantic.[12] Then the two men boarded the steamer *Illinois* for Havana, Cuba, as did William Walker's associate, Parker French, who was returning to the United States. By the time they reached Havana, Rapier had agreed to enter French's service as his personal secretary.[13] The two departed for New Orleans. Meanwhile, Thomas, who

The town of Colon was renamed Aspinwall after American financier and railroad builder William Henry Aspinwall built his Panama Railroad to connect Aspinwall (on the Atlantic side of the Isthmus) with Panama City (on the Pacific side), thus bypassing the two- to four-month trip around Cape Horn, or the dangerous land journey by wagon. The world's first transcontinental railway, the Panama Railroad was key to opening trade up in the West and made Aspinwall an important port city. (SOURCE: PICTURE IN *THE ILLUSTRATED LONDON NEWS*, DECEMBER 30, 1865.)

was yet unwilling to give up his search for a more promising alternative to Nashville, purchased a ticket for New York City.

Many years later, James Thomas recalled how painful it was to observe black workers in Havana. Large, muscular men, bare to the waist, with sweat glistening in the stifling noonday sun, shoveled coal into the holds of the steamships and rolled huge barrels of cargo on and off the merchant ships. They worked under the watchful eye of an overseer, who stood with whip in hand, and they bore the marks of the lash on their backs. They "nearly all showed some sign of being born in Africa, their faces, marked, scarred and other signs of tribe mark," James Thomas observed. "It seemed as if they were bought for the purpose of working them to death, as some people do with Mules."[14]

When Thomas arrived in New York City, his friends barely recognized him. His clothes were ragged, and he was disheveled and unkempt. He purchased a new suit, remained in the city to visit friends, and then, in the late spring of 1856, embarked for the upper Midwest. His dreams of Central America had been dashed; now he traveled through Illinois and Wisconsin, visiting towns for a possible place to settle.[15] He was impressed with the beauty of the countryside, but even though he had worked as a waiter on the *Illinois* to supplement his cash reserve, his funds were low. So he returned to Nashville, temporarily, "with the intention of raising a thousand dollars and going back to Wisconsin."[16]

THE DILEMMA OF JOHN RAPIER SR.

Sally's oldest son, John Rapier Sr., was also wondering if he might fare better in a different location. Rapier had lived in Florence, Alabama, for more than thirty years. He had witnessed the town grow from a tiny hamlet during the 1820s to the fifth-largest city in Alabama in 1850, with a population of nearly eight hundred; he had also observed the large influx of slaves, as Lauderdale County's slave population more than quadrupled to six thousand between 1820 and 1850. As the entrepôt for the Tennessee

River trade, the city saw steamboats arrive with manufactured goods from New Orleans and depart with thousands of bales of cotton for the European market. But unlike Nashville, the town's free black population remained tiny. Indeed, excluding Rapier's own family, the census taker in 1850 listed only three other free blacks in Florence, which was comprised of 458 whites and 327 slaves.[17]

As the town grew and prospered, so too did John Rapier Sr.'s business and property holdings. Despite recurring recessions and the depression of the 1840s, he had been able to make a comfortable living. As early as 1831, he had paid three hundred dollars for a small lot on Court Street, in the main business section; nine years later, as the highest bidder, he purchased an adjacent lot, "together with a white frame dwelling house."[18] Later, he bought several other pieces of real estate.[19] By 1850, Rapier had become a fixture in the town as a dependable, conscientious, and hardworking barber.[20]

Despite his longtime residency, Rapier was troubled, or, as he put it, "Pestard in mind" about the growing number of laws designed to keep blacks subservient.[21] With his wife deceased and his children living elsewhere, he had already started a second family with his slave housekeeper, Lucretia. By 1856, they had four children: Rebecca, Joseph, Thomas, and Charles, all born into slavery due to the legal status of their mother. It would take a special act of the legislature to set them and their mother free, and Rapier felt it best to keep their status quiet, as many residents thought they were already free. Indeed, they were listed as free mulattoes by the census takers. Nonetheless, they were slaves in the eyes of the law, and that made it virtually impossible for

Rapier to provide them with an education or send them away to school, as he had done with his oldest boys when Sally was alive and could take them in. "You have evry Rite to Know I have a fealing for my off spring," he wrote his son John, noting that "they ought to be free and at School."[22] Rapier also wrote that if anything should happen to him, his second family could be placed on the auction block.[23]

Rapier also worried about his chosen occupation. "I am not makeing any money at present," he complained in 1857;[24] "my eyes are geting So I can not See how to Shave."[25] Equally troubling, a new barber named Gowins had moved into town, and was taking away some of Rapier's customers on the grounds that "young People will follow a young Barber."[26] To tell the truth, Rapier confessed, "I hate the name of barber."[27] He admitted in 1857 that he was "more out with Florence at present then Ever before," he told his son John he would try to remain in the town until the end of the year.[28] At that time, he would in all likelihood take Lucretia and his slave family and leave Alabama. But where would they go?

During the early 1850s, West Africa had seemed a possibility. Rapier had subscribed to the *African Repository*, the newspaper of the American Colonization Society, and he had followed the events in the colony of Liberia, founded in 1822 as a refuge for emancipated slaves and free blacks. In the end, however, he had become disillusioned. Members of the society seemed unconcerned with the welfare of black Americans: all that the society's members really wanted was to rid the United States of its free black population. They did not care "if all the free negros in the United States was at the Botom of the Sea [just] So they was out of the United States." In 1854, Rapier wrote a letter to William

McLain, Secretary of the society, canceling his three-year subscription to the society's newspaper. "I am a man of But little learning I hope you will Excuse me on that account, but what I know I Know it as well as any man."[29]

Another possible destination was Canada West. It was, after all, a land of freedom, the so-called "Promised Land." Shortly after his brother Henry had settled in Buxton, John Rapier Sr. had purchased fifty acres in Raleigh Township, Kent County, for forty-four British pounds, and he kept up the property as it slowly appreciated in value. Later, he bought more land in Kent County and three lots in Toronto.[30] He visited the North and Canada on several occasions, staying with his brother Henry and his family, but he finally decided against the move. Henry struggled constantly to make ends meet there and always seemed to be in debt. On one occasion, Henry sent a letter without postage to Rapier's son, noting that he did not have enough money to pay for a stamp. "I like Canada," John Rapier Sr. wrote in 1857, "but I can not See how I can make a liveing in that could [cold] country."[31]

A final alternative was to move to a free state in the West. In fact, he had already advised his son John to settle in "some growing town in an area with natural advantages," where slavery did not exist.[32] John returned the same advice in 1857, urging his father to "move out West and to give Lucretia and the children some Kind of a [chance] for justice."[33] John Sr. replied that he was at that moment making plans to move out "to Some free State."[34] He hoped that his brother and son would join him and that they could be neighbors.[35] The next year he reiterated "I am ankious to quite [quit] Florence my Self but I must Sell first." He planned to sell out to his rival, who had left town but had promised to return and buy him out. "[T]he price we have agreed on is Six Hundred dollars for the house and lot with three hundred down the balance in the next two years."[36]

But the deal never materialized, and despite his plan to sell out and leave, John Rapier Sr. remained in Florence. Notwithstanding his complaints about making a living, he had established himself as the barber of Florence and could earn as much as fifty dollars a month, charging between fifteen and twenty cents for a haircut and additional sums for shaving beards and trimming mustaches.[37] During the first half of 1857, he noted, "my work was good for upwards of three Hundread dollars."[38]

So, in the end, John Rapier Sr. decided that the risks of moving to a new and unfamiliar home were outweighed by the security of his many years in Florence. Even so, he continued to encourage other family members to seek out a better Canaan. Indeed, like his mother before him, he was generous with his savings as well as with his encouragement. Rapier sent various sums of money to his brother Henry in Buxton, Canada West, to defray the cost of educating his sons John Jr. and James, who, at different times, attended school there. "I settle your board with him," he wrote John Jr. in 1856, noting that Henry Thomas's "charges was very Small only Six Shilling per week for 18 months."[39] The expenses for James were greater, however. "I understand he apply him Self closely [to] his Books," Rapier noted in 1857; he *should,* he added, as it was costing him ten dollars a month.[40]

It was remarkable that John Rapier Sr. placed such a high value on education, given his own limited schooling. His firm grasp of the importance of reading and writing was coupled with a keen awareness that statutes in his home state and a number of other southern states denied these opportunities to blacks. He not only urged his boys to study hard, but also counseled them on their behavior. "My Son I hope you will take my advice I have often give you," he wrote John Jr. in 1856, "that is to mind your own business and keep out of bad companey."[41] When he heard that his brother James Thomas was again traveling from one town to another in the upper Midwest, he wrote John Jr.: "I would like very much to See him Settle down for a roling Stone gather no moss remember that my Son."[42]

Always, Rapier knew there were temptations for young men. "I hope you will Save your money and lay it out for land in place of liquor and cigars," he counseled; young men "of all colours" fell into the trap of spending their hard-earned money on frivolous things.[43] Some people fell back on the bottle when they faced adversity, he observed; that only made things worse. He ended one letter to John Jr. in December 1858, by writing:

> in conclusion I want you to look over the year that has Just pass away think of it John how maney that are in thire graves that was alive this time last year and you have been Spard to See 1859 look over the past year my Son and Examion your Self well John and the things you were guilty of that was bad in your Syte [sight] donot be guilty of them any more remember my Son you and I must die you should Keep that before you I pray god to direct you in all things that are right.[44]

Such advice suggested how cautious Rapier was by nature, and that caution extended to his dealings with whites. Nevertheless, on one occasion he probably assisted a slave in gaining his freedom. While visiting Canada, he learned about the death of Sam Ragland, a fugitive slave from Alabama who had acquired a home and four acres of land in the village of York (later a part of Toronto). Ragland died without leaving a will, and the authorities placed his property, worth about five thousand dollars, in escrow until a legal heir could be found. Rapier knew Sam had a brother named Milton, who belonged to Colonel Samuel Ragland, a plantation owner near Florence. When Rapier returned from Canada, he told Colonel Ragland about the property. Deciding to claim the estate, the colonel took John Rapier Sr. and Milton with him to Buffalo. But he hesitated at the Canadian border. Would Canadian authorities give the property up to a slave owner? The colonel decided to remain behind while Milton and Rapier traveled to Toronto, where Milton proved kinship and acquired the property. After returning to Buffalo, Rapier left for Alabama. Milton then went with Colonel Ragland back to Canada, where the colonel hoped to acquire property. But once there, Milton declared that he was on British soil and therefore a free man.[45] What Rapier told Milton is not known, but he almost certainly advised him about what he could do once he was on Canadian soil.

As Rapier approached his fiftieth year, he became increasingly concerned about how to provide for his two sets of children. Like his mother, he had spent his life trying to provide for his children. In 1858, Rapier's large family included his slave wife Lucretia, four slave children, the youngest of whom was two-year-old Charles, and his four grown boys, between the ages of twenty-one and twenty-seven, by Susan, his deceased free black wife. Understandably, he was constantly caught up with various family matters. He also kept in contact and visited with brother James in Nashville and brother Henry in Canada.

Perhaps the most distressing problem involved his son Henry, who left home after a bitter argument and refused to communicate with his father. On a visit to Canada, Rapier read a letter that young Henry had sent from California to his uncle Henry in Canada. Rapier learned that his son was leading a dissolute life.[46] Rapier was also troubled by the behavior of his son James, who was "geting out of harness very much" and had gone on the river also to gamble.[47] "I am not in favor of Boys running the river to make money," John Rapier Sr. wrote. "I would perfear to See a Son of mind on the farm working at 2 Shilling per day then to See him Steam Boating."[48]

His concerns about his son Richard, also in California, were of a different sort. Despite hard work, Richard had lost a substantial portion of his crop to fire when the wind shifted while he was burning off some roughage. The damage cost him eight hundred dollars. The following year, he watched his wheat crop wither during a severe drought. John Rapier Sr. called it "bad luck in farming," noting that this time his son had lost about two thousand dollars.[49]

While he did not play favorites, Rapier felt closest to John Jr., who had attended school in Nashville and Buxton before striking out with his uncle James for Central America. Rapier wrote John Jr. frequently, signing his letters "loveing Father."[50] He complimented him on the affection John showed his younger slave half brothers and sister. He asked him to intervene at various times to influence the behavior of his brothers.[51] The father especially appreciated John's closeness to his stepmother, Lucretia. "Lucretia Send her love an[d] Say She hopes you will do well in this life and that you may be happy in the one to come,"[52] he wrote. He usually ended his letters with a sentiment such as "[Lucretia] request to be remembered to you"[53] or "Lucretia intertain a great opinion of you doing well."[54]

Despite the eighteen-year difference in their ages, Lucretia and John Rapier Sr. got along well. She not only cared for their children, including a fifth child, Susan, born in 1859, but also cleaned, cooked, washed, sewed, and tended the garden. She put up dried fruit, raised chickens, and kept vegetables ready through much of the summer and fall.[55] Rapier also noted how she nursed the children back to health after bouts with the flu[56] and measles, even when she caught the disease herself.[57] He felt frustrated that he could do nothing about his second family's condition as slaves, but realized that any attempt to manumit Lucretia and the children would require him to take them out of the state or send them away. He did break the law by teaching Rebecca and Joseph to read and write, and could have been subject to a heavy fine for this, but he strongly believed that any attempt to free his slave family might do more harm than good.

Raising a young family was a burden, but Rapier was most pained to see his four oldest boys scattered so far afield. Keeping in touch was difficult when letters took several weeks to reach their destination, and downright painful when letters did not bounce back in return. As he wrote John Jr. one summer:

> I am not Satisfide when I See my children Scatard all over the world as they are I can not here any Tyding of your Brother Henry not since he wrote last Summer to his uncle in Canada I Seen that letter and replyed to that letter no answer have I red as yet theas things make me on happy[58]

In a world where the search for Canaan led Rapier's family so far afield, it required constant care to keep in touch.

THE MINNESOTA TERRITORY

Meanwhile, Rapier's son John Jr. was still searching for the Promised Land. After John Rapier Jr. took up the position as the personal secretary of Parker French in Havana, not many months passed before he must have begun to wonder about French's dubious character. The two traveled to New Orleans, New York, and various towns and cities in the North to solicit funds. Alas, French had neglected to tell either Rapier or his audiences the circumstances under which he had left Nicaragua. In truth, William Walker had questioned French's integrity, thereby forcing him to return to the United States.

However, by the time Rapier and French reached the Minnesota Territory, in the late summer of 1856, it was well known that Walker's former minister was no longer to be trusted. Buying bonds from him to support the filibusters in Central America was like throwing money into the river.[59] Even though Rapier must have realized by this time that his companion was an engaging and talented con artist, he continued to work for him. Indeed, when French hired "a company of mechanics" and ventured to Watab, a growing town near St. Cloud, to start a construction company, Rapier not only stayed on but also purchased a piece of land on which to build.[60] Nor did Rapier seem to mind that French was a proslavery Kentuckian who wanted to extend the peculiar institution into Central America.

Rapier quickly learned, however, that loyalty meant little to French. While Rapier was "taken down ill with the winter

Variously described as charming, ambitious, and duplicitous, the one-armed Parker H. French (he lost his right arm in a gunfight) led a group of California volunteers to join Walker's army. In 1855, Walker sent French as an envoy to Washington to obtain recognition for his new regime, but later dismissed him upon learning that he had been convicted of forgery and embezzle. ent in Texas. It was on a return trip to the United States that French hired Rapier as his personal secretary. (SOURCE: COURTESY OF LIBRARY OF CONGRESS.)

fever" in Little Falls and "in this helpless condition Col P H French saw fit to discharge me—Stop my board—and not pay me a dollar of the wages that he owed me." To pay his rent and board, Rapier loaned a silver watch to his landlord with assurance he would pay in full as soon as he got "either work or money."[61]

It was at this point that young Rapier became acquainted with an Englishman named James Long who was interested in opening a hotel in Crow Wing, a thriving town twenty-three miles to the north at the juncture of the Crow Wing and Mississippi rivers. The town was being considered for designation as a postal station to connect it with Superior, Wisconsin. Despite Rapier's financial situation, the two men agreed on a "co-partnership." They were optimistic about the town's prospects and hopeful of finding a building for their venture.[62]

Early on the morning of February 3, 1857, Rapier and Long set out on foot to Crow Wing. Despite a temperature of twenty-five degrees below zero, Rapier described the morning as pleasant, and he found traversing the hard-packed snow relatively easy. As the day wore on, however, the wind increased, and even the tall, lithe Rapier found the going difficult. Gradually he fell behind and, after thirteen miles, collapsed on the drifting snow. His partner pressed ahead about three miles to a tavern, where he fetched a horse and sleigh to carry Rapier to Crow Wing. With the exception of being "a little frozen in the feet, hands, and ears," Rapier survived the ordeal without injury.

The next day, however, Rapier returned to Little Falls, where he settled into a small cabin, vowing to remain "in doors the balance of the winter." In the days that followed, he became obsessed with the weather, the howling winds, drifting snow, and plummeting temperatures. His diary recorded the following notations:

> February 6th "Weather very stormy, and disagreeable, Thermometers this morning have Sunk down to 40° degrees below zero."

February 7th "To day very much like yesterday—Cold, and Windy, Snow flies in Clouds to day . . . The Snow is drifting in masses, an average in depth on the Pra[i]ries 8 or 10 Feet."

February 8th "To day is a Second edition of Yesterday 'gotten up' in stronger style if possible, . . . Cutting winds pierces Your marrow."

February 9th "John,! did you ever breathe, an atmosphere that congealed mercury and caused the fluid in Thermometers to shrink down below (56°) fifty six degrees below Zero!"[63]

When the weather finally broke, Rapier confronted French, but was unable to collect his earnings. He finally received his back pay by promising to accompany French to California. "I will go with him to St Paul & there bid him a final adieu," Rapier wrote, "The dam Scoundrel."[64]

Rapier made good on his promise. After deserting the charming and charismatic charlatan in St. Paul, John found employment as a clerk for shopkeeper Moses Dickson at $12.50 per week; within a few months, he proudly deposited a hundred dollars in a local bank. "I have cut some of my most expensive acquaintances," he admitted, "given up Drinking Smoking & Gambling and enjoy pretty good health in general."[65] Despite a financial downturn that spread through the nation, Rapier could boast by the end of 1858, "I have in the face of a very dull season . . . managed to save since March 28 $200." Let the moralist sing the praises of the "poor but honest" or the "poor but proud," Rapier wrote, but as far as he was concerned, the accumulation of wealth was a "laudable ambition." Whatever anyone said, "we are forced to the conclusion that we must have money."[66]

Rapier may also have earned modest sums for articles he published in local newspapers. Indeed, he took pleasure in speaking out on a diverse range of topics: "Henry Ward Beecher and 'Philo'"; "Winter is Coming"; "The Bottle; or, Snuff and Snuff Dippers"; "A few Words with Republicans"; "Gen. Fillibuster Walker"; and "Reminiscences of a Fillibuster." His articles appeared in the Little Falls *Northern Herald,* St. Paul *Daily Times,* Minnesota *Weekly Times,* and St. Paul *Daily Pioneer and Democrat.*[67] Besides writing on general topics, Rapier took up the cause of black Americans. In an article titled "Can Colored Citizens Preempt?" he chided federal land officials for failing to honor the homestead applications of blacks.[68] His essay brought a rebuttal from the registrar at the land office in Stillwater, who replied that three groups of citizens could live on a tract of land and later claim it as their own: single men over twenty-one; married men whether twenty-one or not; and widows. "Colored persons are not, by any of the United States laws, regarded as citizens, nor can they under any of such laws, as far as I have examined the matter, declare their intentions to become citizens." They were not, therefore, "entitled to the pre-emption right."[69]

Rapier also wrote an article titled "Have Colored Children Rights?" after reading a government report on public schools that indicated that the St. Paul board of education planned to open schools for colored children only "when thirty of them are found who wish instruction." Such a decision, Rapier declared, was unjust and unfair. Did blacks not pay taxes the same as whites? Why should the board consider twenty students less entitled to an education than thirty? He also advised the board to hire a teacher for the black children "of their own race," who would "naturally feel more interested in them and their welfare than any other would."[70]

During his stay in the Midwest, John Rapier Jr. kept up a lively correspondence—perhaps eighty letters over the course of a year—with various members of his family, friends, and a number of young women. Rapier was strikingly handsome: five feet ten inches tall, with long curly hair, a light complexion, high cheekbones, and piercing dark eyes. His erudition, curiosity, self-confidence, and vibrant personality attracted women. To Frances Shelton of Nashville, he sent "passionate love letters," as he called them, and received back from her "protestations of eternal love."[71] His list of "Correspondents" included young women in Tennessee, Alabama, Wisconsin, Pennsylvania, and St. Louis, Missouri.[72] He received most of the "protestations of eternal love" from single free women of color, but two letters reveal that he was also having an affair with a married woman. "I must ask this favor of you, which is to call and see me as often as you can find time, which might be every evening after business hours," a woman named Sarah told him in mid-June 1858; she added a couple of weeks later, "i am going to [separate] myself from my husband in this town" and would let Rapier know of her whereabouts as soon as possible. "I have never Loved as I Love you," she confessed; "it is my only thought."[73]

One of Rapier's primary concerns during his stay in Minnesota was the welfare of his father and his father's slave family. On his visits to Florence, he became a favorite of Lucretia and the slave children; while away, he sent them gifts and kept himself apprised of their activities. In 1858, his father wrote that Thomas, age four, asked "if he was to dream for little John would he come home these are Thom own words you are great favorite with all of them my Son." For his part, John Jr. fretted that Lucretia and his half brothers and sister remained in bondage. In October 1857, he said he planned to visit Florence in order to convince his father "to move out West, and to give Lucretia and the children some Kind of a chance for Justice, and himself peace of mind which of late has been a stranger to his bosom."[74]

As time passed, Rapier found it harder and harder to consider Minnesota as a permanent home. Each winter was proving to be more difficult than the previous. Rapier suffered from a number of illnesses that kept him bedridden for weeks at a time.[75] In 1859, he wrote his cousin Sarah how much he welcomed the coming of spring. "Such a brilliant and dazzling May morning," he reported; in one day a thousand tiny flowers raised their crests and shed their "soft and delicate perfume." During the spring of each year, he was always reminded, "with a sigh," that "God made the country while it was man who built the cities."[76]

He would periodically return to the South to "restore" his health, but as time passed he became increasingly concerned about remaining in such a harsh climate.[77] Even before visiting, he had considered leaving the United States. As early as 1854, he had asked the secretary of the American Colonization Society how to obtain passage on a ship to Liberia.[78] Receiving no response, he wrote again. How much would passage to West Africa cost? What money would be needed once he arrived? Would an agent of the society receive and protect emigrants who assembled at the point of embarkation? "Believe me, Sir, that I am serious in my idea of Emigrating," he asserted; "in this Country I can not live."[79]

In Minnesota, he continued to consider emigration. He was determined to rise above his "low and menial capacity," he noted in his diary in 1857, which could be done only by leaving the United States, where blacks were relegated to "living and drudging for others." But now he came to believe, as did his father, that Liberia was a parched and arid land ruled from afar by merchants and politicians in Baltimore and Washington, D.C. Mexico seemed more to his liking, for there "Colour debars no person from the highest offices within the government."[80] But in 1859 and 1860, Rapier turned his attention to Haiti and Jamaica, seeking information from the Haitian consulate in New York City about the advantages of living there.[81] He also asked a Jamaican resident about that island nation. All refugees from American tyranny, he was told, especially those in Canada, "the creme de la creme of [the] Africo-American population," should emigrate to the Caribbean.[82]

In the fall of 1860, having considered the matter for some time, Rapier booked passage on a steamboat bound for New Orleans and the Caribbean.[83] Canaan would not be found in yet another long, harsh Minnesota winter.

CANADA WEST AND JAMES THOMAS RAPIER

Located a hundred seventy miles southwest of Toronto, in Kent County, the all-black community of Buxton was perhaps the most successful black utopian experiment in the Americas. Founded by William King, an Irish-born Presbyterian minister, the community began in 1849 with sixteen settlers: King and the fifteen Louisiana slaves he had emancipated. The number of residents rose steadily and included a number of fugitive slaves. At first King doubted the wisdom of settling southern slaves in the harsh northland, but he soon praised Buxton blacks for being just as capable as European immigrants in making a new life for themselves.

By the fall of 1856, when eighteen-year-old James Rapier arrived to further his education, the settlement boasted a black population of eight hundred, as well as two sawmills; factories producing shingles, bricks, and potash; a two-story temperance hotel; two churches; two hundred homes; and a thousand acres of cleared and fenced farmland. For many residents, Buxton had truly become a Promised Land.

Like his older brother John, young James Rapier was eager to make money. He hoped to set up an ashery to produce potash, a silvery-white substance used in glassmaking, since prices for the substance had recently soared to as much as fifty dollars per barrel. With one kettle and two assistants he could produce three barrels a week. He could then manufacture potash into pearl ash, a related product, and sell it for six or seven dollars per hundred pounds. He planned to manage the ashery, ship the pearl ash to Montreal, and obtain credit to lay in a supply of retail goods. James also considered investing in real estate, renting farmland, and competing with an unpopular Scotsman who owned a sawmill.[84]

Indeed, young James seemed preoccupied with material things. Money was "devilish scarce," he noted, adding that despite his optimistic plans, it would be difficult to earn two hundred dollars a year. "I like Canada very well but a fellow can not make any money here," he complained; "what signifies a man's liking a place if he can not make some money."[85]

Despite his many activities, Rapier was lonely during those early months in the North. In late January 1857, tucked away in a small cottage by a log fire, he wrote his brother John Jr. of "being all a lone." Outside everything seemed bleak: the snowfall of about twelve inches; tree branches heavy with sleet and rain; soot from the wood fires turning the morning into dusk. Hearing the church bells in the distance made him think of his childhood. Then "all four of us boys were together," he wrote, "we all breathed as one." Sadly, Sally Thomas's family was now scattered abroad "on the face of Earth"; "do you expect ever to see us all together again[?]" he asked John.

> i do not just look where we are at you in the West and myself in the north Henry & Dick in california & Father in Alabama did you ever think how small our Family is[86]

Rapier's premonition proved correct. Indeed, in the future, the family's paths would diverge even more.

Then, in the spring of 1857, a Methodist revival led seventy residents of Buxton, including James and his cousin Sarah, to accept Christ as their personal Savior.[87] "Dear Brother," James wrote John Jr. in April 1857, "I can use the above expression with a better heart than I ever could John by the help of god I have made peace with my savior which you and all must do if you want to see his face in peace." James then assured his older brother that Jesus had died on the Cross as much for him as for the Queen of England or the Czar of Russia. The remainder of the letter was peppered with an abundance of scripture—John 3: "if a man is not born again he cannot see the Kingdom of God"; Isaiah 56: "there is no peace say my God to the wicked"; Paul's letter to Timothy: "Christ came to the world to save the chief of sinners of which he Paul was the chief"; and Second

Founded in 1849, Buxton was the last stop on the Underground Railroad for many fugitive slaves. Organized by Reverend William King, the settlement flourished, and the Buxton Methodist Episcopal Church still stands as a testament to the religious convictions of the original "coloured settlers." (Source: Courtesy of Buxton National Historic Site and Museum, North Buxton, Ontario.)

Corinthians: "behold all old things pass away and new things appear and then one is a new creature."[88]

When John Jr. learned of his brother's newfound piety, he was singularly unimpressed: "Letter from James Buxton—Apl 25," John noted in his diary. "Professed Religion—Wont come West Damn Fool."[89] Later, he protested to James that his "ink absorbing" and "paper destroying" themes were most wearisome. "I write a letter to you and you send me a prayer in reply."[90] Losing patience, he finally asked his brother to exclude any mention of religion from his letters. "Hope he will respect my request and cease his sermonizing or I will be compelled to drop ALL correspondence with him."[91]

Although James acceded to his brother's wishes, his conversion profoundly affected his life. Before coming to Canada, he had gambled, fought, and whored his way up and down the Mississippi on steamboats. He was, as his father said, "geting out of harness very much."[92] Even after his arrival, he continued his rowdy ways in spite of Buxton's strict moral code. He had a fight with Buxton resident William Scott and was afraid he might be asked to leave, "but," he said, "it did not cost me any thing."[93] He admitted to quarreling with other settlers, drinking hard liquor, and entertaining prostitutes. Dark-skinned, tall, and erect, with a broad forehead and pleasant eyes, James Rapier, like his brother John, was a very attractive young man. "I don't Know whether you are acquainted with Sene," he wrote John Jr. in March 1857. She was the younger sister of Elizabeth Johnson alias Burns, "the one which you told me you had one night against a tree." Sene, or Seneth Ann Burns, at age sixteen, was "in the same line of business."[94]

But following his conversion, such profligacy came to an abrupt end. "I never was so mean until I went to New Orleans and the following summer I drank whiskey," he confessed, "and I Know how mean I was before and the spirit of the living god changed me from my old ways."[95] On a visit to see his father nearly eighteen months after his conversion, he was proud to report that "I have not thrown a card in 3 years touched a woman in 2 years smoked nor drunk any Liquor in going on 2 years."[96]

With the acceptance of Christ as his Savior, James began studying in earnest. Attending the William King School, he studied grammar, geography, writing, mathematics, and Old Testa-

*Called before the church elders a few years later on charges of "fornica-
tion," Seneth Ann Burns Hooper (1840–1936) was disciplined but not
forced out of the church, as she appeared penitent and promised "amendment in the future."* (Source: Courtesy of Bryan Prince, North Buxton, Ontario.)

ment Scriptures.[97] He and other Buxton residents were especially
proud of their no-tuition school, which enrolled some one hundred forty students, both black and white. "[W]e have a splendid Teacher," James said. Visitors were also impressed with the
quality of the teachers. Fugitive slave Samuel Ringgold Ward,
who became a prominent abolitionist and visited Buxton, wrote
that the school was so good that whites from surrounding areas
sent their children there rather than to the local public schools.
Thus, Ward said, the students of both races read, recited, and
socialized together without distinction.[98]

"You will think it strange probably to hear that so Ignorant
[a fellow] as I was to be in latin and also studying greek," James

wrote John Jr. in June 1857, but he was studying both languages and phrenology as well.[99] During his second year, he boasted that he could "Knock off a chapter of Caesar as slick as any of them." He also had an excellent grasp of mathematics, and helped the younger children with their lessons. With the possible exception of three other students, two of them white, he had received higher marks in his Latin recitations than any of his classmates.[100]

James eagerly honed his rhetorical skills. "I have been out cutting wood to enliven my spirits and to brighten my Ideas for I have to debate to night according to our appointment and the question is an old one viz which have suffered the most from the Hands of the white man the Indians or the colored men." He and two other classmates planned to argue that Indians had suffered more, while three others took the opposing position. Almost as if laying out the arguments of his opponents, James explained that slavery stultified the mind and repressed the spirit.[101] Consequently, he argued, blacks had little opportunity to improve. Even blacks were often skeptical when another black person attempted to elevate himself: "you cant make no great Lawyer nor Doctor," they would object. "You should go and get a plot of ground and make something to eat." Because whites retained all the power, problems had always been solved by whites, and the answer had always been that "Niggers cannot and never will be anything." But "if each of us would endeavor to do his or her part," he concluded, "we might prove that [the] Problem was solved."[102]

To do his part, he continued his schooling and enrolled in a normal school in Toronto. During the winter of 1862 he complained that he had been thrown out of his situation and was forced to secure credit for his board until the spring. "I have worked hard and I have not made the same progress in the world that some have, but there are those who have made less progress than I have," he wrote; "they may have more money than I have for I have not two Dollars to save my life but I am now very nearly out of debt a good name and a tolerable fair Education." He hoped to work hard, hire himself out, and raise enough money to complete his normal school training.[103]

Apparently he succeeded, for he was hired by William King as a teacher in the Buxton School.[104] As he stepped into the one-room school house built by local residents, James was much impressed. The room was forty-five feet long and thirty feet across, with a fourteen-foot-high ceiling and eight tall windows. The light streamed into the well-constructed edifice, reflecting off the whitewashed stamped-tin walls, the ceiling, and the light brown pine floor. At the far end of the room was a large wood stove. Rapier felt privileged to be selected as the first teacher in the new school, since Reverend King was very particular about who might serve in such a capacity. The students who arrived were both black and white and came from Buxton and the surrounding areas.[105]

During these formative years, James lived with his uncle Henry, aunt Maria, and their growing family. Following his arrival in Buxton in 1851, Henry Thomas had purchased one hundred acres of land, cleared a few acres, and begun a career as a farmer. He had also joined the St. Andrews Presbyterian Church. Along with Wilson Abbott, he raised funds for the Canada Mill and Mercantile Company, the first major black-owned commercial venture in the province. He helped establish a sawmill,

The Buxton School was so successful that whites from surrounding communities sent their children there. Many fugitive slaves were also drawn by its educational opportunities. James Rapier was the first teacher in this school building, erected in 1861, which has been restored to its original form and now stands as a symbol of racial integration and academic excellence. (SOURCE: COURTESY OF BUXTON NATIONAL HISTORIC SITE AND MUSEUM, NORTH BUXTON, ONTARIO.)

gristmill, and general store.[106] Despite these business ventures, Thomas lost a good deal of his wealth in leaving Buffalo so precipitously. He never recovered those losses. Moreover, he and Maria increased their family to seven children: Sarah, Henry, Hannah, Jane, John, Maria, and Richard, the youngest. Meanwhile, they also helped board and house John Rapier Sr.'s sons John Jr. and James for a time.[107]

In 1856, Thomas complained that his "crop was rather Short with the exception of corn that was about half a crop."[108] The next year too he was disappointed, and he remained strapped for

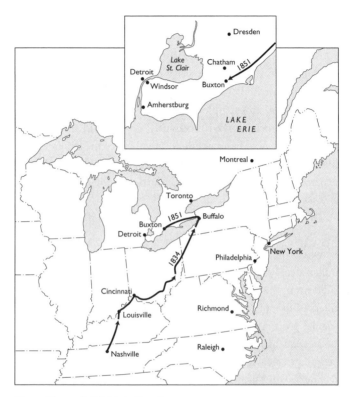

Henry Thomas's Flights to Freedom

cash.[109] He asked his nephew John Jr., then in Minnesota, for a loan "without delay", while his daughter Sarah complained of the "continued monotony [of] Hard *Times*."[110] "I am So poor (owing to bad Luck)," Henry Thomas lamented in 1859, "but few honor me with a prepaid letter, Informing me of their whereabouts & how they fare, fearing I would ask for aid. I am & have been very poor for Some time."[111]

Despite Uncle Henry's poverty, James greatly admired him. "I should like to see him do well," James wrote, "for I believe he is a Clever man."[112] More than any other person, he added, Henry set him an example to lead him "on to the summit." Although his uncle worked incessantly, he also had time to help others; he was kind and gentle to members of his family and to his neighbors. Whenever he had an opportunity, he worked to expand his mind, eagerly reading Harriet Beecher Stowe's *Dred: A Tale of the Great Dismal Swamp*.[113]

Others also thought highly of Henry. During his tour of Buxton in 1861, fugitive slave and black abolitionist William Wells Brown wrote, "My old and intellectual friend, Henry K. Thomas, a man deeply interested in the welfare of his race, has a beautiful farm in the settlement, where he is raising up his children as tillers of the soil, instead of leaving them to the chance of filling menial positions in the city."[114]

Despite his admiration for his uncle Henry, James Rapier yearned to return to the land of his birth. "You can imagine my feelings when I heard that Gen. Beauregard had ordered the firing on Fort Sumter," he confessed some years later. "I listened to the sounds, and though many miles away, I fancied I heard the cannon, in thunder tones, say, 'The year of jubilee has come, return, you exiles, home.'"[115]

Due to the hostilities and the unsettled conditions in the South, it would be three years before James Rapier returned home. But the coming of war did change, in an instant, the calculus of Sally's children and grandchildren, as well as that of all

William Wells Brown (1814–1884), antislavery lecturer, author, and re-former, escaped from slavery in 1834. He became a conductor on the Un-derground Railroad, guiding sixty-nine fugitives to Canada during a sin-gle year. In 1847, he wrote his autobiography, Narrative of William W. Brown, a Fugitive Slave, *the first of more than a dozen books and pam-phlets. During the Civil War, he recruited blacks for the Union Army.* (SOURCE: WILLIAM WELLS BROWN, *NARRATIVE OF WILLIAM W. BROWN, A FUGI-TIVE SLAVE* [LONDON: C. GILPIN, 1849], FRONTISPIECE.)

black Americans. The deteriorating conditions in the South dur-ing the 1850s sent the Thomas and Rapier families searching for their own "Canaans" far beyond the borders of the South: Nicaragua, California, Minnesota, and Canada.

NOTES

1. John Rapier Jr., "Reminiscences of a Fillibuster," Number One, St. Paul [Minnesota] *Pioneer and Democrat*, January 20, 1859, in RTP; William

O. Scroggs, *Filibusters and Financiers: The Story of William Walker and His Associates* (New York: The Macmillan Company, 1916), 139 n.3.

2. Thomas recounted this in a letter a year later. James Thomas to John Rapier Jr., December 23, 1856, RTP.

3. The exact time sequence of events following the December 31 discussion is not clear, but it appears that Thomas remained behind before leaving for New Orleans. John Rapier Jr., "Reminiscences of a Fillibuster," Number One; FTS, 134; *Cohen's New Orleans and Southern Directory* (New Orleans: Daily Delta, 1856), 84.

4. FTS, 134–35.

5. John Rapier Jr., "Reminiscences of a Fillibuster," Numbers Two and Three, St. Paul [Minnesota] *Pioneer and Democrat*, January 26, 1859, February 3, 1859, clippings in RTP.

6. John Rapier Jr., "Reminiscences of a Fillibuster," Number Four, St. Paul [Minnesota] *Pioneer and Democrat,* February 17, 1859, clipping in RTP. Heading for this reminiscence as Number Three is incorrect.

7. FTS, 131, 138; Scroggs, *Filibuster and Financiers,* 9.

8. Description of Greytown and Granada, in John Rapier Jr., "Reminiscences of a Fillibuster," Number Six, St. Paul [Minnesota] *Pioneer and Democrat,* March 10, 1859, clipping in RTP.

9. William Walker, *The War in Nicaragua* (Mobile, Ala.: S. H. Goetzel & Co., 1860; reprint ed., Detroit: Blain Ethridge, 1971), 261; FTS, 138–39; E. Bradford Burns, *Patriarch and Folk: The Emergence of Nicaragua, 1798–1858* (Cambridge: Harvard University Press, 1991), 200–207; Robert E. May, *Manifest Destiny's Underworld: Filibustering in Antebellum America* (Chapel Hill: University of North Carolina Press, 2002).

10. FTS, 139.

11. James Thomas to John Rapier Jr., December 23, 1856, RTP.

12. For a description and brief history of Aspinwall (now Colon), see *The Illustrated London News*, December 30, 1865.

13. On Parker H. French, see Frederick Rosengarten Jr., *Freebooters Must Die: The Life and Death of William Walker, the Most Notorious Filibuster of the Nineteenth Century* (Wayne, Penn.: Haverford House, 1976),

104–105; and Scroggs, *Filibusters and Financiers*, 168–71. See also John Hope Franklin, "The Southern Expansionists of 1846," *Journal of Southern History* 25 (August 1959): 323–38.

14. FTS, 140–42.

15. James Thomas to John Rapier Jr., December 23, 1856, RTP.

16. James Thomas to John Rapier Jr., October 3, 1856, RTP.

17. *The Seventh Census of the United States: 1850* (Washington, D.C.: Robert Armstrong, 1853), 419–22. Two of those listed in his household as free, Lucretia and Rebecca, were in fact slaves.

18. Records of the County Court, Lauderdale County, Ala., Land Deed Records, vol. V (December 31, 1831), 270; ibid., vol. IX (February 20, 1840), 364–65.

19. Records of the County Court, Lauderdale County, Ala., Land Deed Records, vol. XI (May 3, 1844), 7.

20. USMSPC, Lauderdale County, Ala., Florence, 1850, 293.

21. John Rapier Sr. to John Rapier Jr., September 16, 1857, RTP.

22. He ended the sentence with the phrase "at least Some of them," to exclude his infant children. Following the passage of a law in 1860 prohibiting the emancipation of slaves "by any last will and testament, or other instrument," Rapier tried to free Lucretia and four of his children. The case was brought after Union troops had been to the city in 1862. See John Rapier Sr. to John Rapier Jr., September 16, 1857, RTP; *Acts of the Seventh Biennial Session, of the General Assembly of Alabama, held in the City of Montgomery, Commencing on the Second Monday of November 1859* (Montgomery: Shorter and Reid, 1860), 28; USMSPC, Lauderdale County, Ala., Florence, 1850, 293; ibid., 1860, 38, 39; Florence *Gazette*, March 5, 1862.

In 1832, the Alabama legislature passed an act that stated "That any person or persons who shall endeavor or attempt to teach any free person of color, or slave, to spell, read, or write, shall, upon conviction thereof by indictment, be fined in the sum not less than two hundred and fifty dollars nor more than five hundred." *Acts Passed at the Thirteenth Annual Session of the General Assembly of the State of Alabama, Begun and Held in the Town of Tuscaloosa, on the Third Monday in November, One Thousand Eight Hundred and Thirty-one* (Tuscaloosa: Wiley, McGuire & Henry, 1832), 16.

In 1856, the legislature passed a new law prohibiting anyone from teaching "any slave or slaves" to read or write under a penalty of a fine of not less than one hundred dollars and imprisonment in the county jail of not less than three months, "one or both, at the discretion of the jury trying the case." *Acts of the Fifth Biennial Session of the General Assembly of Alabama, Held in the City of Montgomery, Commencing on the Second Monday in November, 1855* (Montgomery: Nates & Lucas, 1856), 50.

23. *The Code of Alabama* (Montgomery, Ala.: Brittan and DeWolf, 1852), 241–45; USMSPC, Lauderdale County, Ala., Florence, 1850, 293. Their family included Rebecca, who was born in 1848; Joseph, who was born in 1852; Thomas in 1854; Charles in 1856; and later Susan, born in 1859. Ibid., 1860, 38, 39.

24. John Rapier Sr. to John Rapier Jr., August 6, 1857, RTP.

25. John Rapier Sr. to John Rapier Jr., March 17, 1857, RTP.

26. John Rapier Sr. to John Rapier Jr., September 16, 1857, RTP.

27. John Rapier Sr. to John Rapier Jr., March 17, 1857, RTP.

28. John Rapier Sr. to John Rapier Jr., September 16, 1857, RTP.

29. John Rapier Sr. to William McLain, January 18, 1854, American Colonization Society Papers, Series I, Vol. 133, part 1, 85, Library of Congress.

30. Assessment Rolls, Raleigh Township, Kent County, 1851, 1853–1857, microfilm, University of Western Ontario, London, Ontario. The Toronto property was mentioned in Rapier's Last Will and Testament. Records of the Chancery Court, Lauderdale County, Ala., Will Record, B (September 13, 1869), 78–80.

31. John Rapier Sr. to John Rapier Jr., September 15, 1856, RTP. To make a living quote in ibid., September 16, 1857, RTP.

32. John Rapier Sr. to John Rapier Jr., September 15, 1856, RTP.

33. Diary of John Rapier Jr., October 7, 1857, RTP.

34. John Rapier Sr. to John Rapier Jr., June 26, 1857, RTP.

35. Ibid.

36. John Rapier Sr. to John Rapier Jr., December 28, 1858, RTP.

37. John Rapier Sr. to John Rapier Jr., June 26, 1857, RTP.

38. John Rapier Sr. to John Rapier Jr., September 16, 1857, RTP.

39. John Rapier Sr. to John Rapier Jr., September 15, 1856, RTP.

40. John Rapier Sr. to John Rapier Jr., August 6, 1857, RTP.

41. John Rapier Sr. to John Rapier Jr., September 15, 1856, RTP.

42. John Rapier Sr. to John Rapier Jr., December 13, 1856, RTP.

43. John Rapier Sr. to John Rapier Jr., June 26, 1857, RTP.

44. John Rapier Sr. to John Rapier Jr., December 28, 1858, RTP.

45. "The Autobiography of William King," Manuscript, King Papers, Public Archives of Canada, Ottawa, Ontario, 355–59; Victor Ullman, *Look to the North Star: The Life of William King* (Boston: Beacon Press 1969), 217–18; Detroit *Tribune*, June 12, 1892. In his autobiography, King dates the incident in 1855, but Milton Ragland, who went to Buxton after claiming his property, purchased land in Canada in 1851. See Register for Sale of Land, Elgin Association, October 21, 1851, in William King Collection, National Archives of Canada, Ottawa, Canada.

46. John Rapier Sr. to John Rapier Jr., September 15, 1856, RTP.

47. John Rapier Sr. to John Rapier Jr., December 13, 1856, RTP.

48. John Rapier Sr. to John Rapier Jr., September 15, 1856, RTP.

49. John Rapier Sr. to John Rapier Jr., August 6, 1857, RTP.

50. John Rapier Sr. to John Rapier Jr., September 15, 1856, RTP; John Rapier Sr. to John Rapier Jr., June 26, 1857, RTP.

51. John Rapier Sr. to John Rapier Jr., December 13, 1856, RTP.

52. John Rapier Sr. to John Rapier Jr., June 26, 1857, RTP.

53. John Rapier Sr. to John Rapier Jr., September 16, 1857, RTP.

54. John Rapier Sr. to John Rapier Jr., August 6, 1857, RTP.

55. John Rapier Sr. to John Rapier Jr., September 15, 1856, RTP.

56. John Rapier Sr. to John Rapier Jr., June 26, 1857, RTP.

57. Ibid.

58. John Rapier Sr. to John Rapier Jr., September 16, 1857, RTP.

59. FTS, 142; Scroggs, *Filibusters and Financiers*, 170–71. This part of French's life is not included in Edward McGowan's "The Strange Eventful History of Parker H. French," appearing in the San Francisco *Daily Evening Post*, January 4, 11, 1879, reprinted as *The Strange Eventful History of Parker H. French*, with notes by Kenneth M. Johnson (Los Angeles: Glen Dawson, 1959).

60. Records of the County Court, Benton County, Minn., Land Deeds, Book B (December 8, 1856), 309–10, County Courthouse, Foley, Minn. He purchased the lot for one hundred dollars and sold it the next year for the same amount. Ibid., Book B (November 4, 1857), 692.

61. Diary of John Rapier Jr., January 18, 1857, RTP.

62. Diary of John Rapier Jr., February 3, 1857, RTP.

63. Diary of John Rapier Jr., February 3–9, 1857, RTP. He asked himself if he should live "in such a region."

64. Diary of John Rapier Jr., February 5, 1857, RTP.

65. Diary of John Rapier Jr., May 30, 1857, RTP.

66. Comments made under "List of Expenses for the year [1858]," in Diary of John Rapier Jr., 1859, RTP.

67. He also wrote about advantages in the West. Little Falls *Northern Herald*, ca. 1857, clipping in RTP; clippings of articles in other newspapers under "My Published Articles," in RTP; "The Bottle; or, Snuff and Snuff Dippers" in St. Paul *Times*, ca. 1858; "Henry Ward Beecher" in St. Paul *Times*, May 25, 1858; "A few Words with Republicans," St. Paul *Times*, November 27, 1858. According to Rapier's notes, the eight articles titled "Reminiscences of a Fillibuster" came out in the St. Paul *Pioneer and Democrat* on January 20, 26, 1859; February 3, 17, 24, 1859; March 10, 17, 1859. The undated final article probably appeared on March 24 or 31, 1859, RTP. In these recollections, he does not examine his relationship with Parker French.

68. St. Paul *Daily Times*, December 11, 1856, quote in Little Falls *Northern Herald*, December 13, 1856, clipping in RTP.

69. Little Falls *Northern Herald*, January 14, 1857; Minnesota *Weekly Times*, January 17, 1857.

70. St. Paul *Times,* ca. July 1858, clipping in RTP.

71. Diary of John Rapier Jr, June 5, 1857; September 15, 24, 1857; December 1857, RTP.

72. FTS, 208; James Thomas to John Rapier Jr., May 3, 1858, RTP; Cyprian Clamorgan, *The Colored Aristocracy of St. Louis* (St. Louis: n.p., 1858; ed. with intro. by Julie Winch, Columbia: University of Missouri Press, 1999), 55–56, 58, 86–87; Diary of John Rapier Jr., 198, RTP; USMSPC, Lauderdale County, Ala., 1860, 71. They included twenty-one-year-old free mulatto Mahala Armistead, of Florence, Ala.; E. I. Stewart in Milwaukee, Wisc.; Sarah Jones, in Harrisburg, Penn.; young Pauline Johnson and Virginia Johnson, of St. Louis, the unmarried daughters of the well-to-do free black barber William Johnson Sr., also of St. Louis, a friend of Rapier's uncle James Thomas.

73. Sarah to John Rapier Jr., June 17, 1858; July 1, 1858, RTP.

74. John Rapier Sr. to John Rapier Jr., December 28, 1858, RTP; Diary of John Rapier Jr., "Letters Written," October 1, 7, 1857, RTP. He planned to return "home" in February.

75. See James Rapier to John Rapier Jr., July 16, 1858, RTP.

76. John Rapier Jr. to Sarah Thomas, May 5, 1859, RTP.

77. For going south to restore his health, see James Rapier to John Rapier Jr., July 16, 1858, RTP.

78. John Rapier Jr. to William McLain, December 28, 1854, American Colonization Society Papers, Series I, Vol. 136, Pt. 1, 454, Library of Congress.

79. John Rapier Jr. to William McLain, March 5, 1855, American Colonization Society Papers, Series I, Vol. 137, Pt. 2, 365, Library of Congress.

80. Diary of John Rapier Jr., October 2, 1857, RTP.

81. Diary of John Rapier Jr., January 4, 1859, under title "Letters Written," RTP.

82. Diary of John Rapier Jr., ca. 1859, RTP.

83. During this period, a number of free blacks emigrated to Haiti. See Robert Reinders, "The Decline of the New Orleans Free Negro in the

Decade before the Civil War," *Journal of Mississippi History* 24 (April 1962): 95–96.

84. James Rapier to John Rapier Jr., March 3, 1857, RTP. For Buxton, see *The Ecclesiastical and Missionary Record,* vol. IX, no. 9 (July 1853): 132, found in Fred Landon Papers, University of Western Ontario, London, Ontario; William King, "The Autobiography of William King," 191, 284, Public Archives of Canada, Ottawa, Ontario; *Fourth Annual Report of the Elgin Association* (Toronto 1853), 7–11; Robin W. Winks, *The Blacks in Canada: A History* (New Haven: Yale University Press, 1971), 209; "The Sixth Annual Report of the Buxton Mission, Presented at the Meeting of Synod in London, June 16th, 1856," *The Ecclesiastical and Missionary Record,* vol. XII, no. 9 (July 1856): 139; *The National Anti-Slavery Standard,* November 7, 1857.

85. James Rapier to John Rapier Jr., March 6, 1857, RTP.

86. James Rapier to John Rapier Jr., January 27, 1857, RTP.

87. James Rapier to John Rapier Jr., April 21, 1857, RTP.

88. Ibid.

89. Diary of John Rapier Jr., May 15, 1857, under "Letters Received," RTP.

90. John Rapier Jr. to James Rapier, September 18, 1857, RTP.

91. Diary of John Rapier Jr., October 7, 1857, RTP.

92. John Rapier Sr. to John Rapier Jr., September 15, 1856, RTP; "geting out of harness" in ibid., December 13, 1856, RTP.

93. James Rapier to John Rapier Jr., January 27, 1857, RTP.

94. James Rapier to John Rapier Jr., March 6, 1857, RTP. Some years later, Seneth Ann Burns had a child out of wedlock (not Rapier's) and was charged with "fornication." Brought before William King and church elders she appeared penitent and the elders told her to "go and sin no more." Rebuke of Seneth Burns, Presbyterian Session, Buxton, Ontario, February 14, 1864, photocopy in possession of Bryan Prince, Buxton National Historic Site and Museum, Buxton, Ontario. Seneth was Bryan Prince's great-great-grandmother. She was born in Lancaster County, Penn., August 26, 1840, the youngest of six children born to Seneth and Samuel Burns. See inscription in *The Holy Bible, Containing Old and New Testaments* (Hartford, Conn.: Silas Andrus, 1828), in possession of Bryan Prince.

95. James Rapier to John Rapier Jr., August 29, 1857, RTP.

96. James Rapier to John Rapier Jr., September 27, 1858, RTP. These were rough estimates. In September 1856, James was still making arrangements to travel to Buxton, but the letter clearly refers to his religious conversion as the watershed in his life.

97. James Rapier to John Rapier Jr., June 26, 1857, RTP.

98. James Rapier to John Rapier Jr., July 29, 1857, RTP; Samuel Ringgold Ward, *Autobiography of a Fugitive Negro: His Anti-Slavery Labors in the United States, Canada and England* (London: John Snow, 1855), 213.

99. James Rapier to John Rapier Jr., June 26, 1857, RTP.

100. James Rapier to John Rapier Jr., February 28, 1858, RTP. In the same letter, he expressed heartfelt thanks to his father.

101. Ibid.

102. Ibid.

103. James Rapier to John Rapier Jr., March 17, 1862, RTP.

104. Little is known about James Rapier's normal school training in Toronto. In 1862, however, his brother wrote that James would graduate in eight months. John Rapier Jr. to James Thomas, February 3, 1862, RTP.

105. The school is currently a tourist attraction. Rapier was listed as a schoolteacher in the Assessment Roll, Raleigh Township, Kent County, 1863, 23.

106. C. Peter Ripley, et al., eds., *The Black Abolitionist Papers, Volume II* 2:164; *Voice of the Fugitive*, September 24, 1851; Assessment Rolls, Raleigh Township, Kent County, 1851, 1853–1857, microfilm, University of Western Ontario, London, Ontario.

107. Census, Kent County, Raleigh Township, Ontario, 1861, National Archives of Canada, Ottawa, Canada.

108. Henry Thomas to John Rapier Jr., October 29, 1856, RTP.

109. James Rapier to John Rapier Jr., June 26, 1857, RTP; Henry Thomas to John Rapier Jr., September 1857, RTP.

110. Henry Thomas to John Rapier Jr., March 13, 1857, RTP; Sarah Thomas to John Rapier Jr., March 10, 1857, RTP.

111. Henry Thomas to John Rapier Jr., January 16, 1859, RTP.

112. James Rapier to John Rapier Jr., June 26, 1857, RTP.

113. Henry Thomas to John Rapier Jr., October 29, 1856, RTP.

114. William Wells Brown, "The Colored People of Canada," in Ripley, et al., eds., *The Black Abolitionist Papers, Volume II*, 475.

115. He made the statement at a celebration following the passage of the Fifteenth Amendment, in Montgomery, Ala., April 26, 1870. *Alabama State Journal*, April 29, 1870.

· Five ·

THE MIDWEST, HAITI,
AND JAMAICA

Aꜱᴛ LTHOUGH YOUNG JAMES RAPIER WAS HOPING TO RETURN south when the Civil War commenced, he had at least found religion and had settled into a steady life teaching in Buxton. His uncle Henry had committed himself to raising his family on a farm. Henry's brother John Rapier Sr., after debating whether or not to leave Florence, had decided to ride out the southern troubles at home. But two of Sally Thomas's family were still birds unwilling to perch. Both her son James Thomas and her grandson John Rapier Jr. continued to feel uncomfortable about worsening conditions in the South, so that when John Jr. took passage from Minnesota heading south along the Mississippi, he intended to return to the Caribbean, where he had traveled with his uncle James Thomas. James, too, was unsettled. But unlike John Rapier Jr., he had not given up on the Midwest.

"The people of Nashville are anxious that I should commence business again," James Thomas acknowledged upon his return from Central America in October 1856, "but I do not like the idea much not at all if I can do better."[1] With regret he noted that "the old town bears no further Charms for me."[2] During the next few weeks he put his real estate up for sale with the firm of Lindsley and Crockett, found temporary employment as a barber at Sulphur Springs, a nearby resort, and made arrangements with David T. Scott, a rich Nashville physician and hotel owner, to accompany him on a trip to the Midwest. "The Dr. has been negotiating for his hotel in Chicago," Thomas noted, "and I understand he has one offered him in St. Paul."[3]

But after arriving in Illinois, Scott decided to turn south to St. Louis, leaving Thomas in Chicago after paying him for his services. Thomas wanted to go on to St. Paul and visit his nephew John Rapier Jr., but an early winter storm detained him in Wisconsin. Despite freezing conditions, he thought the rolling countryside of small farms and one-horse towns picturesque. "I like the appearance of things verry much," he wrote, "but perhaps can be better suited in some of those towns along the [Mississippi] river."[4]

While traveling in Illinois and Wisconsin, Thomas learned about a wave of violence in the South, the "consequence of a rumor (false I have no doubt) that the Negroes had an Insurrection on foot to be carried into effect Christmas." At Dover, in Stewart County, Tennessee, less than seventy-five miles from Nashville, whites hanged nineteen slaves and whipped many more "from a few licks to a few hundred."[5] Thomas blamed the bitterly contested presidential campaign of 1856 for causing the insurrection rumor to be taken seriously. The followers of antislavery Republican John C. Fremont shouted, "Free Speech, Free Press, Free Soil, Free Men, Fremont and Victory." Blacks in Tennessee and elsewhere, both slave and free, followed the campaign and listened to speeches that many white folks thought "the Negroes could get along without hearing."[6] Although Fremont lost, it was in this politically charged atmosphere that someone spread a rumor about slaves plotting a revolt.

"It was all simply Idle and foolish talk," Thomas asserted. Yet no matter how foolish, panicky whites were torturing and hanging "suspicious" blacks. As Thomas traveled up the Cumberland River, returning to Nashville, his steamboat pulled into the ironworks where the hysteria was running high. Thomas had with him a copy of the antislavery novel *Dred: A Tale of the Great Dismal Swamp,* by Harriet Beecher Stowe—an abolitionist hated by many white southerners. At a time when southern legislatures were already taking vigorous measures to prevent any abolitionist literature from being sent into the region, Thomas did not have to think twice about the danger of being caught with such incendiary material. Without calling attention to himself, he let his copy drop overboard, where it sank beneath the dark waters of the Cumberland. "If somebody had said that any particular free Negro had been aiding slaves to run off," Thomas recalled, he would have needed his "strongest friends" to keep him from being hanged.[7]

Returning to check on the status of his real estate, he found Nashville in a state of siege: policemen patrolled the streets; slave patrols rode to farms and plantations day and night; officials closed the black schools, banned slave gatherings, and persecuted black preachers. Even well-known and respected free blacks, if "found in suspicious circumstances," could be arrested and jailed.[8]

Under such conditions, it was remarkable that Thomas was able to find employment. His twenty years of experience and his excellent reputation prompted yet another wealthy white man to ask him to serve as his personal valet and barber on a trip to the North.[9] Thomas accepted the offer even though he had not yet sold his property. By March 1857 he would write to his nephew John Rapier Jr., "During the winter I have spent several weeks in this the city of fires with A young Gentleman who has more money than he wants and is anxious for me to help him use it." In the company of thirty-four-year-old Benjamin Clark, son of a wealthy Davidson County lawyer and planter, James Thomas was staying in a suite of rooms at the Galt House, in Louisville, Kentucky. There was no opera to be seen, but the two men attended the theater, including a performance by the famous actress Eliza Logan. Most of the time, however, "I lay about one or the other of our rooms and give the Chambermaids opportunity to beating in with dusting brushes and broom stocks."

Meanwhile, Thomas's mind was constantly on real estate. He was hoping to "jump the game and begin to make investigations."[10] He was not able to "jump the game" until his companion reached Chicago and paid Thomas for his services. Everywhere in the city people were talking about buying and selling real estate: how much a certain lot or house or building cost, or how much a seller refused for a piece of property. "In many cases," Thomas recalled, "when a man said he would take (and state his price) for a piece of property, The customer would take the advantage and buy at once for fear it might go up during the night."[11]

Believing prices in Chicago were inflated, Thomas followed the river to Keokuk, Iowa, where he found residents equally bent on speculation. After some consideration, he bought a lot in a subdivision called Mason's Lower Addition. "I gave 625 for it," he said in May 1857; "I expect to get 1000 for it next year." Soon after, however, he fell in with fellow Tennessean Jerome S. Ridley, who had amassed a small fortune speculating in undeveloped land along the Mississippi. "He asked me if I had bought anything in Keokuk," Thomas said. "I told him I had bought a lot. He said don't leave any more money here. Prices have reach[d] a point that property cant stand. I have disposed of my interest and am transferring it to Kansas."

Ridley must have been persuasive, for soon Thomas was again on the river, traveling southward to St. Louis, transferring to a smaller boat, and going up the Missouri River to Kansas City. There he booked passage into the Kansas Territory on the *Blackhawk,* whose captain was John Lee, an acquaintance from Thomas's Cumberland River travels. This latter portion of his route was the same that his nephew Richard Rapier had traversed seven years earlier, on his way to California.

INTO "BLEEDING KANSAS"

But the territory had changed a good deal since Richard Rapier traveled overland. Only a year earlier, fighting in Kansas over the issue of slavery had embroiled the nation in a fierce sectional dispute over whether slavery should be permitted in the territories. Since 1820, the Missouri Compromise had ruled that Kansas should keep slavery out, but that measure was repealed in 1854. Instead, the issue was to be settled by a vote under the doctrine of "popular sovereignty." Soon, both southern proslavery advocates and antislavery northerners were pouring into

Kansas, hoping to sway the vote. For a time, rival free-state and slave-state governments vied for power, and violence was common. In 1856, a proslavery mob crossed over from Missouri and attacked Lawrence, a free-state settlement. Shortly after that attack, John Brown raided several proslavery cabins along Pottawatomie Creek, executing several settlers.

When James Thomas arrived in the territory only a year later, the region was still unsettled, and Kansas was further roiled by the speculative mania even greater than that Thomas had seen elsewhere in the Midwest. Advertisements promised that towns still on the drawing boards would soon have courthouses, churches, schools, stores, houses, sidewalks, and tree-lined streets. Buying land in these future town sites would bring great wealth. Caught up in the speculative fervor, Thomas purchased twenty-seven lots in Topeka and Tecumseh, again hoping to turn a quick profit. He also considered settling in Kansas. His "Idea and desire" was to homestead one hundred sixty acres of prairie land, offered by the government to settlers who would improve it, but upon inquiry, he discovered that the homestead "law excluded all except White men or White people."[12] Unable to homestead, he considered buying a farm, for he predicted that fifty thousand immigrants would be arriving in the territory during the spring and summer of 1857.[13]

Thomas had now grown a full beard and carried most of his earthly possessions in a carpetbag. Traveling about the territory, he was surprised by the large number of Indians he saw, including Shawnee, Kaw, Potawatomie, Delaware, and Wyandotte. They were especially numerous around Leavenworth, Kansas City, and Westport, he said. At one point he visited an encampment and shared tea with a Shawnee woman.[14]

Stopping in various towns—including Lawrence, with its antislavery residents, and Lecompton, a center for proslavery settlers—Thomas thought the peculiar institution would never survive in the territory without government assistance. "There appeared to be many more northern men in the territory than southern men and they were still coming in greater numbers," Thomas recalled. "The southern people claimed they were entitled to government protection in their rights to carry their goods, horses, cows, mules, niggers included," wherever they wished.[15]

One evening, during a stopover in Lecompton, Thomas was sleeping in the railroad station, as many did, when he was roused from a deep sleep in the middle of the night by a dozen mean-looking men smelling of cheap whiskey. One of the intruders accused Thomas of being a slave who had asked the man for assistance in escaping. Thomas denied the allegation and fumbled through his carpetbag to show his papers and prove his free status. After what seemed an eternity, the "principal man," described by Thomas only as "a tall, handsome fellow, wearing a hunting shirt," said that Thomas should be released. This and other violent incidents he witnessed or heard about caused him to rethink the possibility of settling in Kansas. It seemed that both northerners and southerners were belligerent toward one another. In many ways, he observed, Kansas was no better than Nicaragua. By July 1857, James Thomas was back in St. Louis.[16]

STEAMBOATING ON THE MISSISSIPPI

The levee was "like a vast warehouse without a roof," James Thomas observed. Drays, wagons, and carriages moved up and down, while hundreds of riverfront workers loaded and un-

" . . . *if you choose to give me a call I would be glad to see you damn it John I cant write any more now you must excuse me with Respect . . .* "

loaded horses, cattle, hogs, mules, corn, hay, and hogsheads of meat, lard, flour, and whiskey from steamboats and packets that stretched up and down the river for some distance. It seemed as if everything from the upper Mississippi, Missouri, and Ohio rivers and their tributaries arrived in St. Louis before moving down "the father of waters" to New Orleans.[17]

Thomas also saw white men prodding black men and women aboard boats destined for the New Orleans market. Everyone knew that the white men were buyers and sellers of slaves. "To the better class of southern people, the nigger trader was most detestable," Thomas recalled.

> After seeing the lot located on [board], he [the slave trader] some-
> times called at the boat's office to inquire if he could not have a
> little better quarters for a likely girl that he had in the lot. Fre-
> quently she was a mulatto or in some case a quadroon. As she was
> supposed to bring a fancy price, she was better cared for than those
> of his lot that would be sold to a planter who would use them for
> plantation work or common labor.[18]

With between nine and ten boats and packets arriving daily, Thomas quickly found employment as a barber on the recently renovated luxury steamboat *William M. Morrison*, a 267-foot, 1,000-ton vessel—John N. Bofinger captain—that ran between St. Louis and New Orleans.[19] The *Morrison*, Thomas recalled, was a floating palace. Its spacious staterooms contained extra wardrobes, washstands, toilets, and mirrors; its main room and dining areas boasted stained-glass windows, exquisitely uphol-stered furniture, Brussels carpets, and sparkling chandeliers.[20] He knew of no other means of travel that combined such comfort, elegance, and freedom for its passengers. "An idea may be formed

St. Louis grew rapidly following the War of 1812, containing a mixture of French, German, Irish, and blacks—slave and free. Despite antagonistic laws and a hostility toward free blacks by many of its citizens, the city harbored a small mulatto elite, often persons of French and African American heritage. (SOURCE: PRINT IN BALLOU'S PICTORIAL DRAWING-ROOM COMPANION, MARCH 14, 1857, COURTESY OF MICHAEL MARLEAU.)

of the high state of finish in her long and brilliant cabins," the St. Louis *Daily Democrat* reported in 1857, by the fact that the stained glass alone, distributed throughout this portion of the boat, cost nearly one thousand dollars. During the six-day trip, the men drank, gambled, dined on fine foods, smoked the best cigars, and discussed the sectional crisis, as the conflict over slavery was being called; the women attended social functions and danced at costume balls.[21]

During layovers in New Orleans, instead of scrambling over freight boxes, wandering through the streets in wide-eyed amazement, and peering through windows, as he had done on his visit as a teenager, Thomas dined out and frequented the opera.[22] Each performance, each audience, seemed more impressive than the previous one. "No city that I have seen in this country has approached near a New Orleans audience on Grand Opera nights, Tuesdays & Thursdays." The blaze of diamonds and the sparkle of full evening dress could not be surpassed.[23] "We had a verry pleasant time up and down," he reported to his nephew John Rapier Jr. in the spring of 1858.[24]

He also noted that no northern city could boast such a prosperous black community. Having visited literally hundreds of towns and cities in the South, North and West, he asserted that blacks in New Orleans enjoyed a higher economic status than any other group of African Americans in the United States. Among them were bondsmen and bondswomen who, as he had done in Nashville, hired themselves out, earned their own wages, came and went as they pleased, and lived outside the

Built in 1856 and eventually acquired by the Confederacy, the steamboat William M. Morrison *accommodated up to two hundred passengers. There is some evidence that young Samuel L. Clemens, or Mark Twain, was a steersman or assistant pilot on the* Morrison *at the time that Thomas worked onboard as a barber. Its captain, John N. Bofinger, was described as having "untiring energy, perseverance and industry" and being "one of the most popular and best boatmen to navigate the Mississippi River."* (Source: Courtesy of Missouri Historical Society, St. Louis, Missouri and from Emerson W. Gould, *Fifty Years on the Mississippi; or, Gould's History of River Navigation,* [St. Louis, Mo.: Nixon-Jones Printing Co., 1889].)

purview and sometimes the control of their owners. Among them also were free people of color who entered the merchant and planter class, acquiring substantial wealth, including slaves. These Creoles of color lived stylishly in tree-lined residential neighborhoods. They vacationed in the North during the summer and sometimes sent their children to Europe for an education.[25]

Nor did Thomas ever recall, in his memoir or letters, any unpleasant racial incident in the Crescent City. There were restrictions to be sure, and most whites believed that he and other black Americans were members of an inferior race, but the regulations and antiblack sentiments seemed less pronounced than in the North. Custom dictated a relaxed intermingling of the races in New Orleans, Thomas said, and if blacks could not enter the dress circle at the opera, they did not seem to care because the boxes set aside in the balcony for wealthy Creoles of color were perhaps as luxurious as the seats below. Thomas never remarked about being asked to leave a theater, or being demeaned because of his race, though he recalled such incidents in the North, and bitterly assailed the hypocrisy of whites who professed to be the black man's best friend but denied him courteous treatment.[26]

At the same time he was not unsympathetic to the plight of less fortunate blacks. During his visit, he passed a building in the lower section of the city bearing a huge sign, MARYLAND AND VIRGINIA NEGROES FOR SALE. He saw black women lined up on dis-

Besides the slaves being shipped on board many of the steamboats plying the western waters, there were also free blacks and hired slaves who worked as deck hands, stewards, barbers, waiters, chambermaids, and cooks, like the one shown here. (SOURCE: HARPER'S NEW MONTHLY MAGAZINE, DECEMBER 1858, P. 7, COURTESY OF MICHAEL MARLEAU.)

play along the sidewalk, black men arranged like pieces of furniture in show windows, and boisterous, cigar-smoking slave brokers scrutinizing, questioning, and handling the human merchandise. He witnessed the sale of slaves who ranged in size and color from towering, purple-black Africans, to lithe, brown-colored Creoles, to shapely, blue-eyed mulattoes. He witnessed the sale of youngsters nine and ten years old. Such scenes reminded him that only a few years earlier he, too, had been human property.[27]

The round trip down to New Orleans and back took about three weeks. During layovers in St. Louis, he found a job working at free black Henry Clamorgan's bathhouse and barbershop, located at Fourth and Pine streets, in the central business district. Clamorgan was from a distinguished family, and it was through him that Thomas met some of the city's most prominent free people of color. They included real-estate speculator and barber William Johnson, who had amassed a small fortune of twenty-one thousand dollars; businessman Cyprian Clamorgan (Henry's half brother), who boasted an even larger estate; and Madame Pelagie Rutgers, the richest free black in Missouri, with holdings worth more than fifty thousand dollars.[28] Thomas soon entered a round of social events with his new friends. He attended concerts, played euchre, frequented private dinner parties, and, as he had in New Orleans, went to the opera and to concerts, including a performance by Italian soprano Ermina Frezzolini, who was touring the United States following rave reviews from Vienna, London, St. Petersburg, Madrid, and Paris.[29]

Gracious and outgoing, Thomas quickly grew in popularity among the city's colored elite. He was "a man of mark," genteel in his manners and attentive to business, Cyprian Clamorgan wrote in 1858 in his booklet *The Colored Aristocracy of St. Louis.*[30] A Tennessean by birth and worth fifteen thousand dollars, Thomas was described by Clamorgan as "a remarkably fine looking man." In terms of character, talent, intelligence, and business acumen, he would do honor to the "proudest white man in the land." As one white gentleman "occupying the front rank of statesmen of the West" noted, the only thing that prevented him from becoming "one of the greatest men of his age was his color."[31]

Shortly before Clamorgan's volume appeared, Thomas saw the famous slave Dred Scott walking along Fourth Street. He had followed Scott's case for years: in 1846, Dred Scott, a Virginia-born slave, had filed suit, claiming he was free because he had lived for nearly nine years in Illinois and the Wisconsin Territory, where slavery was prohibited. Scott's owner had returned to Missouri, but antislavery whites assisted in bringing Scott's suit in St. Louis. A jury in St. Louis declared Scott and his family (they had two children) free, but the Missouri State Supreme Court reversed the decision. In 1854, Scott, who was quasi-free and working as a porter, filed suit in the St. Louis federal court. The case went to the United States Supreme Court where, in March 1857, Chief Justice Roger B. Taney delivered the majority opinion, which declared, in Thomas's words, that the "Negro is a savage and has no rights that a white man is bound to respect." There was no small irony that among the majority on the court was none other than Thomas's own father, John Catron.[32]

During the late 1850s, Thomas grew increasingly weary of his life on the river. Journeying from place to place, month after

Harriett and Dred Scott. (Source: Courtesy of State Historical Society of Missouri, Columbia, Missouri.)

month, year after year, without ever putting down roots, he wrote, was "an ill spent life."[33] Additionally, he had struck up a friendship with the twenty-year-old Antoinette Rutgers, the daughter of the wealthy Pelagie Rutgers.[34] In July 1858, Thomas admitted that he was "thinking of taking charge of some worthy woman."[35] He worried that if he did not get the "matter fixed up before I am 35 or 40 [it] will have to go undone." Thomas, who had turned thirty-two in 1859, opined, "I don't think [passion] burns much after forty." He planned to buy a new suit and surprise Antoinette with a proposal of marriage, he told his nephew John Rapier Jr. Were he "to succeed in that" he might make "Rome howl"—for the Rutgers were Roman Catholic.[36]

Although Thomas had converted to Catholicism and joined Antoinette's church, St. Vincent de Paul, Pelagie Rutgers refused to allow her daughter to marry a former slave. Ironically, the straight-haired and brown-skinned Pelagie had once been a slave herself, but she had married into the Clamorgan clan, and later, as a widow, married free black Louis Rutgers, who left her a substantial estate. Approaching her sixtieth year, she was determined that her daughter marry into one of the old and respected free black families in the city. Despite Antoinette's affection for Thomas, her mother's opposition prevailed.[37] Thomas was saddened by the turn of events, but continued to see Antoinette and spent increasing amounts of time working at Clamorgan's barbershop.

JOHN RAPIER JR. IN THE CARIBBEAN

Although John Rapier Jr. was eight years younger than his uncle James Thomas, the two got along well together. After their trip to Nicaragua, Thomas wrote his nephew regularly. As the secession crisis intensified in the fall of 1860, John Jr. visited his uncle in St. Louis, on his way south from Minnesota, and revealed his latest plans. For a number of years he had contemplated emigrating from the United States, where he felt relegated to the bottom rung of society because of his color. He had now decided to leave the land of his birth.

In December he boarded a ship for Haiti, the first black republic in the Americas. Rapier had been in the Caribbean before, but as the ship reached the channel between the main island of Haiti and the Île de la Govâne, he was struck by the remarkable beauty of the islands. Port-au-Prince was nestled at the end of a long bay at the base of a chain of mountains that rose from the sea. The city appeared well laid out, the streets aligned in an orderly grid fashion.[38]

Once on land, however, Rapier was surprised by the filth and squalor he found almost everywhere and by the rundown cottages that shared the same streets with handsome homes. Even the president's palace, a one-story wooden structure, was surrounded by a crumbling wall and a courtyard overrun with grass and weeds. The streets were filled with refuse and garbage, he observed, forcing the visitor to circumvent "heaps of manure, broken bottles, crockery, and every species of rubbish."[39]

Rapier soon fell in with a wealthy, Cuban-born plantation owner of mixed racial ancestry named Mondesir Errié, who lived alone with his servants in the city in "quite a magnificent house." Errié's young, attractive wife had left him a short time before and had taken up with an aide-de-camp to the Haitian president. "Such instances are very common," Rapier wrote his uncle, "so much so that no one loses Caste by so doing, nor is the circumstance ever referred to, only as 'a good joke on the Old man.' " Lonely and with few friends, Errié invited Rapier to stay with him, and the older man soon became quite fond of his young, energetic, and intelligent American guest. Rapier listened to endless stories about Haiti and its history. He learned that free persons of color from the southern states had risen to positions of prominence there. The minister of the interior, for example, was from Maryland; the chief of police was from South Carolina; and the commander of the port was from Alabama. Rapier also learned about Errié's Haitian relatives, including his grandfather, a half brother of Toussaint L'Overture; and his father, a private secretary to Haiti's first president, Alexandre Petion, who commanded a regiment of mixed-race soldiers during the era of French rule. "Like all mixed bloods," Rapier said of his newfound friend, "he hates the blacks to the death."[40]

To avoid spending his savings, Rapier took a part-time job, but living with Errié meant that his expenses were modest. In addition, things were cheap and the dollar was strong. "I have about 2 hours labor per diem and receive for this $6.00 Spanish per week," he wrote, "and from this I must pay all contingent expenses Board & washing and the other usual expenditures, so at the end of this week I owe only about $1.5 from my pocket."[41]

In January 1861, Errié invited Rapier to visit one of his tobacco plantations, located some twenty-three miles away. Wending their way on donkeys upward over the rugged mountain terrain, Rapier thought about the poverty and squalor of blacks on the island and the privileged position of persons of mixed racial heritage, like him and Errié. They had not gone far when a band of thieves ambushed them. The bandits took not only their donkeys but also their week's supply of provisions. Unharmed, however, Errié and Rapier proceeded on foot, arriving safely at the plantation.[42]

They were greeted by the head man, who invited them into his bamboo hut for supper. Rapier was repulsed by the stench and filth, the man's scantily clad wife and naked children, and the simple fare of roasted plantains.[43] Plantation blacks were "very primitive in all their customs and habits," Rapier wrote. They wore little clothing; they never wore shoes; and they were "pagans in their belief." They prayed to their ancestors and worshiped idols as did their African ancestors; they believed in witchcraft, the evil eye, ghosts, and conjuration. When a person fell ill, Rapier said, the family immediately called for the conjurer, who summoned the devil and demanded that he return the person's health. The conjurer then poured a bowl of milk to the north, one to the south, one to the east, and drank a fourth bowl while facing west. He fell to the ground and wrestled with the devil for an hour, finally "rising and handing a small leather bag to the oldest girl" and explaining that the lost health had been recovered from the devil.[44]

It was not only blacks who repulsed Rapier. He found the mulatto population completely unprincipled. "I am not a strict moralist," he confessed, but the non-black men of Haiti constantly discussed their sexual conquests and often kept several young women as concubines. Both men and women exchanged lovers for a night, or a week. "This is a veritable picture of social life in Port-au-Prince, which comprises the elite of the Island," Rapier wrote, "and from my own observation, and from what I have been told, I have no hesitation in saying that a more degraded, miserable and abandoned set of wretches than the Haytians, never cursed the face of God's earth." Among the fifty-seven births in the city during a two-week period in February, he added, forty-eight were illegitimate.[45]

During the early months of 1861, with Abraham Lincoln elected to the presidency and the states of the Deep South seceding, Rapier was troubled by news he received about his father, John Rapier Sr., in Alabama. A group of recently arrived free black émigrés from Mobile, Alabama, told him that the state's free-black population was about to be sold into slavery or forced to emigrate. "This I do not believe," Rapier correctly surmised, "but one cannot tell what can be, and what can not, in times of revolution."[46] He prayed that his father had seen the storm gathering and had moved with his family out to some free state. Rapier vowed that if he ever had enough money, he would pay for the education of one of his father's slave boys.[47]

The conditions in Haiti also left young John confused about how to weigh the benefits of freedom. "I came here considerably tinctured and spotted with abolitionism, and universal freedom," he confessed to his uncle James Thomas, "but I am now entirely cured of those symptoms of insanity." He was "now ultra pro-slavery, and am satisfied that a greater curse could not be imposed upon the United States or any other country, than the emancipation of the Negro slaves." Once free, he asserted, blacks laid down their shovels and hoes, took up their fiddles, banjos, and tambourines, and devoted their lives to dancing, drinking, and playing, interrupting such activities only to steal something to eat and to support their "time in idleness." If he ever settled in a country where black people predominated, he promised, it would be where they were slaves. This was "sharp language" for a Negro to use, he admitted, "but it is [as] true as strange."[48]

He did not keep his promise, however. In early April, he bade his friend Errié adieu and sailed for Kingston, Jamaica, the capital city of a country where slavery had been abolished nearly a generation earlier. Yet Rapier's reaction to that country was similar to his reaction to Haiti. Jamaica's beauty was unsurpassed, he observed, with majestic mountains, lush green valleys, and fragrant tropical flowers. But "Kingston is certainly the most woe begone City in the West Indies," he wrote three weeks after his arrival; its harbor was nearly deserted, its wharves were rotting and dilapidated, and its "fine fire proof store houses [were] locked up unoccupied." Lying beneath the porticos of deserted houses were crowds of "lazy and sun stricken negroes," half asleep, while groups of "semi-nude women" retailed cakes, pies, and beer. The morals of Kingston were even worse than those of

Haiti, he judged; at least in Port-au-Prince illicit affairs were confined to the homes of the rich, while in the Jamaican capital, immorality could be witnessed "in every form under the heavens, upon nearly every corner, and cross lane."[49]

As he observed more of the city, he continued to criticize the freed slaves and their descendants. "[L]et me repeat it," he wrote his uncle in St. Louis, "that the Negro is a very improvident creature in this latitude."[50] Even as Rapier delighted at what could be found at the central marketplace, including melons, figs, grapes, mangoes, cantaloupes, and "huge pyramids of other delicious fruits," he disparaged those who worked there: old black women with funny turbans; old black men with dilapidated hats; and young men who went about without trousers, jackets, or other articles of clothing, wearing only lengthy "tow shirts" draped over their bodies.

If he found former slaves and their descendants curious and strange, he thought whites and the mulatto elite admirable. The first social circle in Jamaica, he said, consisted of lawyers, doctors, ministers, high-ranking officials, and wealthy planters. They looked upon themselves as aristocrats and never socialized with the second social rank of small shop owners, retail merchants, clerks, Methodist ministers, and Baptist preachers. The third group consisted of mechanics and other unclassified persons "who can put on decent clothing once a week." At the bottom was the one-third of a million blacks who were "rude and savage" and had "no legitimate conceptions of the duties of men and Citizens."[51]

Among those of the first rank were persons of mixed racial origin, who, in Jamaica, Rapier said, "have every thing their own way."[52] He deemed the opening session of the country's Supreme Court "a grand affair." He watched as several officials of mixed race took part in the proceedings: the Honorable Peter Moncrieffe, a griff, or person of three-quarters "Negro blood"[53]; Sir Edward Jordan, a mulatto; and Attorney General Alexander Heslip and his assistant, T. Williams, both persons of mixed race. With one or two exceptions, the lawyers who came before the court were persons of mixed blood, and those exceptions were white. Charles Price, a full-blooded Negro and member of Parliament for Kingston, read the benediction and asked for divine protection of the royal family, while the Honorable William Vickers, also a black man and a former member of the executive council, responded "in the name of Queen." Rapier sat in the audience between two lawyers who, he said, each earned twenty thousand dollars a year. This was heady tonic for a young man who, in the United States, would not be allowed even to enter a county courthouse except as a witness or a prisoner.[54]

Rapier soon found a position assisting Dr. William Beckett, a well-known Canadian dentist who practiced in Kingston. "I am pushing along with all speed possible in my new profession," Rapier wrote, explaining that in a short time he had become as adept as his mentor at lancing gums, applying forceps, and yanking out molars amid "screams of agony." "You should see me sometime have a poor suffering devil with the toothache with his Jaws distended."[55] He also accompanied Beckett to Mandeville, a town about fifty-five miles west of Kingston, where the two men offered their services. Journeying along a winding mountain road, they witnessed some of the most spectacular scenery on the island.

The Road to Mandeville leads to the top of the Manchester Plateau, reaching an elevation of more than two thousand feet. The town of Mandeville was founded as a retreat for colonial officials seeking an escape from the oppressive summer heat. (Source: Courtesy of the National Library of Jamaica, Kingston, Jamaica.)

In Mandeville, Rapier met a Creole widow named Mrs. Nash, a woman "of bewitching beauty" who had lost her husband, an Englishman, shortly after becoming pregnant with twin daughters. Each evening, Rapier rode out on horseback to visit the widow and her daughters, now fifteen, at their villa on the outskirts of town. The group spent many enjoyable hours eating, drinking, and visiting. The daughters were as handsome as they were talented; they sang, danced, painted, sketched, drew, and played musical instruments. Their only drawback, Rapier felt, arose because their mother insisted that they learn to cook, wash, iron, and sew. Such highly cultured young women should not be forced to learn such menial chores, he argued. After a month, Rapier and Beckett traveled to Santa Cruz, on the Black River, to see the most spectacular waterfall on the island, before returning to Kingston.[56]

Rapier's job as a dentist provided him not only a living wage but also an opportunity to meet a number of physicians, including a certain Dr. Scott, who, in early 1862, invited Rapier to read medicine under his direction. Rapier was thrilled, and predicted that in eighteen months he would enter McGill University, in Montreal, or Queen's University, in Toronto. He studied physiology, "medical nomenclature," and, his favorite subject, anatomy. Perhaps he would even study in Dublin, Edinburgh, or London, he conjectured, and earn a decree from the Royal College of Surgeons.[57]

"Kingston is the heaven of prejudice based upon the colour of the skin," he observed, but whites showed "no prejudice toward the mixed bloods." He himself had risen rapidly in Jamaican society. On one occasion, receiving an ink-smeared letter from his brother in Canada, he complained that it was embarrassing: nothing revealed antecedents more than such a letter. Rapier was neither proud, haughty, nor ashamed of his relatives, he insisted, but he was now in a unique situation and associated with a different class of people. It was essential that his acquaintances and others with whom he dealt not learn that his father was once a slave. If they found out, he would be "snubbed by the proud Jamaicans and this, as much as I despise many of their customs, I can not afford."[58]

For a young man, John Rapier Jr.'s experiences in Haiti and Jamaica were disorienting. He had no love for slavery, but the desperate and degraded condition of slaves in the Caribbean troubled him. Like so many other persons of mixed blood, he was accepting of the privileges lighter skin provided him. He was astonished and gratified to find himself treated with respect, even deference, by both white and mulatto associates. He knew he could never receive such public and social approval in the United States. With the opportunity of learning a profession, a path toward more freedom and equality beckoned. Yet those around him shunned lower-class blacks, finding them repugnant. It was both a heady experience, and a confusing one; it was especially difficult not to adopt the views of people who treated him with such respect.

"To tell you the truth a very different kind of f[eeling] and ideas pervades ones heart and head, when he can meet every man on equal terms, and converse without restraint with them upon every topic of the day," Rapier declared on his twenty-sixth birthday, "agreeing and disagreeing, upon themes and subjects just as you think or feel inclined, without feeling all the time that your opinions are only heard because you are a pretty clever nigger, and can read and write—Where you can go to all places of amusement, instruction or interest without a hundred eyes being turned upon you, while their owners are busy wondering what the *hell* is that nigger doing here—"[59]

NOTES

1. James Thomas to John Rapier Jr., October 3, 1856, RTP.
2. James Thomas to John Rapier Jr., November 26, 1856, RTP.
3. James Thomas to John Rapier Jr., November 23, 1856, RTP.
4. Ibid.

5. James Thomas to John Rapier Jr., December 23, 1856, RTP; Harvey Wish, "The Slave Insurrection Panic of 1856," *Journal of Southern History* 5 (May 1939): 211; idem, "American Slavery Insurrection Before 1861," *Journal of Negro History* (July 1937): 299–320.

6. FTS, 88.

7. Ibid., 88–89.

8. Wish, "Slave Insurrection Panic of 1856," 212.

9. James Thomas to John Rapier Jr., December 23, 1856, RTP; James Thomas to John Rapier Jr., March 1, 1857, RTP.

10. James Thomas to John Rapier Jr., March 1, 1857, RTP; USMSPC, Davidson Co., Tenn., Nashville, 1850, 128. Logan was among the most successful actresses in the country. F. Garvin Davenport, *Cultural Life in Nashville on the Eve of the Civil War* (Chapel Hill: University of North Carolina Press, 1941), 121–22.

11. FTS, 144.

12. Ibid., 150.

13. James Thomas to John Rapier Jr., May 11, 1857, RTP.

14. Ibid., FTS, 146, 150–51; George Merrick, *Old Times on the Upper Mississippi: Recollections of a Steamboat Pilot from 1854 to 1863* (Cleveland, Ohio: Arthur H. Clark Co., 1909), 281.

15. FTS, 148–50; James Thomas to John Rapier Jr., May 11, 1857, RTP.

16. FTS, 152; James Thomas to John Rapier Jr., July 27, 1857, RTP.

17. FTS, 108.

18. Ibid., 108, 116.

19. Ibid., 116; William Lass, *A History of Steamboating on the Upper Missouri River* (Lincoln: University of Nebraska Press, 1962), 60; Louis C. Hunter, *Steamboats on the Western Rivers: An Economic and Technological History* (Cambridge: Harvard University Press, 1949), 646. In 1857, 3,443 steamboats arrived in St. Louis, making it the busiest port in the West. Cincinnati and New Orleans each had about 2,700 arrivals.

20. FTS, 116; St. Louis *Daily Democrat,* January 1, 1857. For other material on the *Morrison,* see the *Missouri Democrat,* February 13, 1858, May 28, 1858; and the St. Louis *Leader,* February 13, 1858.

21. FTS, 116; St. Louis *Daily Democrat,* January 1, 1857; Edgar Marquess Branch, Michael B. Frankel, Kenneth M. Sanderson, eds., *Mark Twain's Letters, Volume 1, 1853–1866* (Berkeley: University of California Press, 1988), 387–88.

22. James Thomas to John Rapier Jr., May 3, 1858, RTP.

23. FTS, 111.

24. James Thomas to John Rapier Jr., May 3, 1858, RTP.

25. FTS, 113.

26. Ibid., 109–116.

27. Ibid., 112; Kenneth Stampp, *The Peculiar Institution: Slavery in the Ante-bellum South* (New York: Alfred Knopf, 1956), 263–64.

28. Cyprian Clamorgan, *The Colored Aristocracy of St. Louis,* 14; for William Johnson, see USMSPC, St. Louis., Missouri, Second Ward, 1850, 222; ibid., Fourth Ward, 1860, n.p.

29. James Thomas to John Rapier Jr., May 3, 1858, June 14, 1858, RTP.

30. Clamorgan, *The Colored Aristocracy of St. Louis,* 18.

31. Clamorgan, *The Colored Aristocracy of St. Louis* (reprint ed., introduction by Julie Winch, Columbia: University of Missouri Press, 1999), 59. Clamorgan overstated Thomas's wealth.

32. For Thomas seeing Dred Scott on the street, see "Miscellaneous Notes," RTP; Sanford Levinson, "Slavery in the Canon of Constitutional Law," in Paul Finkelman, ed., *Slavery & the Law* (Madison, Wisconsin: Madison House, 1997), 90–91, 103–104; A. Leon Higginbotham Jr., *Shades of Freedom: Racial Politics and Presumptions of the American Legal Process* (New York: Oxford University Press, 1966), 61–67.

33. James Thomas to John Rapier Jr., January 8, 1859, RTP.

34. Clamorgan, *The Colored Aristocracy of St. Louis,* 49; USMSPC, St. Louis, Mo., Second Ward, 1860, 665; ibid., St. Louis, Mo., Third Ward, 1870, 195 [printed page number]. Antoinette was listed as twenty-two in 1860, and thirty-two in 1870.

35. James Thomas to John Rapier Jr., July 17, 1858, RTP.

36. James Thomas to John Rapier Jr., January 8, 1859, RTP.

37. Clamorgan, *Colored Aristocracy of St. Louis,* 49.

38. New Orleans *Weekly Mirror,* July 9, 1859, cited in Robert Reinders, "The Decline of the New Orleans Free Negro in the Decade before the Civil War," *Journal of Mississippi History* 24 (April 1962): 96. Among the emigrés were free people of color described as "literate and respectable."

39. John Rapier Jr. to James Thomas, January 29, 1861, 16, RTP. See also Spenser St. John, *Hayti or the Black Republic* (London: Smith, Elder, & Co., 1889), 5, 8.

40. John Rapier Jr. to James Thomas, January 29, 1861, RTP.

41. Ibid.

42. Ibid.

43. Ibid.

44. John Rapier Jr. to James Thomas, February 25, 1861, RTP.

45. Ibid.

46. Ibid.

47. John Rapier Jr. to James Thomas, January 29, 1861, RTP.

48. John Rapier Jr. to James Thomas, February 25, 1861, RTP.

49. John Rapier Jr. to James Thomas, April 30, 1861, RTP.

50. John Rapier Jr. to James Thomas, February 18, 1862, RTP.

51. John Rapier Jr. to James Thomas, February 3, 1862, RTP.

52. Ibid.

53. A griff was a person with three-fourths Negro blood, compared with a mulatto, who, in a strict definition, was half white and half black. The term was used in the Caribbean to denote the offspring of a black and a mulatto.

54. John Rapier Jr. to James Thomas, July 28, 1861, RTP.

55. Ibid.

56. John Rapier Jr. to James Thomas, October 17, 1861, RTP.

57. John Rapier Jr. to James Thomas, February 3, 1862, RTP.

58. John Rapier Jr. to James Thomas, April 30, 1861, RTP.

59. John Rapier Jr. to James Thomas, July 28, 1861, RTP.

· Six ·

THIS MIGHTY SCOURGE OF WAR

IT WAS A CLEAR, CHILLY MORNING ON JANUARY 10, 1863 AS JAMES Thomas stood on the deck of the steamboat *Ruth* and watched the Battle of Arkansas Post unfold. He had found work as a barber aboard the *Ruth,* the new elegant passenger steamer. On its maiden voyage, however, the ship had been commandeered by Union general Clinton B. Fisk to carry Union troops to fight against the Confederates along the White and Arkansas rivers. Years later, Thomas recalled how Fisk had walked into the boat's barbershop, raked winnings off a table in the corner where a poker game was in progress, and put the money in a box marked "sanitary commission"—put aside to buy food, clothing, and medical supplies for war refugees. Erect and confident, with deep-set eyes and a full, heavy black beard, Fisk exuded power and authority.[1]

The *Ruth* was among the sixty transports carrying thirty-two thousand infantry, a thousand cavalry, and more than forty pieces of artillery up the Arkansas River. The goal of the Union was to capture Fort Hindman, at Arkansas Post, located on a small bluff on the right bank of the broad, swiftly moving river. The fort served a dual purpose: to control movement into the hinterland and to the state's capital of Little Rock; and to provide a safe haven for attack boats on the Mississippi River.

The battle scene was indeed remarkable. The tranquil countryside, dotted with herds of cattle and fields of cotton and corn, stretched back from the river and stood in sharp contrast to the thousands of Union troops pressing forward in perfect unison. One Confederate soldier recalled that it was "silent except the commands of the Officers," noting that "on, on they come, like an irresistible thunder-bolt, as it dashes unrestrained through the air; to crush the atoms of the sturdiest Oak." The fighting was, said one participant, as "fierce an engagement of six hours as has occurred during the war." Corps commander William T. Sherman noted that Union muskets and guns had "done good execution" as dead men and dead horses lay strewn "very thick" on the ground.[2]

At the end of the second day, a Confederate force of nearly five thousand surrendered. Expressing surprise at the number of Confederate soldiers who were illiterate, James Thomas recalled that the Union troops "captured a few stragglers and all the news they found in the old newspapers was fresh to them and somebody had to read it for them." They gathered around a fellow prisoner who could read and listened to the news from home.[3] The loss of Arkansas Post was a major setback for the Confederacy. It exposed Little Rock and set the stage for the fall of Vicksburg and the opening of the Mississippi River to the Union.

JAMES THOMAS IN ST. LOUIS

Arkansas Post was the only Civil War battle that Thomas witnessed. He spent most of his time during the war working at Clamorgan's, one of the city's most successful barbershops. With short hair the fashion and the price of a haircut up to thirty cents, Thomas earned a good living. His congenial personality and knowledgeable commentary on current events caused him to advance from barber to head barber, and finally to shop manager.

As shop manager, though, he found it difficult to hire other black barbers. What had previously been considered virtually the birthright of persons of color was being taken over, at least in St. Louis, by German immigrants. "In casting around for barbers to hold their trade," Thomas later wrote, barbershop owners "fell upon the Idea of taking some young man from one of the little dutch shops and learning him the American way of serving their patrons." Once German barbers learned the trade, he explained, they moved out on their own and "drew the color line."[4]

Although Thomas tried to hire free blacks, they tended not to stay in the job long, for their situation during the war was unsettled. A "color line" had been drawn on the eve of the war, as white southerners debated the future of free blacks. Most whites believed that slavery was a natural condition for black people and that free people of color set a bad example in a slave society. Indeed, some free blacks, they complained, enticed slaves to run away. In a number of states, influential whites demanded that free blacks be remanded to slavery or forced to leave the state.[5] In Arkansas, this arrangement became law. In Missouri, members of the legislature debated a "free Nigger bill," as Thomas called it, to expel free blacks, and county courts even began gathering blacks in expectation of the bill's being passed. "In rounding up the free people before the court there were many who were Indians, Spaniards, French," Thomas recalled, "whose chocolate colored mothers had lived under the three flags" of

Spain, France, and the United States. In the end, the proposed bill did not pass, and free blacks were permitted to stay.[6]

The beginning of the war in St. Louis was swift and unexpected. James Thomas not only followed events but was also acquainted with some of the participants. A few weeks after the firing on Fort Sumter in April 1861, several officers in the Confederate Missouri State Guard invited Thomas to visit Camp Jackson. Named for the pro-Confederate Missouri governor, Claiborne F. Jackson, the secessionist encampment was located six miles outside St. Louis. Thomas had heard that visitors were very well received there and that the "best wines and liquors were plentiful, cigars abundant." But before he could take the officers up on their invitation, Union captain Nathaniel Lyon launched an attack.[7]

In early May 1861, Lyon disguised himself as a farm woman and entered the camp. While there, he discovered that the state guard was about to launch an assault on the United States Armory in St. Louis. At stake was not only a large store of muskets, powder, cartridge balls, and weapons, but also control of certain industries in the city and, even more important, of the Missouri and Mississippi rivers. On the memorable tenth of May, leaving two companies of regular soldiers behind to guard the armory, Captain Lyon led about six thousand soldiers, including four German Home Guard units, to Camp Jackson. Surrounded by Union forces, the Confederate commander surrendered.[8]

To make a public display of his victory and assert Union authority, Lyon paraded his state guard prisoners into St. Louis and through its streets to the arsenal. As the march began, pro-Confederate civilians jeered and shouted, "Damn the Dutch!"

and "Hurrah for Jeff Davis!" When the column arrived in the city, onlookers began throwing rocks, brickbats, and clods of earth. When a drunken man tried to cross the street by pushing through the front of the column, the troops pushed back, and the man drew a pistol. In the ensuing confusion, the troops opened fire, killing twenty-eight onlookers, two federal soldiers, and three militia prisoners. "The capture of Camp Jackson cast a gloom over the old set," Thomas recalled. "They criticized the dutch harshly." As a result of the incident, many Confederate sympathizers retreated farther south until the end of hostilities.[9]

As Thomas's invitation to Camp Jackson suggested, many of his customers either sympathized with or actively supported the Confederacy. "The old and wealthy families of St. Louis," Thomas wrote, "were all southern in sentiment with few exceptions." Members of those families never admitted their sympathies in public, but when in Thomas's shop, among those of a like mind, they strongly denounced the Republican Party, Abraham Lincoln, and the Union cause. The South was justified in seceding from the Union, they declared, and they would support the Confederacy in any way they could. If they were uncertain of the political persuasion of others in the shop, they referred to Union forces as "our troops," but when among their own set, they remained as ardent as any South Carolina fire-eater.[10]

During the early months of the war, Thomas actually considered supporting the Southern cause. If his customers ever thought he was pro-Union he would have lost a good portion of his income. He also genuinely admired a number of white southerners, including slave owners. The exchange of letters between Thomas and his nephew John Rapier Jr. in Jamaica reveals the ambivalent and inconsistent attitudes among members of the mulatto elite. John, who had previously vowed from Haiti that he would never live in a country where blacks were not slaves, chided his uncle for even considering supporting the South. "I regret that you hint that you wish to enter the secession Camp," Rapier wrote in the fall of 1861, urging his uncle to "do no such thing, for can you not see that the Hand of Him who ruleth the world is directing this war, to His own good purposes." Surely his uncle realized that if slaveholders won the war they would force free blacks to leave the land of their birth. He urged James to stay out of the secessionists' camp; indeed, Rapier told his un-

Following its capture, Camp Jackson, located in the western suburbs of St. Louis, became a drill ground for Union soldiers, as pictured here. (SOURCE: PHOTOGRAPH IN FRANCIS TREVELYAN MILLER, ED., *THE PHOTO-GRAPHIC HISTORY OF THE CIVIL WAR*, 10 VOLS. [NEW YORK: THE REVIEW OF REVIEWS CO., 1911], 1:171–72.)

cle to "avoid it as you would pestilence," predicting that "in the end you will bless your lucky stars that you did not touch the unclean and legitimate offspring of treachery and crime."[11]

In the end, Thomas accepted his nephew's advice. He liked the southern people individually and personally; but collectively and politically, he said, "Dam 'em."[12] But while he would not join the Confederates, Thomas believed that most so-called abolitionists cared little about slaves or free blacks. Some who called themselves abolitionists simply wished to deprive slaveholders of their slaves. He had often heard people say "those slave owners ought to have a chance to work for themselves a while. I have to work. My wife has to work. They are no better than we are. I'd just like to see that thing changed." They cared little about the actual condition of black families, Thomas believed, but envied the comfortable lifestyles of the slaveholding class. Nor did

Union soldiers seem to care about blacks. Many new recruits—young men fresh off the farm—shouted " 'dam the Niggers.' I wish there were no niggers. I am going to fight for the country."[13]

As the war progressed, thousands of black refugees—called contraband of war—streamed into St. Louis. Freed from a lifetime of bondage, they had no food, little clothing, no place to go, nothing to call their own, Thomas wrote. Missionaries, church people, sanitary commission women offered them assistance, but the needs of the refugees were overwhelming. Many suffered from exposure and ill treatment. Indeed, they often suffered as much at the hands of Union soldiers as they did at the hands of Confederates. Navigating the road to freedom in the midst of the fighting was a perilous undertaking. "White and black people gave money and time in trying to make them comfortable and finding something for them to do," Thomas wrote. "Freedom had come to many of them late in life and they found it awkward." Those who had spent a lifetime in bondage struggled to adjust, and the older they were the more difficult this proved. Some had never been to a city; others did not know how to negotiate for wages; still others had few skills they could use to make a living. "The new made citizen had just left the corn and cotton plantations," Thomas explained, "and little they knew about what they had to encounter."[14]

It did not surprise James Thomas that most blacks felt little compulsion to seek revenge against their former owners. Although they had every reason to retaliate against owners who had shown no mercy, who had whipped and beaten them for trivial offenses, and who had sold their loved ones away as punishment, the refugees simply wanted to leave the plantation. In any event, it was often defenseless women and children who were left behind to manage on the home front. Too often, Thomas recalled, their former owners wallowed in self-pity, decrying the disloyalty of their servants. "The infernal 'nigger'," some said, "will be glad to get back where he came from before long"—once he understood what freedom entailed. But such proved not to be the case. Emancipated blacks rarely returned to the plantations of their former owners. Indeed, Thomas said, even the thought of freedom made them "intoxicated."[15]

By April 1862, a year into the war, the chances of blacks experiencing freedom seemed to be expanding. Upriver, along the Tennessee River, General Ulysses S. Grant felt confident there would be no Confederate attack on his position at Pittsburg Landing. Fresh from victories at Fort Henry and Fort Donelson, Grant planned to advance south, seize the Memphis and Charleston Railroad, and cut the western Confederacy's link to the east.[16] Little did he realize that on the evening of April 4, Confederate general Albert Sidney Johnston was moving his troops into position for a surprise attack. Early the following morning, Confederate soldiers stormed through Federal lines and began the Battle of Shiloh, one of the bloodiest and most important of the war. Union troops finally halted the advance, repulsing eleven attacks from their position in "the Hornet's nest."[17] The arrival of Union reinforcements turned the tide. Johnston was mortally wounded, and General P.G.T. Beauregard, second in command, also blamed untested troops, who fled from the field "while the thunder of cannon and the roar and rattle of musketry told them that their brothers were being slaughtered by fresh legions of the enemy."[18] The carnage was immense. Shiloh claimed nearly 24,000 casualties on both sides with 7,300 dead or missing. A crimson-colored pond, acres of bodies heaped upon one another, and the stench of rotting flesh told the grim story.[19]

During the months following the battle, a number of Union officers journeyed to St. Louis for a few days respite. While many seemed to Thomas anxious to promote themselves, strutting about in their dress blues, others were modest and unassuming. On one occasion, Thomas was in a mercantile store when a plain-looking officer, wearing a worn coat and no insignia of rank, entered. Thomas and others had listened to many stories by the store owner about his close friendship with Ulysses Grant, which dated back to Grant's tenure in the city as a captain. When the plainly dressed man asked the merchant if he remembered him, the following exchange took place:

> "Well sir, your face is familiar, but I cant call your name."
> "My name is Grant."
> "O Yes, sure enough. Well I am glad to see you, Mr. Grant, how have you been. I suppose you been down to the front?"
> "Yes."
> "Now tell me Mr. Grant, are you any relation to the Genl."
> "Well, they call me Genl Grant."

Thomas, who was standing nearby, watched the merchant stand dumbfounded as "Mr. Grant" walked off down the street.[20]

The battle of Shiloh, or Pittsburg Landing, as Thomas called it, proved to be a turning point in the western campaign. The Confederates retreated to Corinth, Mississippi, giving up their position in West Tennessee. Soon after, they lost the line of transport provided by the Memphis and Charleston Railroad. With the fall of Memphis, Union troops were poised to move on Vicksburg, gain control of the Mississippi River, and cut the Confederacy in half. There was also the psychological impact of the Union victory. The early boast that one Rebel soldier was equal to ten Federals was no longer heard. Both sides now realized that the war would be long and bloody, silencing those who, as Thomas put it, "expected the war to close after one battle."[21]

In September 1862, President Lincoln signed the Preliminary Emancipation Proclamation, which stated that on January 1, 1863, "all persons held as slaves within any State or designated part of a State the people whereof shall then be in rebellion against the United States shall be then, thenceforward, and forever free."[22] It also called for the enlistment of black troops to fight for the Union. The order thus freed the slaves in areas under Confederate control, where the President had no authority, and failed to free the slaves in areas under Union control, where such authority existed. Even so, the freeing of the slaves and the recruitment of black troops were, in Thomas's estimation, remarkable occurrences. "Where the Negro had been kicked around before, he was now lifted to the highest gift, or elevation," Thomas said, "as his governments protector."[23]

JOHN RAPIER JR.'S CONTINUING ODYSSEY

While James Thomas worked at Clamorgan's barbershop and remained in St. Louis during most of the Civil War, his nephew John Rapier Jr. continued his odyssey, now in pursuit of a career in medicine. His dreams of studying in Scotland, England, or Canada did not materialize, but in the summer of 1862, he returned to the United States to enroll in a school in Ohio. After a year's study there, he spent the following summer "looking around for work to support my college next winter," he wrote his uncle James. He hoped to visit Buxton, yet money was a constant problem; he had saved some for school, but estimated that six months' board would cost fifty dollars, and his books another forty, excluding traveling and other expenses. Moreover, he did not have a decent coat to wear, his breeches were "breechless," and he did not have enough money to buy tobacco for an occasional smoke or to purchase a few bottles of beer "to make me stoical in troublesome times." If his uncle could spare fifty dollars and an old coat, he would appreciate it.[24] His goal, he said, was to enter the University of Michigan Medical School in the autumn.

To his satisfaction, Rapier did manage a journey to Buxton, visiting his brother James Thomas Rapier, his uncle Henry and aunt Maria, and his various cousins, including his favorite, Sarah.[25] Then, in the autumn of 1863, he arrived in Ann Arbor. The requirements for entry into the Department of Medicine and Surgery were stringent. Besides "a good moral and intellectual character, a good English Education, including a proper knowledge of the English Language, and a respectable acquaintance with its literature," each candidate was presumed to be acquainted with the natural sciences, Latin, mathematics, including algebra and geometry, and "current prescriptions." During the autumn and winter, each student was expected to attend four lectures each day. Before each, students would be questioned about the preceding one. In addition, students would spend time in the laboratory analyzing different human tissues under a microscope. On Wednesdays and

Saturdays, they would accompany physicians on their clinic rounds, being present "when examinations are held, prescriptions made, and operations performed." Although the course of study continued for three years, the studies Rapier had completed in Jamaica would allow him to finish in two.[26]

The first of October, Rapier joined 305 fellow students and 32 faculty members to begin the fall session, listing Kingston, Jamaica, as his residence and William Bunce as his preceptor at Ann Arbor. But he quickly encountered trouble. "The University has been thrown into convulsions during the past ten days because an 'American of African descent' dared to present himself as a candidate for admission to the Medical class," Rapier wrote a few weeks later. He was not referring to himself but rather to Al Tucker, a Detroit resident of mixed racial ancestry. Tucker had applied for admission—and was granted it—after he heard about the admission of "a col[']d gentleman from the West Indies." Rapier, regarded as a foreign student, had been admitted regardless of his race. But when Tucker showed up for class, there was a great commotion, Rapier noted, among "the copperhead Students and many unprincipled Republicans." The faculty quickly reversed itself; pandering to the prejudices of the students, they told Tucker that he could not continue.[27] In retaliation, the black community in Detroit launched an attack on Rapier: "They say I pretend to be white when I am nothing but a nigger."[28]

But the term got off to a difficult start for an entirely different reason: a stress-related illness. Six weeks after the start of classes, Rapier was confined to his room with his head "covered with blisters," his eyes swollen nearly shut, and his sight "so dim that I am unable to know whether I am writing on or under the lines." He was taking drugs "every two or three hours." Meanwhile, he had high praise for his roommate, Foster Bodle, a young white man from Darlford, Wisconsin, whom Rapier described as "a bully good fellow" and with whom Rapier shared the same preceptor. It was good that they were compatible, since they spent a great deal of time together, both in class and in their room, where students were expected to do their own cooking.[29]

Rapier found the innumerable lectures, the class routine, and the constant rounds of lab and clinical work "heavy and dull." The unending regimen rarely allowed him any time for himself. He did find temporary relief by writing his family and visiting the local art museum. He particularly delighted in "a full sized" painting by the Flemish Romantic painter Peter Paul Rubens, and in a painting by an unnamed artist titled "Patience Sitting on a Monument Smiling at Grief." Patience was clothed in the "habiliment of woe" resting on the grave of her recently buried husband. Grief, represented as a handsome, dashing cavalier, stood with hat in hand and pointed to a distant carriage, whose horses were chomping at the bit to leave. Rapier thought it a "funny picture" for such a solemn subject. As he and his friends stood before the painting, a young man came up from behind and "startled our party by earnestly exclaiming 'true to life, true to life.'"[30]

Rapier also attended lectures outside the classroom. His favorite of the "distinguished personages" who came to Ann Arbor was Sara Jane Clarke Lippincott, a journalist, poet, and children's story writer, known by her pseudonym, Grace Greenwood. Touring the country to help with the war effort, Greenwood visited hospitals, solicited funds for medical supplies, and worked to assist emanci-

Better known by her pseudonym "Grace Greenwood," Sara Lippincott (1823–1904) was a pioneer female newspaper correspondent who for sixty years sent letters to various newspapers and periodicals recounting her observations of Washington, Europe, and the western United States. (SOURCE: COURTESY OF SPECIAL COLLECTIONS, JACKSON LIBRARY, UNIVERSITY OF NORTH CAROLINA AT GREENSBORO.)

pated slaves. She possessed a sweet, modulated voice as she lectured on "Domestic Life," charming her audiences.[31]

By late winter, however, Rapier had become frustrated by both the unremitting routine and the racial prejudices of those he referred to as "copperhead students." Moreover, he was anxious to practice medicine, and felt that his experiences in Jamaica and his time at the university had sufficiently prepared him. In February 1864, he decided to leave the university a month before completing his first year. He would visit his uncle James in St.

Louis and then enroll in the medical department of Iowa State University, in Keokuk, where he could graduate in June or July rather than the following March.

His plan bore fruit. Within four months of enrolling at Iowa, he graduated with a degree of Doctor of Medicine. The graduation bulletin cited him as being from Jamaica and as planning to become a general practitioner. It noted that most of the other students intended to pursue such specialties as "Inflamation," "Pneumonia," "Tuberculosis," "Hypertrophy of Heart," and "Gangrene."[32]

Before graduating, Rapier wrote to the surgeon general of the United States, expressing his desire to become a medical officer in the army. "I am a native of Alabama," he explained, "and of *African descent*."[33] The response was favorable, for in June 1864, he journeyed to Washington and signed a contract, promising to perform his duties as an officer according to regulations and to keep a complete set of amputating instruments "in good order, and accessible at all times." He would receive one hundred dollars per month and additional pay for service in the field.[34] In short order he became an assistant army surgeon at the Contraband Hospital in Washington, D.C. His job was "to attend such contrabands as require and are not able to procure Medical treatment."[35] Like others who wished to enter government service, Rapier signed a loyalty oath, swearing that he had never voluntarily borne arms against the United States and had never voluntarily given aid, countenance, counsel, or encouragement to persons engaged in armed hostility against the government.[36]

"I never worked so hard, and had so little rest," Rapier confessed in August 1864, "and felt so tired at night as I do now."[37]

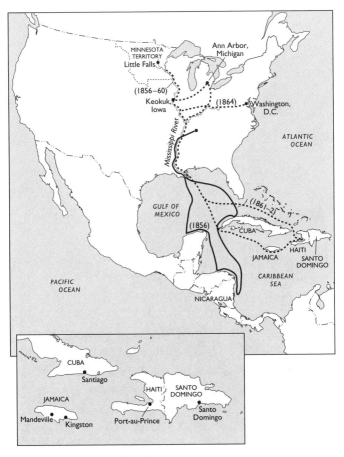

John Rapier Jr.'s Search for Eden

This photograph of John Rapier Jr. was taken during his service as a surgeon and officer in the United States Army. (SOURCE: COURTESY OF THE TALMAN REGIONAL COLLECTION, WELDON LIBRARY, UNIVERSITY OF WESTERN ONTARIO, LONDON, ONTARIO.)

He was speaking of his work at the Freedmen's Hospital, located in a small, one-story frame building in Northwest Washington, D.C. The hospital was founded in 1863 and led for a time by Major Alexander T. Augusta, a black surgeon in the United States Volunteers and one of only eight black army physicians, Rapier included, during the Civil War. It was the only place in the nation's capital where indigent former slaves could receive medical treatment.[38] With so much of the government's effort devoted to treating battlefield casualties, the hospital suffered from a lack of supplies, medicines, beds, even fresh water. Its mortality rate was one out of five patients, which meant that three or four contrabands were dying each day.[39]

Despite such difficulties, Rapier made his daily rounds, in addition to visiting homes in his neighborhood during the evening hours. The population of freedmen and the local residents contracted a wide range of diseases and infections, including smallpox, dysentery, diarrhea, venereal disease, tuberculosis, and fevers. The freedmen entering the city suffered from malnutrition and exposure. Rapier "was ever anxious and ever faithful, as many a poor ex-bondsman can this day testify," one friend asserted. In the stifling heat of summer and bitter cold of winter, Rapier was observed "wending his way amid the homes of the lowly, who needed his professional services."[40]

Rapier was pleasantly surprised that colored men in uniform were "much respected here and in visiting the various departments you receive a military salute from the guard as promptly as if your blood was a [Oliver Otis] Howard"—the Union general and later head of the Freedmen's Bureau.[41] At the same time, Rapier was aware of the prejudices against blacks in the nation's capital. In-

Alexander T. Augusta (1825–1890), surgeon, medical school professor, and practicing physician, received a Bachelor of Medicine degree from the Trinity Medical College of the University of Toronto. He became the surgeon-in-charge of the Freedmen's Hospital in 1863, making him the highest-ranking black officer in the army. After the war, he was offered a faculty position in the medical department of Howard University, the first black offered a faculty position in any American school. (Source: Courtesy of Moorland-Spingarn Research Center, Howard University.)

deed, even in the midst of the Civil War, the city maintained its southern flavor. When a United States senator offered a bill to organize a new city railroad line in 1864, a debate ensued as to whether blacks should be permitted to use the same cars as whites. "As to occupying the same seats with them," one senator said, "all the gentlemanly instincts of the superior race rise up in utter abhorrence of such an idea."[42] On one occasion, Rapier warned his uncle James, who was planning a visit from St. Louis, to give him "due & timely" notice so he might arrange accommodation. In the entire city, he lamented, there was not a single clean and comfortable hotel or public place "for a col^d Gentleman to stop."[43]

Despite a heavy work schedule, Rapier kept in touch with his family. A few days after Christmas 1864, when the Confederacy was clearly dying, Rapier wrote the secretary of the American Missionary Association in New York City on behalf of his nineteen-year-old cousin Sarah Thomas, a teacher in Canada. Although she had spent her life in the North and Canada, she now wished to become an instructor among freedmen in the South. Rapier asked if there were any vacancies for teachers in the association's schools. Sarah "desires to engage in such a mission," he wrote. "Tho' irrelevant," he added, "she is of African extraction."[44]

As an army officer and surgeon, Rapier crossed paths with some of the most prominent blacks in the country. His closest friend was Canadian-born Anderson Ruffin Abbott, whose free black parents migrated in 1835, from Mobile, Alabama, to Toronto. A year younger than Rapier, Abbott had studied at the Oberlin College Preparatory Department and the Toronto School of Medicine before becoming acting assistant surgeon (with the rank of captain) during the war. He helped establish the Freedmen's Hospital. The two men spent a good deal of free time together, and on several occasions may have drunk to excess, though Rapier denied this. "In reference to my indulging in the use of intoxicating drinks in the Matron's room either in company with Dr. Abbott or otherwise," he protested, the assertion was "entirely untrue." Never had he experienced the "peculiar sensation of drunkenness," he told the adjutant general's office when it began an investigation.[45]

Anderson Ruffin Abbott (1837–1913), physician, surgeon, orator, educator, poet, and soldier, was educated at the Elgin settlement in Canada, and in 1861 received a medical degree from the University of Toronto. In 1863, he joined the United States Army, where he reached the rank of lieutenant-colonel. Along with two other Canadians, Alexander T. Augusta and Jerome Riley, he established the Freedmen's (sometimes spelled Freedman's) Hospital. (SOURCE: PHOTOGRAPH COURTESY OF TORONTO PUBLIC LIBRARY.)

In response to another accusation, Rapier defended Abbott when he was accused of taking whiskey to a celebration at the Fifteenth Street Presbyterian Church. Founded in 1841 by John F. Cook, a former slave, the church was a social and cultural center for African Americans. A group gathered there in November 1864 to celebrate "Free Maryland," as Rapier called it, or the implementation of Article XXIV of the new Maryland constitution: "hereafter, in this State, there shall be neither slavery nor involuntary servitude, except in punishment of crime, whereof the party shall have been duly convicted; and all persons held to service or labor as slaves are hereby declared free." Abbott was charged with smuggling hard liquor into the church under the guise of fruit punch. This was a serious offense that constituted conduct unbecoming of an officer. Having accompanied Abbott to the celebration, Rapier wrote that there was no truth to the "malicious and vicious" accusation. Eventually, both charges were dropped.[46]

In addition to being Abbott's close friend, Rapier also socialized with Frederick Douglass, the famous runaway slave who had become a leading abolitionist and women's rights advocate. On August 18, 1864, Rapier heard Douglass speak before "an immense audience" in the district, and the next day was present when Douglass visited the Freedmen's Hospital. With a shock of white hair running back from his forehead, a black mustache, a bushy goatee, penetrating eyes, and an eloquent voice, Douglass was "a fine looking gentleman," Rapier wrote. "He made a fine impression on the public."[47]

That same day, Douglass called on the president at the White House. Lincoln, thinking that he might lose the upcoming elec-

Frederick Douglass (ca. 1817–1895) was born Frederick Bailey, a slave, on the eastern shore of Maryland. He was sent to Baltimore in 1825, and thirteen years later he escaped to freedom and settled in Massachusetts, changing his name to Douglass to avoid detection. There he became an agent for the Massachusetts Anti-Slavery Society and wrote his first au-tobiography, Narrative of the Life of Frederick Douglass, an American Slave. *In 1847, he founded the* North Star, *an antislavery newspaper. Douglass became the most important African American leader during the nineteenth century.* (SOURCE: COURTESY OF LIBRARY OF CONGRESS.)

tion to General George McClellan, the likely candidate of the Democratic Party, fretted that freedom for slaves would remain elusive if a Democrat occupied the White House. He asked Douglass to consult with black leaders and devise a plan to encourage as many slaves as possible in Confederate territories to run away and thus undermine the rebel government.[48] "Did you ever hear such nonsense," Rapier wrote with sarcasm. "The president of the U.S. sending for a 'Nigger' to confer with him on the state of the country." The world had been turned upside down. "I have been invited to take supper with Mr. Douglass to night," he wrote. "I am proud of it."[49] These were heady times for the twenty-nine-year-old Rapier: dining with a man who only hours before had conferred with the president of the United States.

Despite all he had seen and done, Rapier described his first payday in Washington as "the most eventful day of my life." Years of financial strain had finally come to an end. On August 14, 1864, he received a draft for a hundred dollars—minus a $2.50 war tax—for "medical services rendered in the U.S. Government." The check was made out to John H. Rapier, Acting Assistant Surgeon, First Lieutenant, United States Army. Rapier read it several times and confessed that he still could not believe it was true. He planned to mark the occasion by appearing in his full dress blues, complete with gold lace, pointed hat and strap, and sky blue trousers.

He also began to plan his future. As he had during his stay in the Caribbean, Rapier considered where he might further his education and obtain a position. "I have thought of resigning in October for the purpose of attending Lectures in the University of Harvard in Boston," he wrote, "& try for a Surgeons post in the Spring."[50]

He did not resign, however, continuing to make his rounds at the hospital during the final months of the war. In January 1865, Rapier entered the political fray by advocating the commissioning of black soldiers as officers in their own regiments. As one of only eight black surgeons to attain the rank of lieutenant in the army, Rapier realized the difficulties confronting black soldiers who sought to become officers. Although he was highly qualified, it would have been impossible for him to serve as a surgeon in a white unit, or even, for that matter, in a unit of the United States Colored Troops, which were all led by white officers.[51] He also knew that black soldiers prior to June 1864, received less pay than white soldiers; they were, more often than not, assigned to fatigue and labor duty; and they died from disease at a higher rate than did their white counterparts.[52]

If blacks could fight and die for their country, as they had for more than two years, did they not have the right to be led by persons of their own race? Rapier addressed his plea to Tennessee governor Andrew Johnson, who was about to become Lincoln's vice-president. It was a great honor, Rapier wrote, to address his memorial to Johnson requesting that African Americans be commissioned in their own regiments.[53] As a Tennessean, Rapier was familiar with "the liberality that has ever distinguished your political career." Only recently blacks had fought the Confederates at the Battle of Nashville, and even though much of the state was now under Union control, there were bands of Rebels, as one resident complained, "prowling over the country robbing and stealing, murdering good citizens."[54] Black troops, directed by black officers, could track down these guerilla bands and bushwhackers. They could also protect black enlisted men's slave families. Slave owners "turned the women and children out of doors, pulled their cabins down &c, &c—and that there is a great deal of suffering and hardship among the Colored people in consequence."[55] If Johnson ever responded to the letter, there is no record of it.

As the Civil War drew to a close, Rapier remained at his post, ministering to the sick and destitute at the Freedmen's Hospital. He no longer worked for the surgeon general's office but was paid by the Bureau of Refugees, Freedmen, and Abandoned Lands, an agency created by Congress in March 1865 to assist former slaves.[56] He had come a long way from the days of his temporary euphoria in being treated as an equal in Jamaica and professing he would prefer to live in a slave society. He now devoted his energy, indeed nearly every waking hour, to assisting indigent and ill former slaves. As one observer noted, Rapier was "a man whose position, ability and social qualities rendered him a useful and distinguished member of society."[57]

Intelligent, ambitious, and gifted, John Rapier Jr. struggled to reconcile his own contradictory attitudes and feelings. His disparate views might be ascribed to youthful exuberance or intellectual arrogance or could have resulted simply from his writing so frequently and at different times that inconsistences were inevitable. During the war, however, he dedicated himself to the cause of former slaves and devoted his energies to assisting blacks as they made the transition from slavery to freedom.

THE WAR'S END

April 14, 1865 was "the gloomiest day I ever saw," James Thomas recalled. The nation was stunned by the news that Abraham Lincoln had been shot as he watched the play *Our American Cousin* at the Ford's Theatre. Lincoln died the following morning. In St. Louis, the day was cool, overcast, and drizzly. People wandered aimlessly through the muddy streets, unable to believe what they were hearing and reading. The news had a paralyzing effect,

Thomas recalled; people were in shock and kept looking for more information, hoping there had been a mistake.[58] Thomas had come to admire the president greatly, for his determination to preserve the Union, his willingness to free the slaves, and his inspirational words to a war-torn nation. "The people laughed at 'uncle Abes' grammar and the way he said things and used to compare his language with Mr. Jeff Davis, who was a finished scollar," Thomas wrote decades later. "Now we only hear what 'Abe' said, never hear of Jeff."[59]

A few weeks before his assassination, in his Second Inaugural Address, Lincoln had spoken about the meaning of the war. Slavery was a blight on the nation, he said, and God, in his providence, saw fit to remove it forever. Lincoln wished "to bind up the nation's wounds, to care for him who shall have borne the battle and for his widow and his orphan, to do all which may achieve and cherish a just and lasting peace among ourselves and with all nations." "Fondly do we hope, fervently do we pray," he said, "that this mighty scourge of war may speedily pass away."

War had transformed the Tennessee capital. The unhurried town of James Thomas's youth had become a lively, bustling city, with drays and express wagons crowding the streets, peddlers thronging the sidewalks, dock workers scurrying along the wharf, and blue-coated Union soldiers milling about. Unlike many areas of the South, Nashville had experienced a wartime boom. The Confederates evacuated the city in 1862 and never succeeded in recapturing it. The city's prosperity, however, was not shared by black residents. The estimated twelve thousand former slaves who fled to the city during the war suffered from inadequate housing, improper medical care, and malnutrition. "Huddled together, in

This is the last photograph taken of Abraham Lincoln (1809–1865) before his death. He sat before the photographer's lens on April 9, 1865, the day Lee surrendered to Grant, thus ending the Civil War. Despite the slight upturn of his mouth, Lincoln's eyes reveal a deep sadness and weariness. Thomas greatly admired Lincoln and was saddened when he was assassinated by John Wilkes Booth five days after this picture was taken. (SOURCE: PHOTOGRAPH IN FRANCIS TREVELYAN MILLER, ED., *THE PHOTOGRAPHIC HISTORY OF THE CIVIL WAR*, 10 VOLS. [NEW YORK: THE REVIEW OF REVIEWS CO., 1911], 9:257.)

rickety tenements and government houses," one observer noted, "they are deteriorating both physically and morally."[60]

Some residents intended to change the situation for the better. It was only mid-morning and already sultry when nearly one hundred black convention delegates crowded into St. John's Chapel of the African Methodist Church near the Chattanooga Depot on August 7, 1865. Their purpose was to discuss the great changes that had occurred and to write a memorial to the people of Tennessee, encouraging them to give black people the vote. Among those in attendance were several delegates from Nashville: businessman James C. Napier; pastor and former teacher Daniel Wadkins [spelled Watkins in the press]; lawyer Samuel Lowery; James Thomas's old friend, barber Frank Parrish; and James Rapier, who had returned to the South after living so many years in Canada.[61] For Rapier, the year of jubilee was finally at hand, when exiles would be allowed to return home.[62]

Addressing the gathering on the final day, James Rapier made his way confidently among many of his old friends and acquaintances. Blacks had been denied equal rights long enough, he declared; they fully understood the burdens of citizenship and realized, perhaps better than white Americans, that the franchise was both a privilege and a responsibility, without which there would be no true freedom. Nor would granting freedmen the right to vote result in either "social equality" or the Africanization of the state. If ignorance or failure to own property were arguments against granting the right to vote, he said, then many whites should be barred from the polls.[63] Rapier elaborated his ideas in a newspaper column "To the Loyal White Citizens of Tennessee," published a few days later in the Nashville *Daily Press and Times.* "If you urge as a plea for withholding our request, that we were the cause of the late cruel war, which in its march trampled down the civil laws of the land, swept away your cher-

Sally Thomas's grandson James Thomas Rapier emerged as one of the South's most important black leaders during the Reconstruction era. This photograph was taken during his career as an Alabama congressman. (SOURCE: COURTESY OF MOORLAND-SPINGARN RESEARCH CENTER, HOWARD UNIVERSITY.)

ished institutions, devastated your fields, burned your cities and towns, and made a nation of widows and orphans, our answer is, that we are not responsible for these things."[64]

As the delegates left the church, Rapier felt the heavy burden of the past and future upon his shoulders, the memory of his remarkable slave grandmother and the great promise of a new and better life for those freedmen and women who had only recently been considered property. For him and other members of the Thomas-Rapier family, the search for the Promised Land had come full circle. They had struggled to find a new and better life in Canada, Nicaragua, Haiti, Jamaica, the North, and territories in the West, but now they had returned to the South. Twenty-seven-year-old James Rapier, the youngest of the Rapier boys, who had grown up in grandmother Sally Thomas's household, returned to the very city of his youth to assume a position of leadership among his people.

NOTES

1. FTS, 167–68; Francis Trevelyan Miller, ed., *The Photographic History of the Civil War,* 10 vols. (New York: The Review of Reviews Co., 1911), 10:217. Inspired by the British example, the Western Sanitary Commission originated in St. Louis under the direction of James E. Yeatman.

2. Sherman called Arkansas Post "not a Battle but a clean little 'affaire' success perfect." William T. Sherman to Ellen Ewing Sherman, January 12, 1863, in Brooks D. Simpson and Jean V. Berlin, eds., *Sherman's Civil War, Selected Correspondence of William T. Sherman, 1860–1865* (Chapel Hill: University of North Carolina Press, 1999), 353.

3. FTS, 168.

4. Ibid., 85, 86; *Edwards Annual Directory for St. Louis* (St. Louis: Richard Edwards, 1864), 5.

5. FTS, 155.

6. Ibid., 155, 158.

7. Ibid., 160–61.

8. Ibid. Christopher Phillips, *Damned Yankee: The Life of General Nathaniel Lyon* (Columbia: University of Missouri Press, 1990), 187. Thomas estimated the number of troops at nine thousand. Historian Christopher Phillips put the number as indicated in the text.

9. FTS, 161; Phillips, *Damned Yankee,* 191–92.

10. FTS, 156, 165.

11. John Rapier Jr. to James Thomas, October 17, 1861, RTP.

12. FTS, 155.

13. Ibid., 164–65.

14. Ibid., 173.

15. Ibid., 172.

16. John Y. Simon, ed., *The Papers of Ulysses S. Grant, Volume 5: April 1–August 31, 1862* (Carbondale: Southern Illinois University Press, 1973), 5:14.

17. Larry J. Daniel, *Shiloh: The Battle That Changed the Civil War* (New York: Simon & Shuster, 1997), 207–14; James Lee McDonough, *Shiloh—In Hell before Night* (Knoxville: University of Tennessee Press, 1977), 183–89.

18. *Report of General P.G.T. Beauregard,* Confederate States of America, Commanding Army of the Mississippi, April 1862, in Jay Luvaas, Stephen Bowman, Leonard Fullenkamp, *Guide to the Battle of Shiloh* (Lawrence: University Press of Kansas, 1996), 199.

19. Albert Dillahunty, *Shiloh: National Military Park, Tennessee* (Washington, D.C.: National Park Service, 1951), 20.

20. FTS, 167. Grant was in the city on September 25, 1862. John Y. Simon, ed., *The Papers of Ulysses S. Grant, Volume 6: September 1–December 8, 1862* (Carbondale: Southern Illinois University Press, 1973), 6:87–88.

21. FTS, 162.

22. Franklin and Moss Jr., *From Slavery to Freedom,* 686.

23. FTS, 166.

24. John Rapier Jr. to James Thomas, July 8, 1863, RTP. The letter was sent from Fort Wayne, Ind. In March, 1862 he had written from Jamaica that he would leave for America "in July at the latest to continue my medical studies at Toronto." Ibid., March 6, 1862, RTP.

25. John Rapier Jr. to Sarah Thomas, February 7, 1864, RTP.

26. *Catalogue of Officers and Students of the University of Michigan with a Statement of the Course of Instruction in Various Departments for 1864* (Ann Arbor: University of Michigan, 1864), 54–55.

27. John Rapier Jr. to Sarah Thomas, November 12, 1863, RTP.

28. Ibid.

29. John Rapier Jr. to Sarah Thomas, February 7, 1864, RTP; *Catalogue of Officers and Students of the University of Michigan with a Statement of*

the Course of Instruction in Various Departments for 1864 (Ann Arbor: University of Michigan, 1864), 21.

30. John Rapier Jr. to Sarah Thomas, February 7, 1864, RTP; Perry J. Ashley, ed., *Dictionary of Literary Biography, Volume 43: American Newspaper Journalists, 1690–1872* (Detroit, Mich: Gale Research Co., 1985), 303–309.

31. John Rapier Jr. to Sarah Thomas, February 7, 1864, RTP.

32. *Circular and Announcement of the Seventeenth Session of the Medical Department of the Iowa State University Located at the City of Keokuk, Session of 1864–5* (n.p., 1865), 48.

33. John Rapier Jr. to Surgeon General of the United States, April 21, 1864, Records of the Adjutant General's Office, Record Group 94, Medical Officer's File, National Archives.

34. Contract with a Private Physician, Surgeon R. O. Abbot, Medical Director and Dr. John Rapier of St. Louis, Mo., June 29, 1864, Records of the Adjutant General's Office, Record Group 94, Medical Officer's File, National Archives; Ira Berlin, ed., *Freedom: A Documentary History of Emancipation 1861–1867, Series II, The Black Military Experience* (Cambridge: Cambridge University Press, 1982), 311.

35. Appointment, John Rapier Jr., 1864, Records of the Adjutant General's Office, Record Group 94, Medical Officer's File, National Archives.

36. Oath, John Rapier Jr., July 4, 1864, Records of the Adjutant General's Office, Record Group 94, Medical Officer's File, National Archives.

37. John Rapier Jr. to James Thomas, August 19, 1864, RTP.

38. Rayford W. Logan, *Howard University, The First Hundred Years, 1867–1967* (New York: New York University Press, 1969), 40.

39. Thomas Holt, Cassandra Smith-Parker, Rosalyn Terborg-Penn, *A Special Mission: The Story of Freedmen's Hospital, 1862–1962* (Washington, D. C.: Howard University, 1975), 3.

40. The *Christian Recorder,* June 16, 1866.

41. John Rapier Jr. to James Thomas, August 19, 1864, RTP.

42. Evelyn Leasher, ed., *Letter from Washington 1863–1865 by Lois Bryan Adams* (Detroit, Michigan: Wayne State University, 1999), 97.

43. John Rapier Jr. to James Thomas, August 19, 1864, RTP.

44. John Rapier Jr. to George Whipple, December 28, 1864, American Missionary Association Papers, Amistad Research Center, Tulane University, New Orleans.

45. John Rapier Jr. to C. W. Horner, November 28, 1864, Records of the Adjutant General's Office, Record Group 94, Medical Officer's File, National Archives. For Anderson Abbott, see Ripley, et al., *The Black Abolitionist Papers, Volume II*, 2:40.

46. John Rapier Jr. to C. W. Horner, November 28, 1864, Records of the Adjutant General's Office, Record Group 94, Medical Officer's File, National Archives; James McSherry, *History of Maryland* (Baltimore: Baltimore Book Co., 1904), 388–89.

47. John Rapier Jr. to James Thomas, August 19, 1864, RTP.

48. William S. McFeely, *Frederick Douglass* (New York: W.W. Norton, 1991), 231–33; Benjamin Quarles, *The Negro in the Civil War* (Boston: Little, Brown and Company, 1953), 252. "Lincoln treated me as a man," Frederick Douglass proudly proclaimed after the visit.

49. John Rapier Jr. to James Thomas, August 19, 1864, RTP.

50. Ibid.

51. The other seven included Rapier's close friend and confidant Anderson R. Abbott, along with Alexander T. Augusta, John V. DeGrasse, William B. Ellis, William Powell, Charles B. Purvis, and Alpheus Tucker. Joseph T. Glatthaar, *Forged in Battle: The Civil War Alliance of Black Soldiers and White Officers* (New York: Free Press, 1990), 280

52. Ira Berlin, Joseph P. Reidy, Leslie S. Rowland, eds., *Freedom's Soldiers: The Black Military Experience in the Civil War* (Cambridge: Cambridge University Press, 1998), 28–9; Glatthaar, *Forged in Battle*, 174–76.

53. John Rapier Jr. to Andrew Johnson, Governor of Tennessee, January 6, 1865, Andrew Johnson Papers, Library of Congress.

54. John K. Miller to Andrew Johnson, January 30, 1865, in Leroy P. Graf, ed., *The Papers of Andrew Johnson, Volume 7, 1864–1865* (Knoxville: University of Tennessee Press, 1986), 7:446.

55. Reuben D. Mussey to Andrew Johnson, December 29, 1864, in Graf, *The Papers of Andrew Johnson, Volume 7*, 7:367.

56. John Rapier Jr. served as an assistant surgeon in the army from January 29, 1864 until August 21, 1865. Records of the Adjutant General's Office, Record Group 94, Medical Officer's File, National Archives.

57. *The Christian Recorder,* May 17, 1866.

58. FTS, 174.

59. Ibid., 161.

60. Nashville *Dispatch,* July 29, 1865, August 12, 1865, October 12, 1865.

61. The *Colored Tennessean,* August 12, 1865; Nashville *Daily Press and Times,* August 8–14, 1865. Rapier was an active delegate who offered several resolutions and served on the Rules Committee.

62. Rapier made this statement on the passage of the Fifteenth Amendment, in Montgomery, Alabama, on April 26, 1870. The *Alabama State Journal,* April 29, 1870.

63. Nashville *Dispatch,* August 12, 1865; the *Colored Tennessean,* August 17, 1865; Nashville *Daily Press and Times,* August 14, 1865.

64. Nashville *Daily Press and Times,* August 14, 1865; Philip S. Foner and George E. Walker, eds., *Proceedings of the Black National and State Conventions, 1865–1900* (Philadelphia: Temple University Press, 1986), 112–29.

EPILOGUE

JOHN H. RAPIER SR.'S SON **HENRY RAPIER,** WHO LIKE HIS OLDER brother had made the trek to California in the 1850s, proved to be a disappointment to his father. "I See he is a Regular Gamb[l]er," the elder Rapier wrote in September 1856, when he learned that twenty-year-old Henry was going from one camp to another and from town to town in northern California. "I was very Sorry to hear that from his own letter." When a man took up gambling, the father lamented, bad things were bound to follow. Henry's dissolute habits—drinking, fighting, card playing, and taking up with loose women—caught up with him the same month that his father expressed his fears. "An Indictment having been found on the 20th day of September A.D. 1856 in the court of Sessions in the County of Placer [state of California] charging Henry Rapier with the crime of Murder in the 1st degree," the indictment read; the sheriff was ordered to "bring him before the court." Neither the details of the murder nor Henry's fate in court can be found in the sketchy legal records, but two and a half years later, in February 1859, he was arrested and jailed in Marin County, across the bay from San Francisco. The arrest was secured on a warrant for first degree murder.[1] This entry is the last known mention of Henry in the historical record.

One year following the Civil War, while working as a surgeon at the Freedmen's Hospital, **Dr. John H. Rapier Jr.** died suddenly from what was described as a bilious fever. He had not yet reached his thirty-first birthday. *The Christian Recorder,* a Philadelphia newspaper, noted his passing by citing a resolution of the Reunion Literary Club of Washington, D.C., mourning "the loss of one of our most distinguished members, whose gentle, manly deportment, unexceptionable moral character and literary attainments, had secured for himself the esteem and respect of every member of this club, and that his premature death, in the full vigor of faculties, which gave promise of so much usefulness, is the occasion for deep and abiding regret."[2] John Rapier Jr. had packed an immense amount of experience into his thirty-one years. As a youth who had been skeptical of whether blacks could live in conditions other than slavery and dependence, he came to embrace abolitionism and to work to advance both the Union cause and the welfare of former slaves.

Following the war, **John H. Rapier Sr.** continued to live and work in Florence, Alabama, where he had been a barber for nearly forty years. In 1867, when freedmen went to the polls for the first time to elect delegates to a state constitutional convention, the elder Rapier was chosen as a voter registrar for Lauderdale County. "We will endeavor to bring to the consideration of our new duties," the committee that nominated him said, "a solemn sense of the great responsibilities now resting upon us as enfranchised citizens, and entering kindly feelings toward all men, regardless of antecedents, we will enter upon the discharge of our new obligations with a sincere desire to promote peace, harmony, and union."[3]

Two years later, however, illness struck. Rapier's son James wrote: "Father keeps poorly the Dr. had doubts as to his recovery but is more hopeful of him this morning." It was useless, for everything the elder Rapier ate turned into a green liquid and was "ejected by means of vomit." James, who was with his father at the time, told his uncle Henry in Canada that his father "insists on my telling you that he would like to see you very much and how much he would like to be at your house to have Aunt Maria cook him something he can eat." But James could not help thinking that his father would probably never see his brother Henry.[4] His premonition proved correct. Ten days later, at the age of sixty-one, Rapier died of stomach cancer. He bequeathed his real estate and personal property, including cash, to his former slave children, including Susan, Charles, Rebecca, Joseph, and Thomas. As he did not mention his wife, Lucretia, she was probably not still living.[5] An article in his hometown newspaper, the Florence *Journal,* noted that "Uncle John, as he was familiarly known by everyone in Florence, was one of the oldest inhabitants. He was ever respected by the whites as by those of his own color, and it may be truly said that he died respected [by] all classes."[6] Little did the editor or other white townspeople realize that Rapier struggled his entire adult life with the question of whether or not to remain in the South, and he had urged his four free-born sons to emigrate.[7]

~

During the postwar period, Sally's grandson **James Thomas Rapier** continued his efforts in behalf of freedmen and women. Returning to Florence, Alabama, after his eight years in Canada, he presided over the first political gathering of former slaves in northwestern Alabama. Following the passage of the 1867 congressional Reconstruction Acts, he advised blacks to "Proceed with calmness, moderation and intelligence." At the first Republican state convention in Montgomery, he served as chairman of the platform committee and helped draft a plank that called for free speech, free press, free schools, and equal rights for all men without regard to color. His moderate stance during the early period of Reconstruction prompted the conservative press to say "He is, in every particular, except that of race, a superior man."

Shortly after the presidential election of 1868, however, Rapier was driven from politics as well as from his home in Florence by the Ku Klux Klan. Barely escaping with his life, he remained in seclusion for nearly a year. In 1870, he reemerged as the Republican nominee for secretary of state. He lost in the midst of Klan violence, virulent attacks by Democrats, and opposition among white Republicans. As time passed, Rapier grew increasingly radical. He advanced the view that the federal government should help pay for the education of blacks. He called for the formation of a federal bureau to assist black tenant farmers and also organized the Alabama Negro Labor Union. In 1872, he won his party's nomination for Congress from the Second District, which included the capital city of Montgomery. Following a vigorous and violence-free campaign, he won a resounding victory.

Despite this marked success, his personal life remained un-fulfilled. In a letter to his cousin Sarah Thomas, then living in Vicksburg, Mississippi, he lamented that for five years he had been surrounded by people who cared little for him and for whom he cared but little. He was at his office "nearly all the time. Sleep there My associations are wholly of a business character. I have not visited a family since I have been here [in Mont-gomery]." His life appeared to be "innocent of all those social feelings" necessary to make a person happy. "You ask if I intend to marry I reckon I must answer no. I am passed that point of life when men are most anxious to marry The days of poetry are over with me and I am settled down to the stiff prose."[8]

In the Forty-third Congress, James Rapier pushed through a bill to make Montgomery a port of delivery, supported legisla-tion to improve public education in the South, sought to curb violence against freedmen and women, and played an important role in the final passage of the 1875 Civil Rights Act.[9] In a cam-paign marred by violence and retaliation against African Amer-icans, he lost his reelection bids in 1874 and 1876 but continued his struggle for black equality. During the early 1880s, he advo-cated emigration to the West. He even purchased land in Kansas (along the Kansas and Pacific Railroad) to be used for the set-tlement of former slaves. Increasingly, however, his health dete-riorated. Before his dream of emigration could be realized, Rapier died of pulmonary tuberculosis on May 31, 1883, at the age of forty-five. At his bedside was his uncle James Thomas, who took Rapier's body back to St. Louis, where, on June 3, 1883, he was interred in the Thomas family plot at Calvary Cemetery.[10]

During the Civil War, Sally's son **Henry K. Thomas** served in the Buxton militia, and three years after the war he gave up farming and moved to Windsor, Ontario, where he opened a barbershop. His return to barbering was short-lived, however. In 1870, he and his wife, Maria, moved back to the South, to Bovina, Mississippi, a village about ten miles outside of Vicksburg, where they opened a boarding house.[11] In November 1873, he became a justice of the peace and found his way into politics, speaking out and urging former male slaves to go to the polls and vote the Republican ticket.[12] They were citizens of the United States and had a right to vote for any candidate they chose. He declared that the Republican Party was not exclusively black, noting that Ulysses Grant led the party. He told former slaves that they were "to respect the white people and not act against the white people" but that "they have the right to freedom of speech."[13]

It was a turbulent period in Mississippi politics. Determined to wrest the state from so-called "Negro rule," white regulators and militia units attacked blacks throughout the state. In Vicksburg, during a bitterly fought municipal election in August 1874, White Leaguers, as they were called, intimidated and threatened black voters. Two days after the election (won by the white Democrats), Henry Thomas visited Vicksburg to purchase some tobacco, cheese, and other articles. Accosted by a mob of whites, he was held by one of them while several others punched him in the face. In a last desperate effort, Thomas freed himself, ran into a store, and jumped out a back widow, escaping down an alley. He made it to the home of a friend and hid out for the next thirty-six hours before returning stealthily to Bovina. Soon after, Vicksburg White Leaguers shot and killed thirty-five African

Americans in a bloody exchange. Two whites were killed, one possibly by accident.[14]

In the wake of such violence, Congress dispatched an investigating committee to Mississippi. Most blacks were afraid to appear, but Henry Thomas testified that the pretense for the murders was that the colored people were planning to attack whites. His own behavior belied any such notion. Before the killings, he had spoken to an audience of blacks and whites near Bovina, telling them that there was no truth to the rumors. He pointed to the conduct of slaves during the Civil War to illustrate that "colored people had no ill-will, nor any intention to do the white men any harm."

> Q. Since the August election, and about that time, do you know of bands of white men patrolling the country in the day-time and in the night?—
>
> A. I understand from a number of witnesses that they beat and disarmed [freedmen] and threatened them.
>
> Q. And was it at those times that these colored people took to the canes [fields]?—
>
> A. They did leave their houses during that time, a number of them has stated to me.
>
> Q. Since the 7th [of August] has there been a good deal of terror among the colored people in your country?—
>
> A. There has been much. It has pervaded all classes; I believe in my vicinity there are none exempt from it.[15]

Following the reign of terror and the end of Reconstruction, Thomas continued to serve as justice of the peace.[16] In 1880, at age seventy-one, he was listed in the census as a postmaster. For more than thirty-five years he had lived with his wife, who worked as a cook; their twenty-one-year-old son Richard lived with them and taught in the local school.[17] Henry Thomas had journeyed great distances over the years, from Virginia, to Tennessee, to New York, to Ontario, Canada, and back to the South. In 1882, at age seventy-three, he died in Bovina, Mississippi, and was laid to rest there.[18]

Sally Thomas's first grandson, **Richard G. Rapier,** remained in California following the gold rush and continued to farm in Placer County. In 1865, he purchased a small building on East Street in Auburn for three hundred fifty dollars, and, like his father and two uncles before him, opened a barbershop. Three years later, he married Henrietta Stans, and the couple had one son, John, named for his grandfather. As Placer County's population grew, and the economy changed from gold mining to farming, stock raising, fruit growing, lumbering, and tourism at nearby Lake Tahoe, Rapier built up a loyal clientele.[19] While he made an adequate living and expanded his shop to include a bathhouse, he always seemed strapped for cash. "I promise if I ever get hold of money enough I shall certainly come and see you," Dick Rapier wrote his uncle James in St. Louis in 1877, "but to tell you the truth I am poorer to day than I have ever been since I have been in the county." His letters to various members of the Thomas-Rapier family demonstrated a strong interest in the condition of blacks in the South. Even after many years' absence from the region, he still subscribed to the Charleston *News and Courier* and the Montgomery *Advertiser.*

One Saturday in February 1887, while spending the afternoon in the Union Saloon with some friends, Richard Rapier slumped to the floor. He had suffered a cerebral hemorrhage at age fifty-five and never regained consciousness. The "well known Auburn barber," noted the obituary in the *Placer Argus,* died at home a few minutes before eleven Monday night. The funeral was "largely attended, notwithstanding the bad weather," the *Argus* continued, noting that Rapier was of "mixed blood," a "freeman all his days," and lived in Buffalo, New York, during his boyhood. He was "a very intelligent and well informed man" and "well liked by all who knew him."

Before his death, his wife had passed away, and his son, who made no claim against the estate, was living in Portland, Oregon. Richard Rapier possessed a relatively small amount of property. His real estate and personal holdings were auctioned off to cover his debts, and the balance of slightly more than seven hundred dollars, along with "Some family pictures and Certain articles of clothing," were distributed among his five half brothers and half sisters, Lucretia's children, in Florence, Alabama.[20]

A few days before Christmas 1913, a hearse and six horse-drawn carriages moved slowly though the streets of St. Louis to St. Vincent de Paul Catholic Church. A casket was carried up the steps and placed in the vestibule draped with a black pall, and candles were lighted and set on both sides of the bier. "Suscipiat te Christus, qui vocavit te,"* the well-known priest F. J. Moser chanted softly as he sprinkled the coffin with holy water. Then, followed

---

*May Christ who called thee, receive thee.

by six pallbearers and several hundred mourners, Father Moser walked slowly behind a cross-bearer to the altar, where he offered a homily for the deceased. **James P. Thomas,** Sally's youngest son, was a man of wealth, a devout Catholic, and a member of St. Vincent de Paul Church for fifty years. During that time, he and his wife, Antoinette, had contributed to the church in a number of ways. At the conclusion of the two-hour funeral mass, the remains of the deceased were taken to Calvary Cemetery; the priest solemnized the final rites in prayer; and the pallbearers lowered the casket into a grave in the Thomas family plot.[21]

"JAMES P. THOMAS, 87, DIES," read the caption of a front-page article in the conservative St. Louis *Globe-Democrat.* "ST. LOUIS RESIDENT SIXTY-SIX YEARS." The *Globe-Democrat* recounted Thomas's filibustering expedition to Nicaragua, his marriage to Antoinette Rutgers in 1868, following Pelagie Rutgers's death, and the grand opening of his barbershop in the basement of the New Lindell Hotel. Thomas had retired in 1890, moved across the river to Alton, Illinois, and spent his later years writing his memoirs.[22]

Except for misstating his age and the length of time he had lived in St. Louis—he died at eighty-six and had lived in the city fifty-six years—the *Globe-Democrat,* a paper that typically ran derogatory articles about blacks, was accurate in its description of Thomas's life. He had married Antoinette Rutgers at St. Vincent de Paul Catholic Church in a ceremony, one observer wrote, "that has never been surpassed in the city and which those who witnessed it will never forget."[23] The Montgomery [Alabama] *Weekly Advertiser,* under the title "Rich Nigs," added that "Many of the elite of the city were present" and that "The bride has property and money to the value of $400,000."[24]

The estimate was excessive, but in 1870, according to the census, the Thomases were worth an estimated $165,000, the third largest estate held by an African American family in the South.[25] Most of their wealth was in the form of real estate once owned by Pelagie Rutgers, bequeathed to her by her second husband Louis Rutgers, a free man of color who inherited the property from his white father. Although Pelagie stipulated in her will that the real estate would be held in a trust estate for the benefit of her daughter, Thomas took over the management of the real estate, buying, selling, leasing, renting, and renovating apartments and other properties. He also leased a luxury barbershop in downtown St. Louis in 1874, complete with a steam-heating "pipe apparatus," an electric massage bath, a row of leather-upholstered barber's chairs, a wall-length marble-faced mirror, lace curtains, glass chandeliers, and a "German-silver" showcase. He installed three walnut showcases with room for four hundred fifty shaving mugs, and advertised that customers would be treated to "Russian, Turkish, and Cold Water Baths" as well as twelve of the city's finest barbers.[26]

During the 1870s, James Thomas and Antoinette and their growing family—including James, Sarah, Pelagie, Arend John, Joseph, and Anthony—lived in a large and comfortable house on Seventh Street. They decorated it with lace curtains, imported Persian carpets, mahogany furniture, and a rosewood piano. They employed a full-time gardener and a full-time domestic servant, Prussian-born Clara Schoener. Their household in 1870 also included a schoolteacher, a French-born physician, and sev-

This bust of James Thomas was created by the well-known African American sculptor Edmonia Lewis, in Rome in 1874, a few months after Thomas visited the city during his grand tour of Europe. The bust was in private hands for many years, until it was purchased in 2002 by Oberlin College. (SOURCE: PHOTOGRAPH OF BUST COURTESY OF POST ROAD GALLERY, LARCHMONT, NEW YORK.)

The resemblance between James Thomas and United States Supreme Court Justice John Catron can be seen in these two profile pictures. (SOURCE: PHOTOGRAPH OF BUST COURTESY OF POST ROAD GALLERY, LARCHMONT, NEW YORK; PICTURE OF CATRON IN KERMIT L. HALL, ET AL., EDS., *THE OXFORD COMPANION TO THE SUPREME COURT OF THE UNITED STATES* [NEW YORK: OXFORD UNIVERSITY PRESS, 1992], 129–30.)

eral adopted children.[27] In 1873, Thomas made a grand tour in Europe, visiting thirty-two cities in six countries in three months. More than thirty years later, he recalled how he sat up nearly half the night staring at his passport, embossed with "the great American Eagle" and signed by Secretary of State Hamilton Fish. Fifteen years earlier, he could not have crossed the Mississippi River without a voucher from a respectable white person.[28] During his tour of Europe, he stopped in Rome and posed for Edmonia Lewis, the well-known African American sculptress, who sculpted Thomas's bust.

A few years after his retirement, while living in Alton, the depression of 1893 forced Thomas to mortgage much of his and

Born about 1845, near Albany, New York, the daughter of a part African American, part Chippewa woman and a black man from the West Indies, Edmonia Lewis was cared for by her older stepbrother following the death of her parents before she was seven. The stepbrother struck it rich during the California gold rush and sent Lewis to Oberlin College, where she studied painting and drawing. In 1862, she was accused of attempting to poison two white classmates and was forced to leave Oberlin. In 1863, Lewis moved to Boston, where she gained a reputation as a sculptor of busts of prominent abolitionists. In 1865, she emigrated to Rome, Italy, where she set up a studio. It was fashionable for Americans on the Grand Tour to order busts, either of themselves or famous literary and historical figures. With a few interruptions, Lewis remained in Rome until 1909. It is not known when or where she died. (SOURCE: PHOTOGRAPH COURTESY OF THE BOSTON ATHENEUM.)

his wife's property. They were on the road to recovery, however, when a second disaster struck. In 1896, a tornado ripped through St. Louis, killing more than three hundred. One of the worst disasters in the city's history, the twister set down on Rutger Street and razed the block between Seventh and Eighth Streets where Thomas's rental property was located. The "hurricane," as it was called in the press, killed twenty-seven people who lived in Thomas-owned apartments.[29] Inadequately insured, the Thomases never recovered from this second catastrophe.[30]

To make matters worse, after city dwellers cleared away the debris, Antoinette became seriously ill with Bright's disease, an inflamation of the kidneys. "Several times she seemed in imminent danger of passing away," the Alton *Telegraph* noted, but "rallied each time."[31] Continuing to grow weak, she finally suffered a paralytic stroke and died on November 23, 1897, at the age of fifty-nine. "Mrs. Anto[i]nette Thomas Dead," the St. Louis *Post-Dispatch* announced, "the Wealthiest Colored Woman in St. Louis."[32]

Following the funeral, James Thomas moved to Chicago for a time, living with his daughter and son-in-law, but later returned to St. Louis. In later years, prompted by his children, he spent a good deal of time writing his autobiography, his impressions of planters and poor whites, free blacks and slaves, and the tumultuous events leading up to the Civil War. Lacking experience in writing, his style was awkward, even cumbersome, but his memory was sharp and he accurately recalled names, dates, places, and events. Although Thomas extolled black ingenuity, vitality, and industriousness, he also pointed to slaves who trudged sullenly through the streets in chains or who squatted dull-eyed in slave pens. He expressed a genuine admiration for some slaveholders, an incongruity explained less by their ownership of slaves than by their ability to mold their own destiny, exert economic and political power, and offer protection to a few privileged blacks.

Toward the end of his life, Thomas suffered from arthritis and frequent pulmonary infections, illnesses aggravated no doubt by his living conditions. With the comforts of the past only a dim memory, he endured his final years in a dingy, two-room apartment, surrounded by a few scattered pieces of broken furniture, warming himself in the winter next to a small, leaky coal stove. It was a tragic time also because he witnessed the premature death of two of his sons. In the fall of 1913, he contracted influenza, which quickly developed into pneumonia. With Clara Schoener, the domestic servant who been with the family for decades, constantly by his bedside, he grew progressively worse. On December 16, 1913, with virtually nothing left of his once-great estate, James Thomas died.[33] "Chorus Angelorum te suscipiat et cum Lazaro quondam paupero aeternam habeas reqiem," chanted Father Moser as he concluded the funeral mass at St. Vincent de Paul on that December morning. As applied to a former slave, the priest's words had poignant meaning: "May the choir of angels receive them, and with Lazarus, once a beggar, mayest thou have eternal rest."[34]

$\sim$

Sixty-three years after her death during the cholera epidemic of 1850, the legacy of **Sally Thomas** could still be seen in the remarkable career of her youngest son. It could also be seen in the lives of other members of her family. Among her progeny were adventurers, explorers, and men of fortune. There were also professional men: a physician, several entrepreneurs, and a member of Congress. As a slave, Sally devoted her energy and intelligence to protecting and freeing her three sons and to nurturing and guiding her grandchildren. To be sure, she possessed more opportunities than most of her fellow slaves. That is what made her, despite her color and status, an extraordinary figure. The legacy she left for her children and grandchildren was an unremitting determination to become free but in any case to remain independent, fully aware of the importance of that quality in all relations with one's fellow man.

Notes

1. John Rapier Sr. to John Rapier Jr., September 15, 1856, RTP; Records of the Placer County Court, Warrant for Henry Rapier for Murder, September 22, 1856, Placer County Archives, Auburn, California; Arrest of Henry Rapier, February 13, 1859, with ibid.

2. *The Christian Recorder,* June 16, 1866. Rapier died May 17, 1866, in Washington, D.C. Washington *Evening Star,* May 19, 1866. Shortly before his death, he opened an account in the Freedman's Savings and Trust Company Bank in the city, depositing fifty dollars. Records of the Freedman's Savings and Trust Company, Signature Register, January 30, 1866, no. M816, Roll 4, National Archives.

3. "Proceedings of the Meeting of Colored People at Florence, Alabama," April 24, 1867, Wager Swayne Papers, Alabama Department of Archives and History, Montgomery, Alabama.

4. James Rapier to Henry Thomas, September 8, 1869, RTP.

5. Records of the Probate Court, Lauderdale County, Ala., Wills B (September 13, 1869), 78–80.

6. Florence *Journal,* September 23, 1869. He died on Saturday evening, September 18, 1869, with his son James at his side.

7. Florence *Gazette,* March 6, 1862.

8. James Rapier to Sarah Thomas, January 10, 1872, RTP.

9. The port of delivery bill made Montgomery, located on the Alabama River, a federal government port of delivery within the collection district of Mobile. Signed into law in 1874, it authorized the hiring of a deputy collector of customs. Loren Schweninger, *James T. Rapier and Reconstruction* (Chicago: University of Chicago Press, 1978), 124.

10. Records of the Calvary Cemetery, St. Louis, Mo., Lot no. 3, June 3, 1883, St. Louis, Mo. The authors thank Bryan Prince of North Buxton, Canada, for providing us with these records.

11. USMSPC, Warren County, Miss., Vicksburg, Fourth Ward, 1870, 247 [printed page number].

12. Register of Commissions, Secretary of State, Mississippi, 1871–1874, Mississippi Department of Archives and History, Jackson, Miss.

13. United States, Congress, *House Reports,* Forty-third Congress, Second session, no. 265, "Vicksburgh Troubles" (1875), 482–85.

14. Vernon Lane Wharton, *The Negro in Mississippi, 1865–1890* (Chapel Hill: University of North Carolina Press, 1947), 190.

15. United States, Congress, *House Reports,* Forty-third Congress, Second session, no. 265, "Vicksburgh Troubles" (1875), 482–85.

16. Register of Commissions, Secretary of State, Mississippi, 1878–1881, Mississippi Department of Archives and History, Jackson, Miss.

17. USMSPC, Warren County, Miss., Bovina Precinct, Beat no. 4, 1880, 561 [printed page number]. The ages listed in the census are not correct.

18. Fisher Funeral Home Records, Vicksburg, Miss., September 9, 1878–April 1, 1883, typescript prepared by Mary Ragland, 1987, Mississippi Department of Archives and History, Jackson, Miss.

19. Records of the Placer County Court, Indenture, Theresa Bradford and Eliza M. Bradford to Richard Rapier, September 14, 1865, Placer County Archives, Auburn, California; Marriage License, Richard G. Rapier and Henrietta Stans, August 8, 1868, in ibid.; *McKenney's District Directory, for 1879–80, Sacramento, City and County, Amador, Eldorado, Placer*

and Yolo Counties (Sacramento and San Francisco: L. M. McKenney, Publisher, 1879), 436; *City and County Directory Including Sacramento City and County, and Amador, El Dorado, and Placer Counties* (San Francisco: L. M. McKenney & Co., 1884), 498.

20. *Placer Argus,* February 10, 1887; Records of the Probate Court, Placer County, Calif., Probate File, no. 313 (1887), Richard G. Rapier, Placer County Archives, Auburn, Calif. The following documents have been used to reconstruct Richard Rapier's life and death: Proof of Heirship, November 29, 1887; Power of Attorney from Heirs to Thomas Rapier, May 9, 1887; Creditor's Claim, Wills & Huntley News Agents and Variety Store, April 1, 1887, for newspaper subscriptions; Petition for Sale of Personal Property, September 16, 1887; Return and Account of Sale of Real Estate and Petition for Order Confirming Sale, October 11, 1887; Return and Account of Sale of Personal Property and Petition for Confirmation and Approval, October 11, 1887; Final Account of Administrator of the Estate of Richard G. Rapier, November 29, 1887; Petition for Distribution of Estate, November 29, 1887 (at the time of this distribution, all of Richard Rapier's former slave half brothers and sisters were alive and living in Florence, Alabama; they included Rebecca Murdock, wife of Lawson Murdock, and Joseph, Thomas, Charles, and Susan Rapier); Decree for Settling Final Account and Distributing Estate, December 6, 1887, with ibid. The final distribution of Rapier's estate made no mention of his wife but noted that his son, John Rapier, age about twenty, lived in Portland, Oregon. See Petition of Letters of Administration, February 14, 1887, with ibid. In the "Proof of Heirship" presented to the Placer County Court, two long-time residents of Florence testified that they had known Richard's father, John Rapier Sr., well and that none of his three other sons—James, Henry, or John Jr.—was alive. Moreover, they had all died "intestate, and unmarried— and were never married at any time during their lives so that the only heirs at law of Richard G. Rapier" were Lucretia's children.

21. St. Louis *Post Dispatch,* December 17, 1913, 18; St. Louis *Globe-Democrat,* December 17, 1913; Records of the Calvary Cemetery, St. Louis, Missouri, Lot no. 10, December 18, 1913; Sacristy Mortuary Record, St. Vincent de Paul Catholic Church, Funeral Services for James P. Thomas, December 18, 1913; Records of the Probate Court, St. Louis, Mo., Book 68 (January 30, 1914), 682. Thomas died on December 16, 1913, and was

buried two days later. Information about the hearse, carriages, and type of casket was found in the probate record.

22. St. Louis *Globe-Democrat,* December 17, 1913.

23. St. Louis *Times,* February 13, 1868, transcribed copy of article in Miscellaneous Notes, RTP.

24. Montgomery [Alabama] *Weekly Advertiser,* February 25, 1868.

25. USMSPC, St. Louis, Mo., Third Ward, 1870, 196.

26. Records of the County Court, St. Louis, Mo., Deeds, Book 594 (July 11, 1878), 431. This includes the copy of the lease for the barbershop signed June 4, 1874.

27. *Edwards Annual Directory of St. Louis* (St. Louis: Edwards Publishing Company, 1871), 647; USMSPC, St. Louis, Missouri, Third Ward, 1870, 196.

28. FTS, 12–13.

29. St. Louis *Globe,* May 28, 1896; the number who died in the Thomas-owned apartments is found in the St. Louis *Star,* November 29, 1897.

30. FTS, 15.

31. Alton *Telegraph,* November 29, 1897.

32. St. Louis *Post-Dispatch,* November 29, 1897.

33. Records of the County Probate Court, St. Louis, Mo., Wills, Book 68 (January 30, 1914), 682. His personal effects were valued at $1.45, although he did have real estate that provided him with a small income.

34. Records of the Calvary Cemetery, St. Louis, Mo., Lot no. 8, Anthony Thomas, January 24, 1912, and Lot no. 9, Arend J. Thomas, May 27, 1913. Within three weeks after Thomas's death a third son, Joseph F. Thomas, died. Records of the Calvary Cemetery, St. Louis, Mo., Lot no. 9, January 5, 1914; see also, Records of the Probate Court, Madison County, Ill., *Ulysses J. Blair vs. James P. Thomas, James L. R. Thomas, Pelagie S. Blair, Anthony Thomas, et al.,* August 1898, Box 232, County Courthouse, Edwardsville, Ill.; Records of the Probate Court, St. Louis, Mo., Last Will and Testament of James P. Thomas, Book 68 (January 30, 1914), Will no. 42967, City Hall, St. Louis, Mo.

AFTERWORD

Through the Prism of a Black Family

T HE MEMBERS OF THE THOMAS-RAPIER FAMILY WERE EXCEP-
tional individuals. Seeking to examine the complex and complicated nature of race relations and slavery through the lens of literate, industrious, and ambitious slaves and free people of color
offers a number of challenges, not the least of which is to resolve
how much historical significance should be given to a single,
highly unusual family. Since most slaves and free blacks did not
live in towns and cities, hire themselves out, travel to various locations, communicate with one another by letter, or have the
same opportunities as they, it is important to keep their unique
status in mind when discussing the condition of the great majority of their brethren.

In fact it is *because* the Thomas-Rapier family members were in
so many ways unusual that the narrative provides an opportunity
to observe many facets of southern society during the era of slavery. Family members were perceptive observers of the human condition, traveled extensively, and felt a keen sense of kinship (except

for John Rapier Jr. during his stay in the Caribbean) with less fortunate blacks. The narrative thus offers an opportunity to compare and contrast race relations in the southern states with conditions in the North, Canada, the Caribbean, and Central America; and to look at changes over time in various parts of the Americas.

Like most blacks, Sally and members of her family lived with the constant fear that some chance encounter—some untoward incident—might lead to a violent confrontation. She witnessed the harsh treatment of slaves brought into Nashville, either to be sold or already on their way to the burgeoning cotton fields of the Deep South. She knew about the hanging of the slave Jake, who had assaulted and killed his owner, and her son James witnessed the hanging. Owners encouraged such public spectacles, James Thomas recalled, so that their slaves would learn what their fate would be if they assaulted a white man. Even a privileged slave such as Sally knew that racial violence was always lurking near the surface. When she advised her son Henry to run away, she realized the risk both of them would be taking. If he were captured and brought back, the punishment would be severe. If she were deemed a co-conspirator her sentence might be worse. Sally's anxieties were shared by many other slaves who witnessed the brutal treatment of blacks who defied the system.

Family members kept an especially vigilant eye on slave traders. The family knew of slaves and free blacks who had been kidnapped and sold to the Lower South. They had seen slave children sold away from their mothers, mothers sold away from their children, and dispirited blacks crowded together in private jails, auction houses, and slave pens awaiting sale. James Thomas saw slaves on the auction block in Nashville, Richmond, St. Louis, and New Orleans. Passing through Richmond, Virginia, in 1851, he was asked on numerous occasions, "Who do you belong to, boy?" Neither Sally nor James could recite the statistical evidence collected by latter-day historians—that one in three slaves in the Upper South after 1815 was traded out of state, and one in two who fell into the hands of slave traders was separated from a spouse or children—but they witnessed the magnitude firsthand. They also knew about slave owners who had few qualms about turning human property into cash when it suited their purposes. Indeed, the story of the Thomas-Rapier family reveals how important family ties were among blacks, the great lengths to which slaves and free blacks would go to protect loved ones, and the fact that separation, not family stability, was the norm.[1]

The history of the Thomas-Rapier family also demonstrates the great variety of settings and locations in which African Americans lived. Family members traveled to the North, Canada, the West, Central America, and the Caribbean. In various towns and cities in the United States, and in Havana, Port-au-Prince, and Kingston, family members described black and mulatto men and women living and working as slaves and as free people of color. Indeed, as their journeys reveal, there were few locations in the Americas where travelers did not encounter black people. Family members also noted how customs of color, caste, and class differed in the Caribbean, how freedom brought few economic benefits to blacks in the North—where racial prejudice seemed, if anything, more virulent than in the South—and how racial attitudes in Canada and the West appeared to be more tolerant.

Perhaps historians will never know about the true nature of Sally Thomas's sexual relationships with the two different white men who fathered her three sons. Clearly she was an extremely attractive and intelligent woman who used those relationships, as well as her associations with other prominent whites, to protect herself and her family. Whether she accepted or merely endured the advances of a white member of the Thomas family in Virginia, or Judge John Catron, in Tennessee, remains a matter of speculation. The family's mixed racial heritage, however, provides a window into the attitudes and values of persons of mixed racial origin in the antebellum South. What is perhaps most striking is the degree to which members of this family remained sympathetic and loyal to blacks less privileged than they. Sally and James Thomas had slave friends, as did other members of the family. John Rapier Sr., while known and respected as "Uncle John" among whites in Florence, was admired by slaves and former slaves alike, as witnessed by his being chosen to represent freedmen as a voter registrar after the Civil War. Indeed, except for John Rapier Jr. during his stay in the Caribbean, the family exhibited very little color consciousness. Even James Thomas, who mingled with the light-skinned elite in St. Louis, never disparaged or denigrated black people. Indeed, he was more concerned about the reverse; how blacks mocked and made fun of persons of mixed racial heritage.

The ambiguous nature of race relations is another theme illuminated by the activities of the Thomas-Rapier family. Each family member sustained relationships with whites. John Rapier Sr. remained close to white bargeman Richard Rapier, so much so that he took Rapier's surname. As a youngster, John Rapier Jr. became a protégé of a prominent Nashville lawyer, while James Thomas and Henry Thomas served white customers in their barbershops. Yet it is clear that family members viewed whites, even their most loyal customers and "friends," with skepticism and caution. In his personal correspondence (as opposed to his more public autobiography), James Thomas spoke of his customers and traveling companions with a marked indifference or sardonic humor: the son of a rich Davidson County slave owner who had more money than he knew what to do with, or a middle-aged white man, identified only as "the Colonel," who went "on a 'tear' last August," then fell hopelessly "in love with a girl 14 yrs of age." "Why sir," he wrote his nephew John, "it took your Father and Cox both to hold him down."[2]

At the same time it was necessary to rely on whites for protection. When her children were put in jeopardy of being sold, Sally Thomas knew she could count on Ephraim Foster and G. M. Fogg to help her in a time of crisis. James Thomas depended on the elder Foster and on his son Robert, a lawyer; both white men vouched for Thomas's industry, integrity, and good standing in the community. Richard Rapier felt so confident about the integrity of Nashville businessman Madison Barryman Moorman that he entrusted him with his future as they set out for California. Many other skilled slaves and industrious free blacks relied on whites in their communities to testify as to their loyalty, peaceful disposition, and work ethic. Indeed, most free people of color counted on certain whites to stand up for them in case of an emergency. "John you have friends that would go down to the grave with Sorrow to here [hear] that you had come to a disgraceful end," John Rapier Sr. wrote his son in his typical fatherly fashion; "you have Some white friends who ask very often after you."[3] Most free blacks cultivated similar relationships with whites.

And the family's history is shot through with ambiguities in terms of the relationships between whites, blacks, and persons of mixed racial origin. Virtually any generalization about how whites, blacks, and those described as mulattoes interacted seems to miss the mark. Certainly many persons of mixed origin were better off than most of their black brethren, and whites accepted them in certain occupations (such as barbering) more readily than they accepted those of a darker hue. And undoubtedly mulattoes gained their freedom in disproportionate numbers. About two out of five free blacks in the South were listed as "mulattoes" by census takers in 1860, with one out of three in the Upper South and three out of four in the Lower South, compared with 10 percent of the slave population. Projecting this backward in time would reveal a similar disparity. Yet the advantaged status of mulattoes did not protect them from abuse and exploitation. Women of fair complexion from Virginia, Kentucky, Missouri, and Tennessee, James Thomas noted, were in great demand as prostitutes and concubines in Louisiana.

Sally Thomas's children and grandchildren were fortunate to acquire a rudimentary education. "It was surprising to a great many whites to see a colored boy or man with a newspaper," James Thomas recalled. "Often they would ask, 'Can you read?' "[4] It was, as Thomas suggested, unusual for slaves and free blacks (as well as many whites) to be able to read and write. Yet, there was a surprising number of literate slaves and free blacks in the southern states, despite laws and regulations that prohibited teaching of African Americans. In South Carolina, where teaching of slaves was outlawed, a group of slave owners observed that there were literate blacks on virtually every plantation in the state.[5] Although illiterate herself, Sally Thomas recognized the importance of acquiring an education. She made substantial sacrifices to insure that her children and grandchildren became literate, enrolling her youngest son in the Nashville school for blacks and, along with her eldest son, providing room, board, and tuition for two of her grandchildren as they attended the same school. John Rapier Jr. and James Rapier not only learned to read and write there, but also admired their black teacher, Daniel Wadkins, as a role model and mentor.

Family members realized that their values and attitudes were different from those of the great majority of their brethren. Slaves had little incentive to work hard, knowing, as they did, that their labor went into the pockets of their owners. While most slaves did not share the Thomas-Rapier family's remarkable work ethic, it is worth noting that Sally and her children's industry evolved from opportunity. If similar opportunities (quasi-freedom and legal freedom) had been offered to most slaves, they would have responded in much the same manner. Indeed, in the much-studied low country and sea islands of South Carolina and Georgia, slaves responded enthusiastically to the modest incentives of the task system. When their assigned tasks were completed—i.e., hoeing so many rows, planting so much rice, cultivating and harvesting so many bales of cotton—they were permitted to cultivate their own gardens, raise their own livestock, hunt, fish, and sell their own produce. They were seeking a measure of autonomy and independence in much the same way that members of the Thomas-Rapier family struggled to remain self-sufficient.

The pursuit of opportunities by the Thomases and Rapiers illuminates the hidden lives of what contemporaries called "virtually free," "quasi-free," or "nearly free" slaves. That Sally Thomas could remain legally enslaved while renting a house, establishing a business, raising three boys, providing for her grandchildren, and maintaining amicable relations with whites bears testimony to what could be accomplished within the boundaries of slavery. Her youngest son was equally successful as a slave, traveling extensively and managing a profitable business.

Such quasi-freedom was by no means confined to Nashville. Slaves were hired out, hired themselves out, or were permitted to manage businesses in most towns and cities in the southern states. Hiring out was not uncommon in many rural areas. While self-hire was illegal in parts of the South, slave owners ignored or circumvented these prohibitions, especially when they profited from the practice. Slaves were anxious to negotiate their own contracts, live independently of their legal owners, and earn their own livelihoods. They were also ever mindful that being "virtually free" could lead to being actually free.

The vast majority of slave women, of course, could not claim the status of quasi-freedom. Despite Sally Thomas's unique history, however, her life reflects on the situation of other black women who struggled in bondage. Little is known about the first nearly half of her life in Albemarle County, Virginia, but she, like the great majority of slave women, lived on a plantation with a sizable slave labor force. Like many others, she struggled with the advances of a white man, or men, the difficulties of bearing and raising children, and the fears and anxieties of being separated from loved ones. In fact, a constant theme during her first thirty years, and especially after she settled in Nashville, was the reminder that at any moment her children could be taken away from her. She also shared with other slave women the awkward and uncomfortable circumstance of constantly seeing the white father of her children without being able to acknowledge or reveal the children's paternity.

With the exception of James Rapier's conversion to Methodism while in Canada, family members rarely mentioned religion. The closest John Rapier Jr. came to expressing a matter of faith was when he wrote his uncle about his belief that God had ordained the Civil War and that those who supported the North would be vindicated when the liberation of slaves became a reality. John Rapier Sr. invoked God when writing his children—"I pray god," he told his son, "to direct you in all things that are right"—but his faith seemed pragmatic and family oriented.[6] James Thomas joined St. Vincent de Paul Catholic Church in St. Louis (where he later married), but this appeared, at least at the outset, to be a practical decision to gain the hand of Antoinette Rutgers rather than an authentic commitment to Catholicism. And James Rapier's youthful profession of faith dissipated as he matured. Family members did offer observations about the religious activities of slaves and commented about the churches that slaves and free blacks attended. Thomas mentioned how slaves were overcome with joy at various church services and how blacks and whites in one Campbellite church took communion together. But, unlike the great majority of African Americans, who possessed authentic Christian spirituality, most of the members of the Thomas-Rapier family, although at times pious and self-righteous, remained skeptical about religion.

Until recently, scholars paid little attention to the extent to which slaves and free blacks followed political events and campaigns.[7] Indeed, historians of slavery have long assumed that blacks knew or cared little about major political issues. But as the comments of the Thomases and the Rapiers reveal, many black people attended political rallies, listened to speeches, learned about the issues, even supported various candidates. Slaves criticized Andrew Jackson because he did not emancipate slaves following the Battle of New Orleans, as he had promised, while praising him for his opposition to rechartering the bank of the United States. Understanding that the bank provided credit to slave traders reveals a high level of political sophistication.

James Thomas recalled slaves showing up at political meetings, listening to the oratory, and later debating the issues with fellow slaves. He remembered vividly how maids, cooks, waiters, and house servants eavesdropped on political discussions among members of the slaveholding gentry, passing the arguments along to others on the plantation. When the slave Jake was denied the opportunity to attend the great Whig Convention in Nashville, he became unruly, even violent. In short, slaves were far more knowledgeable about political matters, especially issues involving African Americans, than historians have recognized.

The Thomas-Rapier narratives also shed light on the transformation of African American social and cultural values. By the 1830s and 1840s, members of this family looked upon themselves as being quite different from their West African ancestors. As a youngster, James Thomas was struck by this when he came upon African-born slaves dancing in Congo Green, in New Orleans: "thumping on the head of a barrel with a skin stretched over it," chanting, beating sticks together, and making "pieces of tin or some substitute on their legs" jingle. Thomas's sense of being different from the dancers in Congo Green was not unlike the attitudes of the vast majority of blacks who had lived and worked in the South for generations. They differed from West African blacks in speech, dress, manners, mores, religious beliefs, values, and attitudes. John Rapier Sr. and John Rapier Jr. realized as much when they considered resettling in Liberia. Although questioning the motives of the leaders of the American Colonization Society, they felt equally concerned about the conflicts and violence erupting between free blacks from the United States and the native inhabitants of Liberia.

The quest of free blacks for self-sufficiency runs clearly through these narratives. Sally taught her children and grandchildren to work hard and save their money. Her sons did just that, running businesses, saving their extra earnings, and investing in real estate. At times they discussed little else in their correspondence. These values were necessary for survival, especially for John Rapier Sr., who started a second family during the late 1840s and 1850s, and for Henry Thomas, who headed up a large family. In the spring of 1857, James Thomas became caught up in the speculative land frenzy in the West, shortly before the bubble burst and land prices plummeted. His failure to double his money in a short period taught him a lesson he would never forget. Yet the family was in this respect like other free blacks, who devoted most of their time to earning a living. It was a matter of survival and independence.

Last, despite the extraordinary journeys of various members of the Thomas-Rapier family to the North, Canada, the West, Central America, and the Caribbean, they all felt a deep kinship with the South. John Rapier Sr. considered leaving Alabama for many years. He subscribed to the *African Repository* and read about Liberia. He even journeyed to the North and West to investigate possible locations to settle, and purchased fifty acres of land in Canada. In the end, however, he remained in the region of his birth.

It was the insurrection panic of 1856 and the retribution against innocent slaves and free blacks that forced James Thomas out of Tennessee. Only five years before, he had told nine judges in a Davidson County courtroom that if he were compelled, under the existing laws, to leave, he would be "greatly damaged by having to Start anew in some Strange Country & rebuild a character he trusts he has already established in Tennessee." During his years of residency in Canada, Sally's grandson James Rapier felt himself an exile. He prayed that one day he would be able to return to the land of his birth. Having lived in Buffalo, New York, and Buxton, Canada, for more than thirty years, sixty-one-year-old Henry Thomas moved with his family back to the South, settling in Bovina, Mississippi, a black settlement near Vicksburg. However much they wished to extricate themselves from tragic legacies of the past, their roots and traditions were southern, and they probably felt most at home in the South, despite the brutality, violence, oppression, and degradation there. Such tension between flight and southern roots was felt by many other African Americans.

Notes

1. Wright, *African Americans in the Early Republic*, 28, 38.

2. James Thomas to John Rapier Jr., December 18, 1858, RTP. Lawyer Herman Cox (c. 1816–c. 1866) served as a representative of Davidson

County in the Tennessee General Assembly and on the Nashville Board of Aldermen. Robert McBride and Dan Robison, *Biographical Directory of the Tennessee General Assembly* (Nashville: Tennessee State Library and Archives and the Tennessee Historical Commission, 1975).

3. John Rapier Sr. to John Rapier Jr., December 28, 1858, RTP.

4. FTS, 32.

5. Petition of David Hemphill, James Lowry, John McKnight, et al. to the South Carolina Legislature, 1835, in Loren Schweninger, ed., *The Southern Debate Over Slavery: Petitions to Southern Legislatures, 1778–1864* (Urbana: University of Illinois Press, 2001), 153; See Peter Kolchin, *American Slavery 1619–1877* (New York: Hill and Wang, 1993), 129.

6. John Rapier Sr. to John Rapier Jr., December 28, 1858, RTP.

7. See Steven Hahn, *A Nation Under Our Feet: Black Political Struggles in the Rural South from Slavery to the Great Migration* (Cambridge, Mass.: the Belkap Press of Harvard University, 2003), Chapter 1.

About the Sources

In 1948, Chicago physician James Randall White, a native of Nashville and graduate of Fisk University, contacted John Hope Franklin, then teaching at Howard University, about manuscripts in his wife's possession. White explained that his wife, Helen White, was the daughter of Sarah Thomas Brown, the granddaughter of Henry Thomas, and the great-granddaughter of Sally Thomas. The manuscripts included several hundred pages of letters, notes, reminiscences, newspaper clippings, a diary, and a partial autobiography. Sarah Brown's only instruction to her daughter was that she should deposit the collection at "a Negro University."

When the two men met some months later, in Chicago, White asked Franklin to take the box of papers back to Washington, D.C., and deposit them in Founder's Library. Franklin was reluctant to take on such a heavy responsibility but promised to make arrangements for the papers to be turned over to Howard University.

Unfortunately, the partial autobiography, a key to unraveling many aspects of the family's history, was unidentified as to author. In addition, many pages were missing, others were un-numbered or numbered several times, and a few entire sections were apparently lost. Some of the original notes had been copied verbatim into the text, others had been partially copied, while still others had been entirely excluded. Besides these structural problems, most sentences lacked rudimentary punctuation (capitals, periods, quotation marks) and nearly every page contained a stylistic peculiarity, misspelling, or grammatical error. There were also words and phrases commonly used during the early twentieth century (e.g., "the color line," to describe events during the Civil War era). It was not until some years later that we were able to identify James Thomas as the author and fit the various sections together in a coherent fashion.

As it turned out, Thomas's autobiography was one of the few ever written by a former slave and free person of color. Its strengths were unique. It laid bare the texture of urban-slave and free-black life in the Upper South, revealed the internal workings of various black communities, and focused on a group of blacks who had received only passing notice—free and quasi-free persons of mixed racial ancestry. It illuminated the informal relations between blacks and whites; the ability of free blacks to travel from state to state, region to region, country to country; and the social connections among prosperous free people of color. It also suggested how a few privileged African Americans could secure white protectors and fashion their own lives, virtually free from the institutional constraints of slavery. Perhaps most important, Thomas's memory was extremely sharp, his recitation of names, dates, places, and events was uncannily accurate, and while most post–Civil War autobiographies written by former slaves, including Booker T. Washington's classic *Up From Slavery,* concentrated on the period after the Civil War, Thomas focused almost entirely on the era of slavery.

As rich a source as the autobiography proved to be, we needed to be cautious about "memory and distance," as one scholar put it, and to verify Thomas's recollections with contemporary records. It was through the other manuscripts in the Rapier-Thomas papers that we were able to gain a rare inside view of slavery and freedom through the eyes of the participants. The scattered letters, a diary, newspaper articles, and other contemporary material revealed how family members either observed or participated in many of the most important events of their day. In addition, the papers provided firsthand observations of the domestic slave trade, the breakup of black families, violence and resistance, runaways, interracial mixing, class attitudes, insurrection panics, colonization, oppressive laws, slave patrols, severe punishments, and many other subjects. The combination of recollections and contemporary commentary allowed us to speak with some authority about race relations, white society, free blacks, urban life, slavery in different settings, travel in the antebellum North, abolitionism, the proslavery crusade, political campaigns, the "Old-Time Barber Shop," and the attitudes, values, religious beliefs, occupations, and property holdings of free people of color in various sections of the South.

In our quest to trace the history of the Thomas-Rapier family, we were also fortunate to have a wide range of additional primary sources at our disposal. We discovered some of our best information in the dusty basements or record vaults of county courthouses. Among the most exciting finds were the two petitions to the Davidson County Court used in the Prologue to tell the story of James Thomas's emancipation. They were filled with a wealth of pertinent information.

Perhaps nothing is more exciting than finding a probate packet filled with family information. Such was the case when we discovered the probate records for John Rapier Sr. in Lauderdale County, Alabama; for Richard Rapier in Placer County, California; and for James Thomas in St. Louis, Missouri. These files contained, among other documents, wills, inventories, appraisals, affidavits, receipts, bills, vouchers, claims, administrator's reports, court decrees, depositions, and reports of the sale and distribution of property. Besides probate files, other court documents included land deed records, mortgage records, tax assessments, and civil suits. We discovered information on these and other subjects in the county court records of Albemarle County, Virginia; Davidson County, Tennessee; Erie County, New York; Kent County, Ontario, Canada; St. Louis County, Missouri; Madison County, Illinois; Placer County, California; Lauderdale County, Alabama; Lee County, Iowa; and Wabaunsee County, Kansas.

State and federal documents also yielded a good deal of information. The acts of general assemblies and petitions to southern legislatures not only helped us put our narrative into historical context but also on occasion gave us information on specific family members. John Rapier Sr., for example, obtained his freedom when the Alabama General Assembly passed an act of emancipation in his behalf. He also petitioned the assembly to make sure his four boys would receive his property following his death. Two other family members testified before select

House and Senate committees of Congress concerning violence in the southern states. John Rapier Jr.'s medical officer's file at the National Archives in the Records of the Adjutant General's Office contains pertinent information about his activities as a physician in the nation's capital during the final year of the Civil War.

Perhaps the most unexpected discoveries came while we were perusing the United States Manuscript Population Censuses, now available through several decades into the twentieth century. Finding Sally Thomas listed in Nashville in 1840, and her son and grandson a decade later, was extraordinary, but the census returns provided glimpses of virtually every family member at one time or another. The returns were especially helpful in our tracking down the whereabouts of Henry Thomas after the Civil War. Several Buxton residents recalled that there were rumors that he and his family had moved to Mississippi. Upon further investigation, we found that he had indeed settled a few miles to the east of Vicksburg, in the black community of Bovina. Henry was listed in the 1870 and 1880 censuses with his wife, Maria, and son Richard. In addition, the Fisher Funeral Home Records of Vicksburg, Mississippi, contained the following: "Thomas, H. K. (Col.)" died November 9, 1882, age "73 years 19 days." We could now correct the year of his birth (most primary and secondary sources listed it as 1817 rather than 1809).

City directories from Nashville, Buffalo, Florence, Placer County, and St. Louis; newspaper articles before and after the Civil War; state and local convention minutes; the personal papers of a few prominent whites, including those of Ephraim Foster and John Catron; the autobiography of Buxton's founder,

William King; and entries in biographical dictionaries and encyclopedias also yielded important information. In short, we examined a broad range of primary sources at the local, state, and federal levels, and a variety of other primary source materials, in seeking to create our narrative.

The great strength of these sources is that they were written not to show the evils of slavery or to offer recollections of a childhood in bondage (as was the case with Depression-era reminiscences), but rather for reasons of their own, which were neither didactic nor polemical. Consequently, the sources provide immediate, verifiable, and objective firsthand information about a wide range of subjects relating to slavery and freedom in the Old South. The picture that emerges differs sharply from older interpretations of slavery constructed by U. B. Phillips and others and by the black culture and community scholars of the 1970s and 1980s. Indeed, the anxiety, fear, brutality, and wrenching pain of bondage in a remarkable way merge with hope, achievement, and success. In this way, the family's history reveals both the multifaceted, ambiguous nature of slavery and the complicated and peculiar nature of freedom.

APPENDIX 1

Petitions of Ephraim Foster and James Thomas to the Davidson County Court, 1851

The petitions below provide a window into the legal system of the South and reveal the importance of white support for a black person seeking to gain his freedom. The laws in the various southern states differed in this regard, and in a few states of the Deep South it was virtually impossible for slaves to acquire their freedom at the time Foster and Thomas presented their petitions to the Davidson County Court. It was extremely important to have the sanction of law to prove one's freedom, and many free blacks carried their "freedom papers" on their person at all times. Thomas, in fact, had a copy of his papers stolen by a robber who broke into his house on Deaderick Street following the death of his mother. He remained anxious for some time until he secured a replacement.

In the matter of the freedom of a boy of color named James Thomas

In the County Court for the County of Davidson in the State of Tennessee, March Term 1851. Present Joseph H McEwen chairman, Hawes Graves, Henry M Hutton E A Raworth, Josiah Ferriss, L. B Davidson, Robert Greene, W L Barry & Isaac Paul Esquires, Judges of said Court & Justices of the Peace for said

County—The following memorial was presented to wit: Ephraim H Foster, a citizen of said County, respectfully shows unto your worships that he is now and has been since the 20th day of January 1834 the legal owner of a certain mulatto Slave called James Thomas who was born in said County of Davidson in the month of October 1827 and has resided therein all his life, When a youth, your petitioner States, that said Slave was placed in a barbers Shop, where he remained until he had learned his trade well; and having followed it ever since, he is now an adept in his business, and profitably employed therein.

Your petitioner further Shows, that said Slave has always maintained a most exemplary character,—he is industrious, honest, moral, & humble & polite & in fact has so conducted himself as to gain the confidence & the respect, the good wishes and the constant patronage of all who know him, Believing therefore as your petitioner faithfully does, that said Slave James, is a man of great worth in his place & that he would, as a free man, make a valuable, honest & excellent citizen, he prays your worships, on this his petition to decree the freedom of said negro James, according to acts of assembly in such cases made and provided.

[signed] E H Foster

Whereupon, present the Justices there of as aforesaid, the said Court, having examined the reasons set forth in said petition of said Foster and being of opinion that according to the same, would be consistent with the interest and policy of the State do order their chairman to report said petition and it is done accordingly

[signed] J H McEwen chairman

Whereupon, the premises considered, said Court is ready and willing to acceede to said petition, and to emancipate said slave James, on said Foster first entering into bond with good security, according to the act of 1831, chapter 112. And now at the same time the said Foster having entered into bond with Alex Allison his security according to said Law, the Court nine Justices thereof being present and concurring therein, does order, adjudge & [decree] . . . that Said Slave James, otherwise Called James Thomas, be emancipated, and forever set free, according to the terms & conditions specified in said act.

In the County Court for the County of Davidson in the State of Tennessee March Term 1851

The petition of James otherwise called James Thomas, a free man of color humbly represents, that at the present term of this worshipful Court he has, by a Kind Judgement & decree thereof in his favor, been emancipated & forever set free—The petitioner further shows, that he is a native of this State being born and having always resided in said County of Davidson & being now Twenty three years of age.

Your petitioner further Shows, that he has led a moral & industrious life, and has, as he hopes, deported himself in such manner, as to engage the confidence, the assistance & the good wishes of the Society in which he lives—In his early years your petitioner was placed in a barbers Shop, and having learned his trade, is now honestly and profitably employed in his shop in the town of Nashville, where he has a large [clientele] & is trying to make a living by faithful attention to his business. If he is compelled, under the existing laws, to remove out of the State, he will be greatly damaged by having to Start anew in some Strange Country & rebuild a character he trusts he has already established in Tennessee.

The premises considered, your petitioner humbly prays that by an order & decree of your worships he may be allowed & permitted to remain in said County of Davidson, exempt from the pains & penalties imposed by law upon free people of color, emancipated since the year 1831, and that on complying with its conditions, he may have all the priveledges & benefits confered upon such persons by the act of 1842.

James otherwise called James Thomas,

County Court for the County of Davidson in the State of Tennessee March term 1851

In the matter of James, otherwise called James Thomas a free man of color and a barber by trade. Decree

It appearing to the Court that the petitioner was born in the State of Tennessee, that he has resided therein before the 1st January 1836 and ever since his birth, and that he is a man of good character and ought to be permitted to reside in said County of Davidson It further appearing that said petitioner has given bond and security in this court, according to the terms of the Statute in such cases made and provided, This Court does thereupon order, adjudge and decree, that said James Thomas shall be permitted to reside in said County, upon the conditions prescribed by law, exempted from the penalties imposed by the act of 1831, chapter 102, & other penalties and conditions imposed on free persons of color, removing to or residing in this State.

Whereupon the said James Thomas in court here gave bond in the Sum of Five Hundred dollars, with E H Foster and E A Raworth his securities.

Source: Records of the Davidson County Court, Minute Book E (March 1851), 134–35, Metropolitan Nashville–Davidson County Archives, Nashville, Tenn.

APPENDIX 2

John Rapier Sr. to Richard Rapier, April 8, 1845

Most blacks and many whites in the South during the time of slavery were illiterate. Not only are the small number of letters by John Rapier Sr. and other family members unique in this respect, but they reveal the deep feelings the Thomases and Rapiers felt toward one another. The elder Rapier, as seen in this letter, was a consummate father, informing, advising, supporting, cautioning, and cajoling. The letter below also reports on the slaves and free blacks that entered their lives.

Florence Alabama   april 8th 1845

Dear son I have red your last letter I am truly Glad to hear of you all enjoying good health I would have wrote before this but i have been looking for a letter from nashville to hear how they are all doing i were at nashville in January last to see them all mother looks as young as she did 8 years ago and works as hard and hardly take the time to talk to you James is with frank Parish this year and has the promise of twelve dollars per month and he is taken lessons with jordan mc Gowin on the violin James will make a man of musick I think he seems to be very fond of it John has wrote me two letter and he writes very plain for a boy of his age and practice and has as much taste for reading as any child I know off and very good in arithmetic and your brother James reads well for a little Boy henry has become very tired of home and has promised me if i will let him go to school that he will be a good boy and try and learn he is very anctious to go to buffalo this summer with me when i Come to see you all and perhaps I will leave he is very good child at the present time but he will not study his book i am in hopes you will study your Book well and try and give your father satisfaction I am in hopes you will show me that you have not Been in Buffalo all this time for nothing and that I can hold you up as and example to your little Brothers much depend on your course of conduct my son and i am in hopes Richard you have that much Knowledge to see it i am well please with your hand writing and i hope your studys are as much improved richard you are Blessed if will look at your situation that you have kind relation who are anctious to see you grow up an ornament to society and it will do them good to hear others speak well of y[ou] Richard i hope you will do all that your uncle and aunt will request of you for they will not make you do anything wrong from What i have heard my sister she is a lady and i hope you will treat her as if she were your mother if you do that you will please me very much when i see her she will not have any fault of you My dear Sister i am in hopes you are not dissatisfied with richard make him mind you and obey you in all things that is my wish that you would treat him as a child of your own Dear Brother I shall come to see you some time this summer iff life last and no preventing providence i want you to make richard write in may i see from your letter he is doing very well at school keep him where he can learn that is my wish we have had no snow all the winter not as much as would cover the ground i have a fine prospect of a good garden at the present most of the things are up and growing I am still keeping house by myself an[d] i have become use to it i have seen Levi Lewis since he has Come home and he is well pleased with his trip that he had last summer give my respects to Mr Butler and family all of friends in Buffalo I hope i shall have the pleasure of seeing them all this summer write me word how is trade with you I tried to Get James to come and see you this spring But he would not consent to [go] Frank Clerk and head workman he is . . . [torn page] But i do not like the Business myself when you write let me know how is alabama and Tennessee money in Buffalo in the way of money I do not know what way i shall come this summer yet i had some of thought of coming by the way of Pittsburgh henry is more than anctious to see you all and promise that he will try and please you if i will let him stay my health is as usual

I am yours truly

[signed] John H. Rapier

Source: John Rapier Sr. to Richard Rapier, April 8, 1845, RTP.

Appendix 3

John Rapier Jr. to James Thomas, July 28, 1861

John Rapier Jr. was a precocious child and prolific writer as a young adult. Here he struggles with his attitudes about race and color while living in a society that, unlike the United States, granted him many privileges because he was a person of mixed racial ancestry. He confesses that being treated as an equal has a profound effect on "ones heart and head." Later, of course, he changed his stance, working tirelessly as a physician to improve the condition of former slaves during the Civil War.

Kingston Jamaica July 28th 1861

James P Thomas Esqr
St Louis Missouri

Dear Uncle, since my last letter to you [illegible word] . . . and the mail Packets have been propitious, and I have received two letters from Father, besides I have also heard from James and Uncle Henry. James' letters are always enigmas for me to solve and his mode of addressing letters are about as lucid as the fellow who wishing to write to Sir Humphrey Davy, addressed him "Zrumphrty davi". If you ever should write to him, hint that it does [not] depend entirely on the quantity of ink that you use, but something on the manner of applying it to the paper, that secures a decent and legible address. You know me too well, to enter into any arguments to prove that I am neither proud nor haughty, nor ashamed of my relatives, but I am now somewhat differently situated in life, and commingle with a different class of people than heretofore, and therefore it is highly essential that I should leave no gap by which my former position would become exposed, or I would be snubbed by the proud Jamaicans and this, as much as I despise many of their customs, I can not afford, Nothing goes as readily to prove the antecedents, and associates of a man, as the Kind of correspondents he has, if his letters are neatly addressed, and written so that ~~you~~ he can read an extract occasionally to ~~your~~ his associates. it helps ~~you~~ him wonderfully and vice versa.

I feel a delicacy in telling this to James but he does spread the damnest quantity of ink of anybody I know of.

To tell you the truth a very different kind of f[eeling] and ideas pervades ones heart and head, when he can meet every man on equal terms, and converse without restraint with them upon every topic of the day—agreeing and disagreeing, upon themes and subjects just as you think or feel inclined, without feeling all the time that your opinions are only heard because you are a pretty clever nigger, and can read and write—Where you can go to all places of amusement, instruction or interest without a hundred eyes being turned upon you, while their owners are busy wondering what the *hell* is that nigger doing here—The Supreme Court sat last week in this City. I attended the opening of it, for this be it known is nothing less than a grand affair—The Chief Justice Sir Bryan presided, assisted by Justice Moncrief a griff and

Sir Edward Jordan a mulatto, The attorney Genl Hon Mr Heslip a mulatto, was assisted by T Williams Esqr of the same complexion, all the lawyers with one or two exceptions were mixed bloods, and these exceptions were whites—Hon Charles Price a full-blooded negro, and member of Parliament for this City read the usual formula for the Divine protection of the Royal Family, while Hon Mr Vickars of the Late Executive Council, of the same [general] origin responded in the name of Queen—I occupied a seat between two *Barristers* outside of the bar, whose income from their practice is said (each) to amount to $20,000—per annuum—If that had been in a little county court in Kansas I would not have been permitted to enter only as a Prisoner, or witness—

The odds are greatly in the mulattoes favour in this country, indeed they are the rulers, and even the Governorship of the Island it is said will pass into the hands of either Sir Edward Jordan, or the Hon Richard Hill, sometime during the next year—

Mrs Gov Darling gives her "at homes" every Friday evening where the ebony faces of the sons of Africa may be seen in horrid proximity to the cheeks of Caucasia's fairest daughters, as they whirl away in the giddy waltz or indulge their light fantastic [illegible word] . . . in intricacies of the Redown Lancers Mazour Ra [sic] and the other fashionable and popular dances. such things do not often occur in Atchison to do any good, that is not as any body knows on—

The Hon Charles Price, through the intercession of a Friend procured me a ticket to the last "at home" as my wardrobe was scanty, and my purse still more so, I had to forego the brilliant pleasure that I would have had in a room where a live *Lord* breathed with me on equality the same atmosphere, and who knows but might had between my own fingers plebian as they are the palm of a titled Lady's hand. Will if this had happen you just bet I would a give it one squeeze anyway—

Some of these days you may be invited to some Gove[r]nors ball, and for fear that you may not have a better opportunity of learning the routine of dress let me tell what is full costume in Jamaica. White Cravat Dress coat & pants (black) white satin vest patent leather congress boots, and a clean shirt—if you are found wanting in any of these ~~the~~ indispensable articles the major Doms will politely inform you that you are *outre* and therefore inadmissable—

I also had the pleasure a few evenings since of visiting the Grand Lodge of Jamaica that had its session in this City last week. It has a splendid affair over 300 Master workmen were present arranged under their different Lodges—I was attached for the evening to the Sussex Lodge, or else I could not have been admitted, as none are permitted to enter on such occasions unless vouched for, and adopted by some represented Lodge We were entertained in a handsome manner by the G[rand] M[aster] in a Lecture, in which he said a great deal about one Hiram Abiff, said to be a widows son. But as you have met Hiram under somewhat mysterious circumstances, I will not say anymore about it. But I can not thus dismiss the supper that followed which were given by the Grand Lodge to all *Masters* Masons and let me tell you when we were called from [forth] to refreshment, in all that number not a single brother was found who refused to obey the sound of the gavel But the Junior Master had much trouble to prevent many of his brethren from converting the hours of refreshment into excess and intemperance, particularly in the eating line—I feel hungry every time I think about that supper—we adjourn at 2 am after one of the most convivial evenings that ever fell to my lot.

I am pushing along with all speed possible in my new profession of Dentist, you should see me sometime have a poor devil suffering with the toothache with his Jaws distended, lance in hand dissected around the molar preparatory to applying the forceps. And then to hear such screams of agony as I can wring out of mouths, It is wonderful indeed perfectly astonishing that I who have been but a few months in the profession can make my patients bellow louder, hold on to the tooth faster and longer, and finally wrench it out with more of the Jawbone sticking than my master who has spent years in the profession. Arn't you proud of your promising nephew—When I see you I will just pull out two of your front teeth to show you how it is done—

The greatest trouble I have is to wonder how and where I will get my "Kit" to work with in December, I may even need them in October, as my master talks of leaving the Island in the latter month for South America—You must try, *and do* some thing for me that I may be enabled to weather the point, and meet successfully the exigencies of the case. News from Hayti is dull, and gloomy, six Spanish men of war, were only prevented 2 weeks ago by the streneous efforts of the British Consul, and the energetic protest of U.S. Commercial Agent from reducing Port-au Prince to ashes. Alleging as a cause that certain Haytiens and exiled Dominicans had insulted the Spanish flag in the Dominican frontier [final part of letter missing] . . .

Source: John Rapier Jr. to James Thomas, July 28, 1861, RTP.

SELECTED BIBLIOGRAPHY ON SLAVERY

Aptheker, Herbert. *American Negro Slave Revolts.* New York: Columbia University Press, 1943.

Bancroft, Frederic. *Slave Trading in the Old South.* Baltimore: J. H. Furst Co., 1931.

Berlin, Ira. *Many Thousands Gone: The First Two Centuries of Slavery in North America.* Cambridge: Harvard University Press, 1998.

———. *Slaves Without Masters: The Free Negro in the Antebellum South.* New York: Pantheon Books, 1974.

Blassingame, John. *The Slave Community: Plantation Life in the Antebellum South.* New York: Oxford University Press, 1972; rev. ed., 1979.

Dew, Charles. *Bond of Iron: Master and Slave and Buffalo Forge.* New York: W. W. Norton and Company, 1994.

Dusinberre, William. *Them Dark Days: Slavery in the American Rice Swamps.* New York: Oxford University Press, 1996.

Egerton, Douglas R. *Gabriel's Rebellion: The Virginia Slave Conspiracies of 1800 and 1802.* Chapel Hill: University of North Carolina Press, 1993.

Fox-Genovese, Elizabeth. *Within the Plantation Household: Black and White Women of the Old South.* Chapel Hill: University of North Carolina Press, 1988.

Franklin, John Hope. *The Free Negro in North Carolina, 1790–1860.* Chapel Hill: University of North Carolina Press, 1943.

———, and Schweninger, Loren. *Runaway Slaves: Rebels on the Plantation.* New York: Oxford University Press, 1999.

Gara, Larry. *The Liberty Line: The Legend of the Underground Railroad.* Lexington: University of Kentucky Press, 1961.

Genovese, Eugene. *Roll, Jordan, Roll: The World the Slaves Made.* New York: Pantheon Books, 1974.

Hadden, Sally E. *Slave Patrols: Law and Violence in Virginia and the Carolinas.* Cambridge: Harvard University Press, 2001.

Johnson, Walter. *Soul by Soul: Life Inside the Antebellum Slave Market.* Cambridge: Harvard University Press, 1999.

Jordan, Withrop. *White Over Black: American Attitudes Toward the Negro, 1550–1812.* Chapel Hill: University of North Carolina Press, 1968.

Joyner, Charles. *Down by the Riverside: A South Carolina Slave Community.* Urbana: University of Illinois Press, 1984.

Kolchin, Peter. *American Slavery, 1619–1877.* New York: Hill and Wang, 1993.

Litwack, Leon F. *Been in the Storm So Long: The Aftermath of Slavery.* New York: Alfred A. Knopf, 1979.

Malone, Ann Patton. *Sweet Chariot: Slave Family and Household Structure in Nineteenth-Century Louisiana.* Chapel Hill: University of North Carolina Press, 1992.

Morris, Thomas D. *Southern Slavery and the Law, 1619–1860.* Chapel Hill: University of North Carolina Press, 1996.

Mullin, Gerald M. *Flight and Rebellion: Slave Resistance in Eighteenth-Century Virginia.* New York: Oxford University Press, 1972.

Phillips, Ulrich B. *American Negro Slavery: A Survey of the Supply, Employment and Control of Negro Labor as Determined by the Plantation Regime.* New York: D. Appleton and Co., 1918.

Raboteau, Albert J. *Slave Religion: The "Invisible Institution" in the Antebellum South.* New York: Oxford University Press, 1978.

Schweninger, Loren, ed., *The Southern Debate over Slavery, Volume 1, Petitions to Southern Legislatures, 1778–1864.* Urbana: University of Illinois Press, 2001.

Stampp, Kenneth. *The Peculiar Institution: Slavery in the Ante-Bellum South.* New York: Alfred A. Knopf, 1956.

Tadman, Michael. *Speculators and Slaves: Masters and Slaves in the Old South.* Madison: University of Wisconsin Press, 1989.

White, Deborah. *Ar'n't I a Woman? Female Slaves in the Plantation South.* New York: W. W. Norton and Company, 1985.

INDEX

For members of the Thomas-Rapier family, see pp. xvi-xvii, The Descendants of Sally Thomas.